Caroline Keen holds a PhD from the School of Oriental and African Studies (SOAS), University of London.

PRINCELY INDIA AND THE BRITISH

Political Development and the
Operation of Empire

Caroline Keen

I.B. TAURIS

LONDON · NEW YORK

Published in 2012 by I.B.Tauris & Co Ltd
6 Salem Road, London W2 4BU
175 Fifth Avenue, New York NY 10010
www.ibtauris.com

Distributed in the United States and Canada
Exclusively by Palgrave Macmillan
175 Fifth Avenue, New York NY 10010

International Library of Colonial History 1

ISBN 978 1 84885 878 7

A full CIP record for this book is available from the British Library
A full CIP record for this book is available from the Library of Congress

Library of Congress catalog card: available

Typeset by Newgen Publishers, Chennai
Printed and bound in Great Britain by CPI Antony Rowe, Chippenham

CONTENTS

ABBREVIATIONS

ADC	Aide-de-Camp
AGG	Agent to the Governor-General
Asst. AGG	Assistant to the Agent to the Governor-General
CI	Central India
FD	Foreign Department
GoI	Government of India
IOR	India Office Records
Lt. Gov.	Lieutenant-Governor
NWP	North-West Provinces
Offg.	Officiating
PCI	Political Correspondence with India (IOR)
Pol.	Political
PP	Parliamentary Papers (IOR)
PSCI	Political and Secret Correspondence with India (IOR)
R/1 and R/2	Crown Representative Records (IOR)
Res.	Resident
Sec.	Secretary
Sec. Govt.	Secretary to the Government
SoS	Secretary of State (for India)

MAP

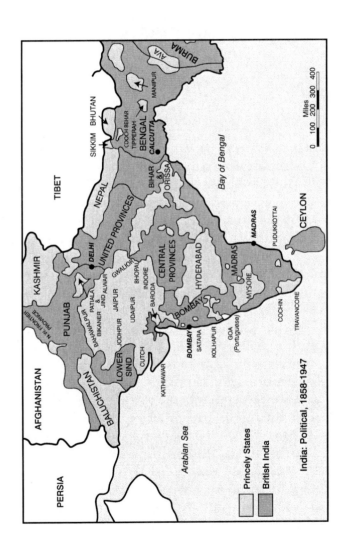

India: Political, 1858-1947

ACKNOWLEDGEMENTS

This book has been long in coming to fruition. The original research started late in the 1980s under the wise guidance of Philip Woods and Peter Marshall and was furthered in its earliest stages by generous input from Stephen Ashton, Barbara Ramusack, Ian Copland, Robin Jeffery and James Manor. At SOAS it emerged as a doctoral thesis in 2003 with the expert navigation of Avril Powell and Peter Robb. Since then it has been substantially rewritten to accommodate new material, to make it more relevant to the general reader and to take account of the new developments in the historiography of princely India which have occurred over the past ten years. During this period of gestation I owe particular thanks to the solicitous staff overseeing the Oriental and India Office Collections at the British Library where I was a fixture and fitting, to Richard Bingle, to the various participants in the research symposium on the history of the princely states at the University of Southampton in 2005, to the staff of the Institute of Historical Research and to the backing and encouragement of Miles Taylor who spurred me on to publication. Jo Godfrey has been a highly supportive editor and Ian McDonald copyedited the manuscript with much care. Finally I owe many thanks to my husband Nigel and my sons, Dominic and Thomas, for their help and interest. They have co-habited with members of the Indian Political Service for a considerable time with great tolerance.

PREFACE

Princely India and the British maps out British policy towards the Indian princes and their states from 1858 to 1909 and examines in detail different facets of the operation of indirect rule during that period. The years 1858 and 1909 both marked a significant change in British attitude towards the rulers. In 1858 a conciliatory approach was urged as a recognition of princely aid in the Indian Mutiny, and in 1909 a policy of *laissez-faire* was adopted in an attempt to secure the loyalty of the princes in the face of emerging Indian nationalism.

The book challenges the view held by a number of modern historians[1] that the latter decades of the nineteenth century constituted a golden age for the princes, during which they received considerable assistance and encouragement from the paramount power within a deliberate strategy to form alliances between Britain and influential Indians. It makes it clear that, on the contrary, British ideological motives for westernisation and 'civilisation', coupled with the need to curb costs and promote efficient government, resulted in a significant loss of princely power over the period. While monographs dealing with the subject usually centre on princely rule in one state, and often see 1947 as the rupture which changed the governance of the states, this book's coverage spans a number of princely states in which notably different circumstances existed and is focused on an earlier stage of princely development which has been little researched. The time frame of the narrative is of great significance since the period covered proved to be a crucial stage of transition from traditional to modern rule for the first generation of westernised rulers.

Recently published works on the princely states of a general, reference nature, namely Barbara Ramusack's *The Indian Princes and Their States* (2004) and *India's Princely States: People, Princes and Colonialism* (eds) Waltraud Ernst and Biswamoy Pati (2007), have a broad temporal span and cover a wide range of states' issues. However this study is firmly centred on the stage of the palace, drawing much-needed attention to men (and women) such as British political officers and residents, tutors, Indian ministers and members of the *zenana*, and the way in which these, often neglected, actors played a major role in influencing the actions, beliefs and styles of rule of a number of princes. It reflects the political importance of subjects that have been hitherto sidelined in the prevailing historiography, which favours the 'subaltern' subject as opposed to the elite, and British India rather than princely India. Moreover by providing an awareness of the powerful intermediaries that influenced colonial government, the book moves away from the presumption that British relations with the princely states were dictated from the metropolis. In drawing attention to the adaptability and nuances of indirect rule it rejects the view that there was little scope for negotiation or resistance, questioning the validity of prevalent historical accounts which adopt a stereotypical view of Indian rulers and their states subject to an inflexible imperialist authority.

The book makes extensive use of archival sources, in particular the India Office Records held at the British Library and the private papers of British officials who served in India and London, in order to fill a substantial gap in the knowledge of the operation of British influence and to open up a number of new questions on its intricacies and style. It adopts the thematic construction of a princely life cycle, using the situation of one ruler or another as an extended illustration of various stages of the life cycle – not only because a particular case was better documented than others but also because it proved to be a more interesting and revealing example of the workings of indirect rule during the period. The first section examines the position of the British in determining disputed successions to Indian princely thrones. The second section deals with the first generation of rulers to be exposed to a western education, either under an English tutor attached to a court or at one of the new princely colleges. The third section looks at marriages of Indian rulers and the extent to which royal women were empowered by British rule. The fourth section tackles the administration of a state under an adult ruler and the relative success of political officers in turning Indian princes from traditional rulers into westernised administrators. The final section studies changes in princely status as a result of the establishment of a British imperial hierarchy and considers British efforts to find an appropriate role for the princes in an imperial context. Inevitably, the major states tend to feature most frequently in that they attracted the greatest British attention.

INTRODUCTION

THE INDIAN STATES AND THE BRITISH

The States

Before 1947, two-fifths of the Indian subcontinent was not British territory and two-ninths of its inhabitants were not British subjects. This territory was divided into over 600 individual states which were governed by hereditary princes of varying rank, owing allegiance to the British Crown. The states displayed a great diversity in terms of size, population and revenue. Collectively they covered an area of nearly 600,000 square miles with a population of just over 80 million. Individually they ranged from Hyderabad, the principal state, with an area of 82,698 square miles and a population of over 14 million, to the tiny Kathiawar state of Veja-no-ness with an area of about three-tenths of a square mile and a population of 184. In general, however, statistics indicate the 'insignificance of the overwhelming majority of states' and only 28 had a population of over 500,000.[1]

There was a great diversity also in the irregular geographical distribution of the states. In Rajputana, for example, the states were few and of a comparatively large size, while in central and western India they were small and very numerous. The explanation for these irregularities lay partly in the policies pursued by the British at various times and partly in a course of events over which they had exerted no control.

At the beginning of the eighteenth century over much of the subcontinent's huge land mass from Jammu and Kashmir in the north to the upland plateau of the Deccan in the south, the Mughal dynasty at Delhi fought to maintain the position of dominance achieved by Emperor Akbar in the second half of the sixteenth century. Thereafter the decline of Mughal imperial power quickened. Provincial governors in Awadh, Bengal and the Deccan consolidated their own regional bases of power in the aftermath of the Persian and, later, the Afghan invasions of 1759–61. In 1757 the British seized control of the rich province of Bengal and, after a brief rearguard action in defence of the core area of Delhi, the Mughal emperor submitted in 1784 to the 'protection' of the Maratha war chief, Scindia. With the defeat of the Marathas in 1803 Delhi was occupied by the British, and the Mughal emperor was reduced in European eyes to the status of a 'tinsel sovereign'.[2]

In some areas of India a stronger power had destroyed newcomers and petty ancient dynasties before the arrival of the British. During the second half of the eighteenth century the ground had been cleared in the south of India by the Nizam of Hyderabad, the Nawab of the Carnatic and Haider Ali, the Muslim usurper of Mysore, whose patrimony was expanded by Tipu Sultan. When the Carnatic fell under British control and Tipu Sultan was finally overthrown in 1799, large united territories had to be disposed of either by annexation or, as in the case of Mysore, by restitution to a former dynasty. The situation was different in central and western India. This area was under the control of the Marathas, a loose confederacy of five military units under the nominal leadership of the Peshwa who controlled western India from his capital at Poona. The other four units were led by the Gaekwar of Baroda, the Bhonsle Raja of Nagpur, the Maharaja of Gwalior and the Maharaja of Indore. By the end of the eighteenth century the five chiefs of the confederacy were interested solely in personal gain and regarded each other as rivals in a struggle for supremacy. As a result territories in central and western India were constantly changing hands until 1818, when the Maratha chiefs came under British control. The numerous petty states in that area stood in marked contrast to the situation in Rajputana where, despite Maratha intrusions, 17 states preserved their separate political existence. The most significant of these were Mewar (Udaipur), Jodhpur (Marwar), Jaipur and Bikaner.[3]

The physical characteristics of the states displayed the same degree of diversity. Much of Rajputana was desert, while in the deep south Travancore possessed tropical vegetation. Hyderabad and Mysore were rich in mineral resources, contrasting in their wealth with the poverty of the hill states of the Punjab in north-western India and the agriculturalists of Kathiawar in the west. Equally diverse were the varieties of population and religion. The primitive and mostly animistic tribes of the Assam states and Manipur on the Burmese frontier contrasted with the wealthy Muslim aristocracy of Hyderabad and the proud nobles of Rajputana. In Jammu and Kashmir in the far north, the prince was Hindu and the population largely Muslim. In Hyderabad, the reverse was the case.[4]

Coalitions of a clan, groups of clans or military allies had created many of the states. To achieve stability a newly established ruler often provided internal allies with grants to collect land revenue from areas within the conquered land, thereby creating a landed nobility. As a result many of the states exhibited feudal conditions. Land was divided into two categories: *khalsa* and non-*khalsa*. In the *khalsa* areas, the land revenue and various administrative departments were administered centrally. The non-*khalsa* areas consisted of numerous estates or *jagirs*, the incumbents of which, known as *jagirdars*, exercised considerable authority in judicial and police administration.[5] In central India numerous minor Rajput chiefs, known as *thakurs*, existed as feudatories of the great Maratha princes, Scindia of Gwalior and Holkar of Indore. The *thakurs* were often descendants of nobles who had ruled the territory before the arrival of the invading Marathas, and their relations with their new overlords were frequently a source of bitter discontent.[6] A different situation existed in Rajputana where the states were traditionally regarded as the property of a territorial nobility, not the individual prince who was only *primus inter pares*. In Udaipur, 28 principal nobles commanded the subsidiary allegiance of nearly one-third of the population, and their estates comprised just over half the area of the entire state. A similar situation existed in Hyderabad, where only half of the land was *khalsa*.

As the most powerful of the elite, the ruler of a state generated the income to maintain an administration from taxes on land that was designated as *khalsa* and from indirect levies such as customs, salt and stamp taxes. When government functions were limited, a prince had a minimal administration led by a diwan, or chief minister, to supervise the collection of taxes. Other officers headed departments of finance, military affairs, the judiciary and household affairs. From the mid-nineteenth century onwards a few states such as Travancore, Mysore and Baroda established departments of public works and education. The revenue department had immediate jurisdiction over *khalsa* lands, which paid land revenues directly to the ruler, while *jagirdars* collected the land revenue from areas beyond the control of state administration. Larger states were divided into divisions, under which were districts, but, as in British India, the state structure often did not penetrate into local society below the district level. Village headmen (*patels*), accountants (*patwaris*) and councils were responsible for the collection and payment of revenues to state-appointed officers or revenue contractors. More powerful *jagirdars* had their own revenue officers but, like the British and the princes, usually did not collect revenue directly from peasant cultivators or tenants but from local intermediaries.[7]

The judicial system 'reflected both the autocratic nature of states and their narrow infiltration into local society'. Caste *panchayats*, village headmen and religious leaders settled most civil and some criminal disputes at the local level. In larger states the lowest-level revenue collector, either a state-appointed officer named a *tahsildar* or *amildar*, or a relatively autonomous *jagirdar*, decided revenue claims and other civil disputes. By the early twentieth century appeals went to district courts and then to a high court of the state located in the capital, or in some smaller states to a consolidated regional court. In many cases the ruler was the highest court of appeal both in civil and criminal cases and frequently approved death sentences. Therefore 'the intervention of the ruler at the highest level and revenue authorities at the lowest sharply reduced the independence of the judiciary'.[8]

The Ascent of the Resident

The British first established their contact with India in 1600 when Elizabeth I gave the East India Company its charter. This commercial organisation controlled British affairs in India for just over 250 years, after which it was superseded by the Government of India in the form of a colonial government responsible to a minister in London. During its existence the East India Company did in fact rule, although its rule developed slowly and its commercial activities took preference for some considerable time. A charter of Charles II in 1661 gave the Company power to make peace or war 'with any Prince not Christian' and from this charter the practice grew of making treaties of peace and defensive alliances, the first being anti-piracy treaties with the western Indian maritime states of Savantwadi (1730) and Janjira (1733).[9] This treaty-making power was exercised by delegation through the Company's representatives in India until 1773, when parliament decreed that, unless an emergency existed, approval had to be obtained from London. Directed by a governor-general, the organisation in India (consisting of a small council of traders who eventually became civil servants) was based in Calcutta and controlled by the Court of Directors in London.

The British adopted and perfected the mechanism of the subsidiary alliance. In return for a tribute or 'subsidy', or the lease of productive territories, the Company engaged to support a ruler against his enemies and to maintain their own troops in his lands as garrisons. For example, by 1763 British naval and financial superiority had virtually banished French power from the coast and helped Muhammed Ali Wallajah to consolidate his position as Nawab of Arcot in the Carnatic. Powerful bonds of dependency were tied, which were ultimately to strangle Arcot and draw the British into direct administrative control of the Tamil country. In the north the Nawab of Awadh, Shuja-ud-Daula, agreed to a subsidiary treaty in 1765. These types of schemes were to be adopted many times over the whole subcontinent in the next half century as a mode of securing a stable frontier for British commercial interests and payment for Company troops. In practice, however, alliances put intolerable strains on fragile Indian states whose rulers were never certain of the amount of their revenue from month to month. Shortfalls in subsidiary payments faced the British with mutinies among their own unpaid troops and led to piecemeal annexation in order to stabilise the financial situation. In the view of Christopher Bayly it is 'ironic that the subsidiary alliance system, designed to set bounds to British territorial intervention, in fact pointed to its unlimited extension'.[10]

The Mughal Empire had its own diplomatic conventions and regulations to which the Company had to conform, at least in part. A Mughal official was expected to send a personal agent, a *vakil*, to represent him before the Emperor in the official's absence. Mughal officials also posted *vakils* to each other, particularly to other regional courts, in order to look after their interests.[11] The title of 'resident' given to a Company representative in a state was particularly appropriate in the light of the Company's peculiar role as far as the British and Mughal sovereigns were concerned. As a chartered company it could not appoint full ambassadors or deal with sovereigns on the basis of *de jure* equality. Moreover the Company's position within the Mughal Empire could never be regularised within the practice of international law of the day. From 1772, the Company formally acknowledged Mughal sovereignty and at the same time acknowledged the sovereignty of the British Crown, although the Council of the Governor-General agreed that to make the latter recognition public in India would create anti-Company feeling. Appointing a 'resident' instead of an 'ambassador' had advantages to the Company not only of lower cost but also of raising fewer questions of ceremony and precedence.[12]

Although official policy called for intervention in external, not internal, affairs of states, in fact residents followed Company interests above all others and on occasions engaged in deep intervention in domestic matters. After the ruling gaekwar's death in 1800, a long succession struggle in Baroda ensued. One faction enlisted the military support of the Company, for which the new ruler was forced to guarantee valuable territories as security and on his failure to meet the arrears upon his debt was forced to give up the territories permanently to the Company. In Hyderabad an arrangement worked out in 1809 and sustained until 1843 gave the British the right to influence the choice of successor to the diwanship. The resident and the governor-general discussed the strengths and weaknesses of each possible candidate and the resident then attempted to channel all business of state through the diwan. Following the last Mysore War of 1799 the Company re-established the Travancore residency, and between 1811 and 1814 the resident played a major role in the state administration, thereafter operating under an imposed chief minister who simply carried out British instructions in what has been termed a 'Dominant Resident' relationship between resident and ruler.[13] However when it suited Company policy, internal intervention was minimal. In the first half of the nineteenth century requests from the rulers of Awadh and Gwalior for Company assistance in the form of British troops and revenue officials to reform the administration were refused on the grounds that the Company could offer no more than the advice of the resident.[14]

While, during this period, there were major disputes between the Company and a number of rulers, the British remained committed to supporting them either within their states or as dependants of the Company. There remained the underlying assumption that there was a legitimacy attached to the princes as a whole, even if such legitimacy was overridden by the circumstances of the day. On most occasions the British attempted to preserve a local ruler under indirect rule. Where they deposed an incumbent they continued to accord him titles, dignity and what they considered to be an appropriate pension even in exile. Following the fourth and final war with Mysore and two wars with the Marathas, in addition to a number of minor armed conflicts, the Company restored most of the defeated rulers to their thrones. Where it deposed a particular ruler, he was usually replaced with a relative, as was the case with the Nawab of Arcot in 1799. In Mysore in 1799, the British carefully drafted a treaty stipulating that the Company was giving the state to a scion of the ousted Hindu dynasty but reserved the right to interfere in the administration should the state be threatened by misrule. Michael Fisher points out that the case of Mysore illustrates the contradictions of the situation. On the one hand the British tended towards indirect rule with a respect for India's hereditary rulers, which required a relatively low investment of manpower and money. On the other hand the British felt an obligation to provide 'moral' and efficient administration for the people of India. In Mysore, more conspicuously than in most other states, the conflict between the two resulted in 'a condition between direct and indirect rule'.[15]

The Company attempted to isolate states from each other by inserting residents as an exclusive medium for political communication. Residents negotiated treaties binding most rulers to communicate officially with each other only through residencies, and British surveillance over rulers and courts established an enforced monopoly on interstate political communication.[16] Starting in 1792 the Company induced some 55 states individually to agree by treaty to channel all foreign policy contacts through their residents. A typical treaty stipulated that the ruler in question abjured any 'negotiation or political correspondence with any European or native power without the consent of the said Company'.[17] While the Company did not literally forbid rulers from maintaining a foreign policy, it did insist that all communications passed through its hands and met with its approval. By 1840 some 31 rulers had handed over their official political interaction to their residents. Among the first were Awadh, Mysore, Hyderabad, Gwalior and Cochin, followed by others in Rajputana and central and western India.

Inevitably, behind a resident's advice to a ruler lay the 'practically invincible military power of the Company'.[18] In a crucial move to shift the financial burden of this power onto the princes, the Company established subsidiary forces in several states. As well as reducing expenditure this action placed disciplined troops under the immediate control of the resident and, since the troops largely replaced the ruler's own armies, the resident thus commanded the most potent military force in the state. In exchange for organising and disbursing funds for subsidiary forces the Company acquired substantial resources from states. In some cases a ruler paid subsidies in cash as a 'tribute', but in most cases land revenue from territory would be assigned in order to pay the subsidy. Hyderabad, for example, ceded the disputed Madras coastal area of the Northern Circars in 1766 in exchange for the use of Company troops, and in 1814 the Company established the 'Russell Contingent' in the same state (named after the then Resident, Henry Russell) and took the rich territory of Berar to pay for it. Many of the Company's choicest territories came from such arrangements, as when Awadh ceded half of its lands in 1801. By controlling the military forces within a state and building a constituency of courtiers, administrators, landholders and members of the general populace, residents were able to accomplish many of the purposes of the Company.

Rulers quickly recognised the danger to their authority that the establishment of a residency tended to entail. Into the early nineteenth century more powerful rulers retained the capacity to block or terminate a residency when it suited their policies. A few rulers entirely refused the residency system. In the eighteenth century Haider Ali and Tipu Sultan were particularly anxious to avoid having a resident at the Mysore court and, after conflicts over the role of the British in their particular states, the Nawab of Awadh and the Raja of Travancore succeeded in obtaining the temporary abolition of their residencies. In some cases rulers or supporters resorted to extreme tactics to remove the resident, attacking the residency with force of arms. In the early nineteenth century political agents were attacked or killed in Banaras, Travancore, Nagpur, Poona, Jaipur and Sind, and several residencies, most prominently Delhi and Lucknow, were destroyed or besieged in 1857.[19]

Strategies and tactics employed by various rulers and officials did much to shape indirect rule. The variety among treaties suggests the manner in which each state was able to affect its individual relationship with the British. While many of the same phrases occur in a number of treaties concluded before the Mutiny, there are striking differences as well, as one or another ruler objected to or insisted upon a certain provision. Local practices varied also, reflecting the peculiar relationship between ruler and resident. The strategy of a ruler or official would be matched by Company strategy and different tactics resulted in a range of outcomes, leading to the acquisition of new powers or lands at the hand of Britain or to loss of territory, rights or even throne.

From the outset the British maintained that it was impossible to achieve a precise definition of the paramountcy[20] they exercised over the Indian states. The treaties which had been concluded could never be regarded as definitive simply because 'no such agreement could survive indefinitely in its original form'.[21] Sir William Lee-Warner, a leading authority on paramountcy at the end of the nineteenth century, wrote that 'Even if the whole body of Indian treaties, engagements and *sanads* were carefully compiled, with a view to extracting from them a catalogue of the obligations or duties that might be held to be common to all, the list would be incomplete'.[22] In order to deal with changing needs and circumstances a body of political practice or usage was gradually built up. Such usage was employed primarily to promote imperial interests and to supply imperial needs, as in the case of laws relating to the construction of roads and railways and the development of commercial policy, and frequently new principles established in relations with one state were subsequently taken to apply to all states. In practice, therefore, the operation of paramountcy meant that 'the full extent of British interference in the Home Departments of the states has never and never can be defined'.[23]

The British Debate

By the nineteenth century the religious and social mores of the British precluded them from any form of partnership with the indigenous community, unlike their Mughal predecessors who, through informal treaties and matrimonial relations, established close links with rulers such as the princes of Rajputana. There was much suspicion and mistrust as the British adopted a policy of keeping the princes at arm's length from the government and isolated from each other. Under the British system of tutelage the rulers had no hope of achieving either fame or distinction. Confined to their own territories and with no prospect of advancement, they began to lose the compulsion to maintain decent and orderly standards of administration and instead became increasingly dependent upon British guarantees. Under British protection the princes were not only secure from foreign or domestic enemies but also 'free to govern in an arbitrary manner, defying the wishes of their subjects with impunity'.[24]

One of the most forthright critics of the subsidiary system was Sir Thomas Munro, Governor of Madras between 1820 and 1827. Munro respected indigenous customs and institutions and wished to preserve them in order to conciliate all sections of Indian society. Britain's role in India, he believed, should be confined to the provision of sound and efficient government. In 1817 he expressed his view to the Governor-General Lord Hastings:

> There are many weighty objections to the employment of a sub-sidiary force. It has a natural tendency to render the government of every country in which it exists weak and oppressive; to extinguish all honourable spirit among the higher classes of society and to degrade and impoverish the whole people.[25]

The misgivings of Munro were shared by the liberal reformers of the early Victorian era. From the end of the eighteenth century until the Mutiny in 1857, the position of the Indian privileged classes was consistently criticised by supporters of Jeremy Bentham's utilitarianism. The philosophical root of liberalism in India is best exemplified by the work of the early nineteenth-century Benthamite James Mill, an East India Company examiner, and his fellow examiner and son, John Stuart Mill. The elder Mill in his somewhat plodding *History of British India* and the younger in *On Liberty* and *Considerations of Representative Government* argued that 'civilisation' was a universal goal, on the path to which every people and society could be measured.[26] With some slight differences of opinion the Mills believed that Britain stood at the pinnacle of the hierarchy of world civilisation while India and other oriental and 'coloured' regions ranked near the bottom. India specifically had taken 'but a few of the earliest steps in the progress to civilisation'.[27] However it needed only a different environment to induce most Indians to become self-governing, rational and energetic. In the case of the princely states, the Company had so far singularly failed to create such an environment. The military power of the British had secured the authority of native rulers over their people without at the same time providing the checks and balances to ensure that their rule was fair and benevolent.

James Mill demanded a revolution in Indian society carried through by the operation of 'good government', 'just laws' and a 'scientific' system of taxation. 'Clearness, certainty, promptitude, cheapness' in British administration would, he believed, provide 'a complete deliverance' for the individual from the tyranny of priests and aristocrats, so that India would be placed on the path of 'improvement'.[28] Mill's utilitarian argument would have borne much less weight had it not been able to harness the contempt of evangelical Christians for the personal conduct and character of the native ruling classes it opposed on political and economic grounds. Convinced that western civilisation was superior and inspired by the belief that Britain had a moral obligation to change Indian society, utilitarian and evangelical reformers were equally appalled to learn that British policy encouraged princely misgovernment. They found themselves converted, despite their pacifist and anti-imperial sentiments, into apostles of annexation. Mill was among the first to demand that Britain put an end to princely rule. Not to enhance Britain's imperial glory, he told a House of Commons Committee in 1832, but to secure the happiness of the people, the Indian states should be taken over:

> Unless you take the collection of the revenue into your hands, and appoint your own collectors, with your own people to supervise those collectors, you may be perfectly sure the people will be plundered. In like manner, there will be no justice unless you administer it.[29]

The views of the annexationists, however, were by no means universally endorsed. Mountstuart Elphinstone and Sir John Malcolm were prominent among those who disagreed with the criticism of the subsidiary system and who strenuously opposed the idea of bringing princely rule to an end. Elphinstone, with experience as resident at Poona and Governor of Bombay, believed that such decay and stagnation as existed in the states was due not to the subsidiary system but to what he described as the 'ephemeral character of Asiatic governments'. Elphinstone also warned any would-be annexationists that the stability of Britain's existing possessions in India was to a large extent dependent upon the maintenance of princely territories which afforded 'a refuge to all those whose habits of war, intrigue, or depradation [sic] make them incapable of keeping quiet in ours'.[30] In this respect he was supported by Malcolm, who succeeded him as Governor of Bombay and in 1832 declared that he was

decidedly of the opinion that the tranquillity, not to say the
security of our vast Oriental possessions is involved in the preservation of the native principalities which are dependent upon
us for protection ... their coexistence with our rule is of itself
a source of political strength the value of which will never be
known until it is lost.[31]

Malcolm recognised that territorial expansion and the introduction of
western reforms were probably inevitable but warned of serious reper-
cussions if they were not accompanied by restraint. He stressed that
'We must try to march slow time if we cannot halt and to support,
at least for a period, what is left of native rank and power. Its dissolution, to be safe, must be gradual, and we must make, before that crisis
comes, a change in some sort of our principles of administration'.[32]

An examination of the 25 years preceding the Mutiny reveals that
little heed was paid to the warnings of Elphinstone and Malcolm.
However it has been argued that even during this period the British
were not fully committed to a policy of annexing the states. The
Board of Control and the Court of Directors in London were basically
opposed to any further territorial expansion other than that dictated
by political or military necessity. Successive governors-general at the
start of their administrations were also opposed to expansion, but local
circumstances, together with the urge to check abuses as and when
they occurred, frequently led them to abandon their earlier views.
Lord Bentinck, governor-general between 1828 and 1835, was at first
a non-interventionist as far as the states were concerned. He believed
that there was already too much 'petty interference', particularly in
the private lives of the princes, and even advocated the removal of
political officers from all states except those in which subsidiary troops
were stationed. However Bentinck soon found himself threatening the
errant ruler of Awadh that he would have to forfeit his throne unless
he mended his ways. Furthermore, he placed Mysore under British
administration following a rebellion in 1831 and annexed the state of
Coorg in 1834 on the grounds of misgovernment.[33]

It was not, however, until the time of Lord Dalhousie,
governor-general between 1848 and 1856, that annexation became a

salient feature of British policy. Convinced of the superiority of British rule and the degeneracy of the Indian states, Dalhousie stated his views at the start of his administration in August 1848:

> I cannot conceive it possible for anyone to dispute the policy of taking advantage of every just opportunity which presents itself for consolidating the territories which already belong to us, by taking possession of States that may lapse in the midst of them; for thus getting rid of those petty intervening principalities, which may be made a means of annoyance, but which can never, I venture to think, be a source of strength, for adding to the resources of the public treasury, and for extending the uniform application of our system of government to those whose best interests, we sincerely believe, will be promoted thereby.[34]

The device which Dalhousie used to gain possession of seven states in seven years was the 'doctrine of lapse', giving the government the right to take over a state if a prince died without heirs, a situation which is discussed in further depth in the chapter on succession. Dalhousie specifically limited the application of this right to dependent states created by the British Government or owing their existence to it. However, the governor-general wielded the doctrine of lapse so extensively as to arouse suspicion even among the most ancient Hindu princes. He was restrained by the Home Government from taking over the small semi-independent Rajput state of Kerauli, but, of the seven states he did annex, Satara, Jhansi and Nagpur were Maratha principalities of the first rank.

In addition to the doctrine of lapse, Dalhousie's administration also abolished the pensions and titles of erstwhile ruling families. Even Bahadur Shah II, the last of the Mughal emperors, was informed that the imperial title would lapse upon his death. The climax of the expansionist phase came in 1856 with the annexation of Awadh upon the grounds of misrule. Awadh was in drastic need of reform, yet the resident, W. H. Sleeman, did not believe that it should be annexed outright and warned the governor-general of the possible consequences of annexing states:

If we succeed in sweeping them all away or absorbing them, we shall be at the mercy of our native army, and they shall see it, and accidents may possibly occur to unite them, or a great proportion of them, in some desperate act ... the best provision against it seems to me to be the maintenance of native rulers, whose confidence and affection can be engaged, and administration improved under judicious management.[35]

However, the Governor-General's Council and the government in London feared that civil war might ensue in Awadh. The subsequent annexation of the state in February 1856 coincided with the end of Dalhousie's administration and, as an example of current British policy towards the rulers, contributed largely to the unrest from which the Indian Mutiny emerged the following year.

The loyalty of the reigning princes during the revolt clearly demonstrated the potential of the Indian states as a political force in support of British rule. Dalhousie's successor, Lord Canning, was urged by the Home Government to spare no effort in rewarding the princes who had given active assistance. In a despatch to Sir Charles Wood, who had become Secretary of State for India in June 1859, the governor-general agreed that the 'safety of our rule is increased not diminished by the maintenance of Native Chiefs well affected to us'. During the Mutiny 'patches of native government' such as Gwalior, Hyderabad, Patiala, Rampur and Rewah had, according to Canning, 'served as breakwaters to the storm which would otherwise have swept over us'. He believed that 'should the day come when India shall be threatened by an external enemy, or when the interests of England elsewhere may require that her Eastern Empire shall incur more than ordinary risks, one of our best mainstays will be found in these Native States'.[36] The policy of annexation could no longer be continued. For the first time under British rule it appeared that the princes were to be given a permanent position as part of the British Empire.

It has been suggested that the British, who had started their rule as 'outsiders', became 'insiders' by vesting in their monarch the sovereignty of India through an amnesty document, the Government of India Act.[37] This new relationship between the British monarch, her

Indian subjects and the native princes was published in all principal centres of British rule on 1 November 1858. In the proclamation Queen Victoria, who was of the opinion that the Indian rulers had been mistreated in the years preceding the Mutiny, assured the princes that 'their rights, dignity and honour', as well as the control over their territorial possessions, would be respected and that the queen 'was bound to the natives of Our Indian territories by the same obligations of duty which binds us to all our other subjects'. All her Indian subjects were to be secure in the practice of their religions. They were to enjoy 'the equal and impartial protection of the law' and 'due regard would be paid to the ancient rights, usages and customs of India'. Works of 'public utility and improvement' were to be promoted and they 'should enjoy that social advancement which can only be secured by internal peace and good government'.[38] Miles Taylor considers that the role played by Victoria and Albert in the 1858 Act, and subsequent transfer of power from the East India Company to the Crown, has been largely overlooked and that in both instances 'Victoria is revealed to be less a modern icon of Empire and more a European-style monarch, exercising a considerable sway of personal influence'.[39] To ensure the continuation of her active participation in Indian affairs the queen made the specific demands that the Secretary of State for India should have the power to override the Council of India, that the Crown be shown all despatches relating to India and that all government proclamations in India be made in Victoria's name.[40]

For the Government of India, it is clear that the policy to cease annexation was to a great extent one of expediency under current conditions. As Canning was aware, while India now seemed fairly secure, at least in a military sense, there was no room for complacency. Hatred of Europeans had increased as a result of the Mutiny, and another European war, as in 1854, might find India denuded of British troops.[41] Economically a policy of detente with loyal princes and landlords made good sense. The campaigns of 1857–8, following hard on an expensive programme of public works under Dalhousie, had saddled the British with a legacy of debt. In 1858–9 the budget deficit was 14 million *lakhs*, in 1859–60 nine million.[42] The government was incapable of taking on new administrative burdens, at least for the foreseeable future. 'Our officers', explained Canning, 'are

too few for the work which they have on their hands. Accession of territory will not make it easier to discharge our already existing duties in the
administration of justice, the prosecution of public works, and in many
other ways'. Most importantly, Canning regarded the princes as the natural leaders of Indian society, with 'a hold over the feelings and hearts of
the common herd which they cannot bequeath to us'.[43]

To show British generosity to the rulers overall 'an act of general
and substantial grace' was needed. The specific measure that Canning
proposed was to give 'an assurance to every Chief above the rank of
Jagheerdar, who now governs his own territory,... that on failure of
natural heirs his adoption of a successor ... will be recognised'. No
other innovation, he assured Wood, would capture the confidence of
the princes so successfully and 'give a character of immovability to
the policy which it initiates'.[44] Both at home and from the Viceroy's
Council, Canning's proposal evoked a favourable response. Council
member Sir Bartle Frere described the effects of the measure in glow-
ing terms and told Canning that it would 'do more for tranquillity
and good government in India than years of legislation and successful
campaigns'. No avid reformer, Sir Bartle felt few pangs of conscience
at the thought of millions left under Indian rule: 'Every real advantage to the people which can be expected from our rule can be secured
through a Native ruler, with the aid of an English Political Agent of
average ability, more surely, easily, and cheaply than by any form of
direct administration with which I am acquainted'.[45]

Sir Charles Wood was less optimistic over the future of the states,
but he recognised the value of attaching to Britain those 'influential
classes' who would deprive 'the active and stirring elements' in India
of possible leaders.[46] In a despatch of July 1860 he authorised the issue
of adoption *sanads* to all sovereign chiefs under British protection: 'It
is not by the extension of our Empire that its permanence is to be
secured, but by the character of British rule in the territories already
committed to our care, and by practically demonstrating that we are
as willing to respect the rights of others as we are capable of maintaining our own'.[47]

The measure was well received by some sections of the Indian
people for different reasons. It appeared that 'the states were islands

of self-government in a sea of alien rule'.[48] They provided an outlet for political ambition denied in British India and an example of the ability of Indians to rule themselves. As early as August 1858 the *Hindu Patriot* had advocated recognition of the right of adoption and went on to recommend that the princes be freed from the surveillance of British residents. India, the newspaper suggested, should be organised on a federal basis, with the various states and provinces left free to manage their own internal affairs.[49] With considerably more vehemence the vernacular Bengali press deplored British interference in the princely states, and one newspaper asserted in 1863 that despite adoption 'there is no independence allowed to Native Rajas'.[50]

However, not only in government correspondence but also in public addresses to rulers at *durbars*, Canning justified any such interference by stressing that the British Government had a duty to the people of the native states, as much as to the rulers and their families. The government would always consider it a right of the paramount power to intervene in the affairs of the native states to ensure elementary good government according to the principles of British rule in the country.[51] Indeed the recognition of adoption was by no means to prevent the British Government from interfering in princely affairs. Canning made it plain in April 1860 that, with annexation repudiated, intervention was a necessary deterrent to the opportunities now available for gross misrule. In explaining the adoption procedure to Wood, the viceroy[52] declared, 'The proposed measure will not debar the Government of India from stepping in to set right such serious abuses in a native Government as may threaten any part of the country with anarchy or disturbance, nor from assuming temporary change of a Native State when there shall be sufficient reason to do so'.[53]

The issue of *sanads* of adoption has often been represented as indicative of a determination to put an end to Britain's career of annexation in India, however during the 1860s the tide of post-Mutiny reaction began to ebb. Lord Elgin, viceroy from 1862 to 1863, was to some extent in agreement with his departmental heads, such as Sir Henry Durand, that Canning's assessment of imperial priorities had been warped by the trauma of 1857. Writing to Wood in September 1862, he wondered whether the direction which British policy had taken under Canning was 'altogether correct' and whether 'that portion of it which was a policy of circumstance should not have been distinguished from that which was a policy of principle'. Elgin was sure that his predecessor had 'never intended to let the chiefs get the bit into their mouths' and that 'his policy of deference to the authority of native chiefs was only a means to an end, that end being the establishment of the British Raj in India'. The viceroy concluded, 'It may perhaps turn out that a time of peace is better fitted to one of revolution for the discovery of the true theory according to which our relations with native states ought to be conducted'.[54]

The attention given to the Indian rulers in the aftermath of the Mutiny was no accident, for it rested on the British conclusion that the Indian people were not yet ready for James Mill's implanting of western conceptions of justice and freedom and needed reassurance in the reinforcement of a traditional form of rule. In the following decades the British turned to the indigenous royalty of the subcontinent to legitimise the colonial position. Having taken on the princes as clients, the British now had a vested interest in seeing that they acted responsibly and in a manner which would do credit to their patronage. The conduit through which British policy was delivered to the states was the Political Department of the Government of India.

The Man on the Spot

Those men best equipped to formulate the 'true theory' of governing states were undoubtedly the members of the political branch of the Company. This branch, having evolved over the years, consisted of residents, when there was only one state involved, and political agents, who usually each had a group of minor states in their charge, under the control of the agent to the governor-general at the local political agency. During periods of the greatest British expansion in the early nineteenth century the post of political officer had attracted the most ambitious of Company servants. However, following 1858, much of the appeal of the political branch faded when routine replaced dynamism and glamour, as a result of the new British policy of stabilising relations with Indian states, and by the 1870s increased administrative importance had been placed upon political officers. Moreover, by the very nature of his duties the political agent often found himself isolated for long periods from the company of Europeans in conditions which, even by the standards of British India, were primitive and uncomfortable. In such locations political officers and rulers were highly reliant upon their relationships with each other, relationships which were heavily influenced by their social, cultural and educational backgrounds, their personal temperaments and their previous experience. Sir Lepel Griffin, Agent to the Governor-General in Central India from 1881 to 1888, stressed the value of recruiting 'patient, intelligent, self-reliant and discreet' officers, as 'the political agent is often the only Englishman with whom chief and people come in contact'. Such an officer was 'their last and surest refuge against oppression, with the result that the people in India most attached to the Government, and most ready to obey its slightest wish, are often to be found among the population of native States'.[55]

After the Mutiny politicals were overwhelmingly military men recruited from the Staff Corps of the Indian Army.[56] In stark contrast to the other main branches of government, revenue and justice, civilians comprised only a small part of the service. The main reason behind the post-Mutiny preference for military rather than civilian personnel in political posts was one of economy. Man for man, Staff Corps officers cost less than civilians, 'perhaps as much as Rs. 1,000 a month less for men of equal standing'.[57] Moreover salary scales in the two services were calculated differently. In the Indian Civil Service, a man's pay was determined by his length of service; in the Political Service,[58] by the importance of his appointment. A satisfactory time-scale system was not introduced until the second decade of the twentieth century and, owing to the shortage of command posts, promotional opportunities for most officers were extremely limited. In 1873 the Governor of Bombay noted that the 'prizes of the Political Department are so few that the majority of Political officers can expect to rise to no higher pay than Rs. 1,200 [monthly]', roughly equivalent to £120.[59] The financial prospects of the Political Service declined further during the last decades of the century as a consequence of inflation. The cost of living in India, particularly for Europeans, increased sharply from the 1880s and despite meagre increases in civil salaries the real wages of Indian public servants were lower in 1900 than they had been at any time since the Mutiny. Embittered by long-standing grievances over pay and promotion, the rank and file of the service retained little faith in the good intentions of the Political Secretariat, despite the fact that the finance department and Whitehall were responsible for major decisions in these areas.

The most important part of the application form for the Political Service was the section devoted to comments from the candidate's commanding officer. High on the list of information solicited were queries about the applicant's popularity, horsemanship and sporting ability. Significantly, referees, whether commanding officers or senior men in the government, almost never mentioned the mental ability of their proteges. Admittedly applicants had to have passed all their army examinations plus a test in Hindustani, but in view of the departmental prejudice against civilians it seems likely that book-learning and related skills were not highly thought of by the men who administered the selection process. Even William Lee-Warner, one of the most cerebral of nineteenth-century Indian civilians, when asked by the Adjutant-General to draw up a list of desirable qualifications for political employees, settled for the social factor: 'A Pol. Officer has to deal with ruling chiefs and nobles in his capacity as representative of the British Govt.; it therefore follows that he should be a gentleman'.[60]

As a result intellectually the Political Service fell far short of the standard of the Indian Civil Service, which itself did not always maintain a particularly rigorous selection process for candidates. On the other hand there was probably something to be said for the government's argument that political work required more than just intellectual agility. Most of the *durbars* in the mid-nineteenth century were still run on basically paternal lines by high-caste officials skilled in courtly intrigue. In this relatively unbureaucratic world, a political officer who surrounded himself with files was unlikely to make headway.[61] To win the confidence of the rulers personal contact was essential. The men who succeeded most at this task were invariably 'those with the most magnetic personalities: extroverts and sporting types, sensitive to the cultural milieu of the courts but strong-willed enough to resist the temptations inherent in the environment'.[62]

Except for civilian members of the Political Service, who worked for three years in the 'revenue line' before joining up, political officers received no special administrative or judicial training. Armed only with manuals, grammars and legal texts, they were despatched into the field to learn their trade by experience. Much depended on the individual coming to terms with his social environment. Months or even years might be spent in building up the right contacts, mastering a new vernacular if a political agent came from a different region and becoming familiar with the customs and prejudices of the people. Length of tenure could have an important bearing on a political agent's performance. It was surprising, therefore, that the transfer of political officers tended to become increasingly more frequent. In 1877 political appointments in Bombay averaged over a duration of four years; by 1901 the average had fallen by half to just over two years. The reason for this apparent paradox was the government's fear, confirmed by costly experience, that 'too long an exposure to the problems and personalities of one state or region might encourage an unhealthy spirit of partisanship' among the officers concerned.[63]

A political agent posted to a large agency comprising many small states had on the whole a much tougher assignment than one appointed to a single state agency or residency. Not only were there more *durbars* to be won over but also there were the sheer physical problems of getting around such a large area, especially in the type of terrain commonly encountered in central India and Orissa where many of the small states were located. The annual winter tour, which was supposed to put political officers in continuous touch with their agency, was too brief to be good for more than 'showing the flag'. Moreover by the late nineteenth century the *durbars* were often sufficiently cognisant of the workings of the political system to make sure that for the duration of his stay the political agent failed to unearth information which might reflect unfavourably on the ruling regime. Some political agents may have been able to surmount these obstacles, but 'judging from the paucity and naivety of much of the information contained in the periodic summaries which were filed with the Secretariat, they were probably in the minority'.[64] By the twentieth century there was a groundswell of dissatisfaction with existing procedures of training and recruitment. Even by its own standards the Political Service had failed to attract enough men of a sufficiently high calibre from the Indian Civil Service and, more importantly, from the Staff Corps of the Indian Army, which was naturally reluctant to release its best young regimental officers for civil employment.

Secretariat officials were frequently criticised for being out of touch with their political officers on the ground. In the nineteenth century the Government of India saw no incongruity in appointing men to the Political Secretariat without benefit of a practical apprenticeship in the states. Charles Gonne, political secretary in the Bombay Government for a record term of 20 years (1864–84), never set foot in a native state in an official capacity during his entire Indian career. His celebrated successor, William Lee-Warner, served only 18 months in Kolhapur prior to taking over as political secretary. The secretariat was a closed shop to the vast majority of members of the Political Service, who were destined to spend their careers exclusively in subordinate stations. Feelings of hostility and frustration towards the secretariat were exacerbated by what the subordinate men saw as 'a gradual and deliberate erosion of their power and authority'.[65]

Adding to local officers' sense of powerlessness was the dramatic improvement in communications which occurred during the late nineteenth century. Prior to 1870 not many states were linked to headquarters by the telegraph, and almost none by the railway. As a result the man on the spot was frequently compelled to take the initiative in committing government to a particular course of action. During the 1870s, and still more in the 1880s and 1890s, a network of railways and telegraph lines was constructed across the country, some financed by the states themselves, with the result that the political officer became more and more a mere channel of communication between the British Government and the ruler. Although still an important link in the chain of command, he could no longer maintain a regular influence on the course of imperial policy and was increasingly stifled by bureaucracy.

Crown Representative records display a marked change over the final 30 years of the century; the intimate, paternalistic approach of resident to ruler alters to a more fractious, less patient tone as the officer concerned is beset by an increasingly sophisticated administration on one hand and the scrutiny of his superiors on the other. At the same time, a highly fluid situation developed in many states. A number of rulers tried to redefine their position through negotiation, evasion or contestation, and official views shifted over time in response to the changing interests and outlook of the British in India.[66] With a lack of consistent policy emanating from senior levels of the Government of India as to a clear-cut role for the future of the princes, the rulers and their British advisors on the spot frequently appeared as 'people whose plans were often formulated on the run, or in the dark because of lack of knowledge ... struggling valiantly to "muddle through"'.[67]

1

SUCCESSION

The process of succession was not regulated in India before British rule and was often highly questionable in the successor states to the Mughal Empire. Due to the fluidity of inheritance laws Muslim rulers tended to emerge from a large body of favourites connected with a dead ruler's harem and concubines, and even in Hindu royal families an eldest son might not succeed if he proved to be incapable of fulfilling the strenuous demands of leadership. A prince had the prerogative of choosing among his sons for his heir, and the rules of descent could be and were manipulated in the face of contingency. Moreover in the case of a disputed succession a successful candidate frequently required the support of an outside power with the inevitable strings attached. Under Mughal rule there was a great variety of such outside powers, large and small, with different agendas to fulfil. In contrast in the last decades of the nineteenth century the British were able, given the opportunity, to manipulate the rules of descent with the single-minded, unconditional purpose of arriving at their desired form of westernised government in the Indian states.

In the latter part of the nineteenth century the Government of India never relinquished its right to sanction royal successions, and in the cause of instigating 'good government' took advantage of every available opportunity to install candidates of its choice. There was a concerted effort on the part of political officers during the period to settle the matter of succession prior to a ruler's death, and of those successions which were disputed the vast majority was resolved with none of the infighting and bloodletting which had occurred as a matter of course between various branches of royal families before British rule. Wars of succession such as those in Bhopal in 1742 and in Jaipur in 1743 ceased to occur. No doubt the lack of conflict was largely due to the late eighteenth- and early nineteenth-century British guarantees to princes to fulfil both their internal and external defence requirements, thereby ensuring that the usurper of a legitimate heir to a *gadi*[1] would feel the full force of British military power. The granting of adoption *sanads* to some princes was another significant factor. By making the succession process more standardised, the cases of disputed inheritance were much reduced. However the absence of bloodshed is also indicative of the fact that royal rulers and their families were remarkably quiescent in accepting without challenge the ruling of the paramount power when it came to successions. Through lack of opposition the British were enabled, principally through the enthronement of young, responsive candidates, to take a leading role as early as possible in the princely life cycle, a position which was maintained with great determination through the control of royal education and marriage.

Early Succession Issues

The East India Company took an early step in asserting a degree of interference in the internal affairs of Indian states through its interest in the succession of rulers. To some extent the Company was assuming the mantle of the significant powers, the principal *sanad*-holders[2] of the Mughal Empire who entered a succession dispute to support the legitimacy of one candidate for a princely throne and, if the candidate were successful, to exact a tribute. This strategy was used dozens of times in the eighteenth century with a wide variety of groups as the outside power. Dost Mohammed Khan of Bhopal used it against the Rajput houses of western Malwa, and in the Bhopal succession of 1728 it was ultimately the *sanad*-grantor, the Nizam of Hyderabad, who decided which of Dost Mohammed's two eligible sons was to succeed him. The subordinate treaties made by the French and British with

Indian states towards the end of the century were 'simply European terms for a very common indigenous phenomenon'.[3]

As was the case for the major *sanad*-holders under Mughal rule, the potential scope for intervention by a resident in a succession remained broad partly because of political conditions within many states. The line of inheritance for most Indian dynasties followed no absolute or clear rule. Male rulers customarily engaged in sexual relations with a variety of types of wives and concubines, the offspring of whom made claims to their common father's estate. Problems were caused also by adoption in the case of wives who failed to produce a son and heir. Robbins Burling, having examined successions in several principal Maratha houses, concluded that

> Sons had a greater claim than brothers, elder brothers had prec-
> edence over younger brothers, and natural sons had a stronger
> claim than adopted sons. Except for the exclusive rights of the
> male line, however, none of these priorities were absolute.[4]

Residents, acting as an independent force, frequently held the balance of power among the various pretenders to a throne, each of whom might hold the loyalty of only a small faction in the court or army as his basis of support within the state. Therefore upon the death of a ruler the resident, and the Company's political and military force which he represented, could often prove the arbiter of succession, to the political or financial advantage of the Company. Even before its first appointment of residents in 1764 the Company involved itself in the succession of Indian dynasties in both the Carnatic and Bengal. The sanction of successions within states provided an admirable oppor-tunity for the tightening of British control. A ruler who owed his accession to the tacit or active approval of the Company incurred an obligation which affected his relationship with the resident. Moreover since the nomination of a successor depended on the blessing of the Company, potential heirs saw the resident as an 'assessor, whose good reports might prove vital to their future prospects'.[5]

The level of the Company's interference in succession reached its peak with the 'doctrine of lapse'. Although it did not originate with

Lord Dalhousie, this measure was exercised by him most frequently and extensively. British recognition was given as a matter of course to heirs in the direct line of succession, but when a prince died without heirs the government assumed the right to take over his state. Ordinarily a prince was able to avert this fate by adopting a son who succeeded to the throne as if he were the legal heir. Dalhousie's innovation lay in consistently refusing to sanction such adoptions, stating that on all occasions 'where heirs natural shall fail, the territory should be made to lapse and adoption should not be permitted, excepting in those cases in which some strong political reason may render it necessary to depart from the general rule'.[6]

A heated debate in Britain and among the British in India was engendered over whether such action was justified on the basis of the interpretation of Hindu, Muslim, British or international law.[7] The details of the application of the doctrine varied considerably. The rajas of Satara and Jhansi had both adopted sons prior to their deaths (in 1847 and 1853 respectively). Despite these formal adoptions, the Company refused to acknowledge the adopted sons as heirs and, in the case of Satara, the governor-general further justified annexation on the grounds that the Company had created the state and, when it served the Company's convenience, it could be annexed as 'a practical, administrative consolidation'.[8] In the case of Nagpur, the ruler had no son, natural or adopted, and the Company annexed the state on the raja's death in 1853. The Company also annexed a number of smaller states under the doctrine when justified by its own administrative purposes, awaiting the death of the incumbent ruler as a convenient point to take over his state.

The Company even asserted its right to determine the succession to the Mughal imperial dynasty. To the Company the reigning emperor, Bahadur Shah II, represented a vestige of the old political order. Although the Company wished to eliminate the emperor's remaining political authority, it was unwilling to do so abruptly. As a result, the resident at Delhi reached an agreement in 1852 with the heir apparent that the Company would recognise his claim against those of his brothers in return for a lesser political status. In exchange for the support of the Company, he agreed 'to accept a reduced title (from Padshah,

'Emperor', to Shahzada, 'King's son'), meet the governor-general in ceremonies symbolising equality, and transfer the imperial palace (the Red Fort) to the Company, taking residence elsewhere'.[9] In 1856, however, the Company obtained the opportunity to further degrade the Mughal dynasty when the heir apparent predeceased his father. The Company refused to recognise the emperor's choice of another son as heir. Indeed, it determined to abolish the dynasty altogether on the death of Bahadur Shah. This proposed blatant interference in the imperial succession did much to raise public hostility to the Company in 1857, when the emperor proved a major focal point for the uprising against the British.

After 1857 the British Crown took over the government of India from the Company, and to all intents and purposes returned to a policy of indirect rule. In order to safeguard the dynasties of the princes, the viceroy, Lord Canning, dispensed with the doctrine of lapse and, as discussed in the introduction, in 1862 bestowed adoption *sanads* upon rulers above the rank of *jagirdar* who guaranteed to maintain the loyalty expressed in their treaties. In his study of Indian princely history during the period, Bhupen Qanungo states that although the adoption *sanads* bound the states as never before in 'ties of good faith and goodwill' to the British Government, in no way did they diminish the position of power which the British had assumed in the days of the doctrine of lapse. The paramount power was still the ultimate arbiter in cases of a native ruler dying without a natural heir. No treaties between equal powers, only *sanads* or grants, 'and these explicitly conditional and revocable', contained the assurance of the British Government regarding succession by adoptions. Qanungo contends that

> In accepting Canning's adoption *sanads*, the Native Rulers were accepting, by clear implication, the hitherto disputed claim of the Government that, as Paramount Power, it had the right to decide the validity of a succession to a *gadi*, to sanction a succession, and to intervene in a Native State to settle a disputed succession.[10]

Thus the total legal effect of such *sanads* was to emphasise the power of the Government of India 'in matters relating to life and death' over every state.[11] Writing in January 1875 the secretary of state, Lord Salisbury, summed up the situation in his advice to the viceroy, Lord Northbrook:

> It should be impressed on the minds of the feudatories that their privileges under the Proclamation and the Sunnud are contingent on their good behaviour and that misconduct releases the Paramount Power from special obligation, and will not merely involve the supersession of the offender. If their misconduct took the form of rebellion, it would probably involve annexation; and in a lesser degree it involves the adjustment of the succession, not according to their customs, but according to the discretion of the Paramount Power.[12]

Although less than 200 *sanads* were issued, the 400 or 500 states which did not receive such a written guarantee from the British Government were all given to understand by the tone of official utterances on the subject that the paramount power wished 'to perpetuate all loyal states' and to acknowledge adopted successors to their *gadis* on the failure of natural heirs. Thereafter there was no dispute about the right to adopt. But often, when a prince died leaving an adopted son, 'collaterals would weigh in with petitions drafted by the most eminent lawyers in India alleging a flaw here or there in the adoption and pressing their own claims'.[13] If there had been no adoption, the case was further complicated. It required some legal ability and a good knowledge of local conditions and personalities to advise on such cases, which, if the state was of importance, were not finally settled by the viceroy but referred to the Secretary of State for India.

In larger and more powerful states, lost opportunities to regulate successions were much regretted by the British. In Gwalior in 1877 the birth of a son was seen by Salisbury as a disappointment, as the secretary of state had hoped that Maharaja Jayaji Rao Scindia's prejudice against adopting 'would ultimately place it in the power of the British Government to divide his state in two before providing for the succession'.[14] In 1875 at the time of the selection of a successor to the late Maharaja of Alwar in Rajputana, dismay was expressed by the India Office that by omitting to regrant the state on a formal basis by an adoption *sanad* or otherwise, a chance had been lost of 'placing the relations between the British Government and Ulwur State on a footing less anomalous and unsuited to the present condition than is possible under existing treaties with that State'. Under similar circumstances, it was suggested, the British Government should not only recognise a succession on general grounds, but should also attach conditions which would give the paramount power 'a fair equivalent' for the external protection and internal support which it provided. Although the confiscation of a state was ruled out following the Mutiny, the British could exercise much power in applying such conditions, and it was stressed that the Indian rulers should be taught to look upon the restoration of native rule as 'a favour, not a right'.[15]

The Legal Position

In 1886 in a paper on various principles applying to political relations with Indian states, Sir William Lee-Warner clarified the policy which had arisen during the decades following the granting of adoption *sanads*. Theoretically in the event of a ruler dying without natural heirs and without exercising the powers of adoption conferred upon him, the doctrine of lapse might legally operate. Under these circumstances the declared policy of the Queen's Proclamation protected the integrity of the state, however 'the rights of the reigning dynasty' were no longer secured by formal agreement. Lee-Warner stressed that 'The perpetuation of Native rule is wider than the perpetuation of the houses of Native rulers, and it is based on grounds of general policy, not on an exclusive regard for individual claims'. It was to be 'a policy and not a pledge', to be 'administered subject to conditions' and 'of course capable of exceptions under the pressure of adequate exigency'.[16]

In Lee-Warner's view there was a 'wide and fundamental difference between escheat and confiscation' and the attachment of conditions to the restoration of native rule in states such as Mysore or Baroda after the deposition of their respective rulers. In adoptions or successions guaranteed by *sanad* the minimum of interference was exercised, but in the 'selection' of a successor a wider play was allowed to the Government of India. The distinction between adoption and selection was of great importance. The Government of India was bound by Canning's *sanads* to recognise an adoption made by a ruler in accordance with Hindu law and the 'customs of the house'. Where there was no valid adoption, as, for example, in the case of the heir to a deposed ruler, the government could either recognise an invalid adoption or exercise its own selection. In all cases the sanction of the British Government was necessary before any succession could be proclaimed, therefore 'every endeavour should be made to induce a ruler to settle the succession in his lifetime by making an adoption, or choosing a successor in accordance with his *Sanads*'.[17]

Where there was the possibility of a British selection of a successor, as in the case of Mysore, British policy was under great scrutiny. The transfer of Mysore back from British to princely rule had been under consideration since 1861 when Krishnaraja Wadiyar, the former maharaja deposed in 1831 upon grounds of misgovernment, petitioned Lord Canning for the restoration of his powers.[18] Both Canning and his successor, Lord Lawrence, played for time in the hope that Mysore could be incorporated into British India upon the maharaja's death. However in 1865 the maharaja adopted an heir. The British were under no obligation to recognise the adoption, for Mysore had not been under princely rule when Canning bestowed adoption *sanads* upon the princes. Both the viceroy and the secretary of state, Sir Charles Wood, were prepared to withhold recognition, but Wood retired from office in 1866 and the Liberal Government of which he had been a member was defeated in the same year. In 1867 Lord Cranborne, the Conservative secretary of state whose respect for the Indian princes was 'a frequent source of irritation to Lawrence', pledged that the state would be restored to native rule.[19]

In 1879, when considering how best to effect the transfer to the maharaja's successor, Chamarajendra Wadiyar, the Government of India prepared a draft Instrument of Transfer including detailed restrictions upon the powers of the adopted prince and expressed the wish that they might serve as a precedent to be adopted in all cases of states emerging from minority periods.[20] These restrictions came into force in Mysore in 1881 upon the young ruler's investiture, but a more general application of them was disallowed by the secretary of state, Lord Cranbrook, who considered that they would be interpreted as an unwarranted revision of the treaties with the states. Mysore was used as a showcase for British policy towards the states in the late nineteenth century, helped to a great extent by the existing strong British presence in the administration. British politicians both in Britain and India were well aware of the importance placed by Indians upon the future of the young adopted heir and of the question mark hanging over the restoration.[21]

Conscious of the highly sensitive nature of post-Mutiny princely successions, of which Mysore was an example, the Government of India made it patently clear that it wished to be thoroughly briefed in any case of disputed succession and that such matters were not to be concluded locally without further consultation. In 1885 the Bombay Government reported that a decision had been arrived at in the case of the death of the Nawab of Savanur and the succession of his cousin, Abdul Tabriz Khan. There were several claimants to the *gadi* and the local government had been guided by the opinion of its legal officer, submitting no information as to whether or not the succession was in accordance with the wishes of the late nawab's choice. William Lee-Warner stressed that 'We have generally held that in recognising a distant succession the customs of the family, the wishes of the deceased or his widow, and the qualifications of the selected successor, are the main factors in a decision', particularly where an adoption *sanad* had been given, as in the case of Savanur.[22] Lee-Warner hoped that it would be possible for the Government of India to support the local government's decision, but equally that no action should be taken which might 'compromise the free selection of the Government of India'. In his opinion, 'If there was time to refer to the legal advisers there was time to refer to the Government of India'. Whereas in Hindu law there were separate rules which regulated successions to 'Principalities and Kingdoms', works on Muslim law did not contain such rules. Therefore claims by contending parties needed to be decided upon after consultation with a 'competent' law officer.[23] The viceroy eventually accepted the succession of Abdul Tabriz Khan, but the point had been made.[24]

The Government of India, despite its ostensible adherence to the rule of law, fought hard to maintain its right to act as adjudicator in cases such as that of Savanur. A memorandum to the Marquis of Hartington, Secretary of State for India, from the Viceroy's Council in 1880 set out frankly the objections of the council to the referral to the high courts of 'disputed questions of laws or fact' that might arise in political cases. In the opinion of the Government of India points of native law and local and family custom arose in many cases, and it was hard to see how it would be possible to 'define or circumscribe' cases in which reference was made to the high courts. In central India and Rajputana constant questions were arising of succession, tribute and boundary, and it was likely that the defeated party would urge that justice was denied to him until the claim was fairly argued out before a court of law. Discontented parties frequently sent agents to Calcutta to consult lawyers, British or native, in order to argue their client's case before agents to the governor-general. If legislation were enacted allowing accessibility to the high courts in disputed questions, professional advisers would concentrate their efforts upon obtaining submission of their case to the presidency courts[25] and would demand papers and correspondence (including records in state archives) to be produced in court, a request which could rarely be refused. Therefore the proposed enactment would materially affect not only the jurisdiction of rulers but also the influence exercised by political officers and the Government of India in upholding the authority and responsibility of rulers and in dealing with disputes which might otherwise lead to disorder.[26]

The council appreciated that it might be argued that the practice of referring all disputed questions of law to a court of justice would introduce stability and uniformity into the 'fluctuating and irregular mass of usages and traditional precedents' involved in the regulation of succession disputes. However stereotyping laws that governed successions to states and the various jurisdictions that a ruler exercised in his territory could also radically change the relations between a state and the Government of India. The effect of moulding constitutional laws would lead to a tendency of states to subside gradually into 'proprietary sovereignties'. It would not only curtail the discretion of the

Government of India in the free exercise of its influence to choose 'fit and qualified' rulers, but it would also diminish the share now held by the leading men of the principal states in the determination of such questions, of which they were normally the best judges. Whereas the point of law was usually a subordinate element in the determination of cases of high importance to the constitution of a state, this element would acquire predominance if a practice of referral were to prevail. A decision in a succession case which followed the 'wishes and votes' of leading *sirdars* and others was often arbitrary and independent of fixed rules. This kind of consideration would be likely to fall into disrepute or neglect if matters were to be decided, as the high court would decide them, by the same principle as that governing the devolution of property. Moreover when a case of this kind was referred to a court of law it was inevitably followed by litigation. Two hostile parties would face each other, and frequently those parties would be the government and 'its own feudatories', which would be extremely damaging to the influence of political officers and the existing good feeling between such officers and the rulers to whom they were attached.[27]

However, despite the heed which the above memorandum suggested should be paid to the wishes and votes of leading *sirdars*, such wishes and votes were not intended to challenge the power of the Government of India. It was pointed out in 1885 when the Maharawat of Pratapgarh died without an heir that the custom prevailed in some Rajput states of electing a successor before government orders had been received. Sirdars and officials sometimes carried out a ceremony of investiture in order that the *gadi* was not left empty even for a single day, and there was no break in the 'direction of general business or trade'. The Government of India considered that ceremonies of this kind ought to be discouraged, since they conferred no right and tended to 'keep alive mistaken ideas as to the source from which Native States derive their authority', producing 'much practical embarrassment' for the government.[28] Nevertheless, in view of the fact that there was a requirement in Rajputana to settle a succession as quickly as possible, if a highly competent political officer were present it was accepted that he could confer with the royal women and principal nobles rather than referring the matter to the Government of India. In the case of the somewhat unclear Mewar succession in 1884, the resident, Colonel C. K. M. Walter, described how the maharanis summoned all the principal *sirdars* and officials to the door of the *zenana*, where a unanimous decision was announced in favour of Fateh Singh becoming maharana.[29] The Government of India praised the 'care and forethought' of Colonel Walter in dealing with the question, recognising that 'An officer of less experience might have been at a loss how to act or advise under such circumstances'.[30]

Minorities

The channels of British influence upon Indian rulers were both direct and indirect. The political agent not only advised in the matter of a prince's education but also was frequently involved in the setting up of a provisional administration until the ruler attained his powers, usually at 18. As the paramount power, the government reserved the right if the new ruler happened to be a minor to take steps to safeguard his patrimony during his minority. Minority rule provided the occasion for strong, often creative, intervention and laid the basis for subsequent influence. The policy governing British relations with the Indian princes in the latter part of the nineteenth century determined that 'intimate British involvement in all but the largest states would not be allowed to continue beyond a ruler's majority, when the established patterns of administration would continue under the supervision of the adult raja'. Therefore if changes were to be made in the administrative basis of a state under minority rule, they could not simply be introduced by the authority of the agent but would have to be 'deeply ingrained in the bureaucracy'. Any advances in the administration would otherwise be artificial and easily removed or adapted when British participation was reduced.[31] The minority administration was an exact replica of the larger administrative machinery existing in British India. The Government of India with a regency or minority council under its control usually reorganised the state government already in force, which was frequently outmoded and medieval in many respects, and cautiously introduced its own administrative ideas.

Since British policy was to appoint a political officer to a council of regency[32] or to approve its membership, thus maintaining a position whereby British economic and political interests could be furthered, there were obvious advantages to the choice of an heir who was as young as possible. In Baroda, for example, the deposition of the gaekwar, Malhar Rao,[33] in 1875 provided an ideal opportunity for British sanction of the adoption of a minor to give more lengthy British control over a major state. Northbrook admitted that there would be

> a distinct advantage to the Baroda state in a minority, for the sink of iniquity surrounding the old Court can be thoroughly purged, and we must be content to bear the further attack of having set up a doubtful claim for the purpose of being able virtually to direct the administration of Baroda during a long minority.[34]

Malhar Rao was replaced by a 12-year-old boy, Sayaji Rao, son of a village headman from an obscure lineage of the Gaekwar family living in Maharashtra. Despite his immediate inability to rule due to his age it was stressed in British official documents that extensive enquiries had been carried out into claims to the succession made by various members of the ruling family, and copper plates and family documents had indisputably proved Sayaji Rao to be the most desirable candidate.[35] British reluctance to surrender its newly found power in the state was illustrated by the fact that, even after the gaekwar had been installed for nearly two years, there was a strong recommendation from the Government of India that no alteration should be made in the constitution of the Baroda Agency for at least a further two years. This recommendation was in agreement with Northbrook's minute of March 1876, stating that 'Baroda State should remain under the control of the Governor-General in Council... This conclusion is founded on considerations affecting the State and its administration; and also on grounds of general policy'.[36]

In the case of Hyderabad, a state equal in gun ranking to Baroda,[37] British policy towards succession was carefully worked out in advance. In an official despatch of 1877 the secretary of state expressed his agreement with the Government of India that because the nizam was a minor the paramount power acting on his behalf might 'justly' make the selection of a successor upon the failure of lineal heirs. It was considered that the Muslim civil law of inheritance furnished 'scanty materials for a conclusion as to the succession to a regality', moreover the terms used by Lord Canning in his *sanad* measure did not 'possess that precision which would constitute a guide under all circumstances'. By these terms much was left to the decision of the paramount power upon each case as it occurred, and the secretary of state was not of the opinion that it was desirable 'to supply the blank which Lord Canning has left, by the establishment of a new rule, or the creation of a precedent binding the future action of the Government'.[38]

A political advantage might be derived by recognising in the reigning nizam a right of selection, which the Government of India would practically exercise, but this convenience would be purchased at the cost of vesting in a future nizam a new prerogative which might not be exercised with discretion. To retain as much British power as possible within Hyderabad it was considered wiser to recognise the most suitable candidate 'as an act of favour – but carefully avoiding the admission of any right'. It was emphatically not the intention of the secretary of state to give a decision which would be taken as a precedent for other Muslim states under similar circumstances; each case which presented serious difficulty was to be reported for separate consideration.[39]

The desirability of gaining increased control in a state, albeit one considerably smaller than Hyderabad, was apparent in the case of Pudukkottai in south India, where the British were prepared to challenge the local establishment by bending the rules of succession to suit their needs.[40] In 1877 recognition was given to the adoption by the Raja of Pudukkottai of his daughter's son as heir, in supersession of the claims of the son of the raja's deceased brother. The contention had been made by officials of the state that there had been no failure of natural heirs to allow such an adoption, and this action was therefore 'opposed to the customs of the Rajah's family'. However the result of the proposed adoption would be a prolonged minority, during which the state would be under British management, whereas on the raja's fairly imminent death, the nephew would be 'a young man with (probably) no training, save what he has got from priests, courtiers and dancing girls'. It was therefore agreed that the Government of India would comply with the raja's request, although 'Recognition should be based not on strict interpretation of the *sunnud*, but consideration of general policy'.[41]

The Pudukkottai succession was not an isolated example of official enthusiasm to introduce 'good government' through the education of young princes in British hands. Following the death of Sidi Ibrahim Khan, the Nawab of Janjira, in 1879, the leading *sirdars* of the state elected the ruler's illegitimate son to the vacant *gadi*, 'no doubt as a fresh assertion of right of control over the administration of the state'. However on the grounds that the education of Ahmed Khan, the only legitimate son of Sidi Ibrahim, had been expressly provided for in an agreement of 1870, the Government of India turned down the *sirdars'* request. The young prince would not be allowed to assume the administration until he was 21 and had finished his education at Rajkumar College.[42] The choice as successor of a young, malleable prince who could be transformed into an effective ruler and an active prop to the British Government was seen to be ample justification for sanctioning a succession which ignored local feeling.

Minority rule was also the goal in the state of Idar in western India.[43] In 1901, following the death of the maharaja without male issue one of his widows, the Chavhan Rani, claimed to be two months pregnant. The political agent was aware of the fact that if the pregnancy were true and resulted in the birth of a male heir, the succession would be in direct line. If not, the next course of action would be the recognition of the nearest collateral, Jagatsinghji of Sawar, a distant relative of the late maharaja, a man of between 55 and 60 years old and 'neither by training nor by education a desirable successor to the *gadi* of as important a state as Idar'.

The Government of Bombay recognised the advantage of using the precedent of the Baroda succession, in which sanction was granted to the widow of the late ruler to adopt, 'within certain limitations', irrespective of any collateral's claim. If this policy were adopted in Idar, the senior maharani would probably be willing to adopt Jagatsinghji's son in place of his father. The financial position of the state was so dire that it was felt that the longer the period of 'nursing' under British control the better. Under Jagatsinghji the administration would be likely to deteriorate and security for the heavy debts due to the government would be 'appreciably decreased'. In the circumstances it would be most desirable to have a long minority, either if the maharani's pregnancy resulted in a male heir or if there were an adopted son, in order that from the start a scheme could be drawn up for reforming the administration and setting the finances of the state upon a sound basis. However it was admitted that imperial levies on states would not help such measures. In the event of a collateral or an adopted son succeeding, the state would be liable for a further payment of about Rs. 400,000 for *nazar*,[44] which, on top of a loan contracted during the famine of 1899, would bring Idar's debt to the Government of India to ten *lakhs* of rupees.[45]

Finally it was decided that the government of Idar would be better handed over to a proven administrator rather than a minority council. The Rathors of Jodhpur were closely related to the rulers of Idar, and while the other claimants were trying to make good their claims with the viceroy, Pratap Singh, the third son of the ruler of Jodhpur, appealed directly to Queen Victoria, sending her a cable saying simply, 'Idar is mine'.[46] Despite the loss of an opportunity for minority rule, the Government of India conceded that Pratap Singh was able to claim 'a substantial share of credit for the prosperity, self development and good government in Marwar' and fulfilled the requirements of the official maxim

> that, where there are no direct or lineal heirs to a Chiefship, and when no real and valid adoption has been made, the succession must be determined by selection, the principal considerations being the personal fitness of the nominee and the general interests of the State.[47]

The British desire for room to manoeuvre in the general interest of princely subjects was in some cases helped by the particular conditions of inheritance existing in some states. Successions in Travancore (and Cochin) on the south-west coast of India differed from other states in that they followed Marumakatayam law, by which descent was mat-rilineal and only female children of the family were able to carry on the succession. In 1899 the Travancore royal family consisted of four members, the rani, aged 51, the maharaja, aged 42, the elaya raja, aged 32 and his brother, aged 28. It was clear that the family would become extinct unless there was an adoption and the choice fell on two girls, aged three and four, whose mothers were daughters of the sister of the rani and therefore blood relations.

The elaya raja saw no need to adopt until the lifetime of the last remaining male and considered that the children were too young; how-ever, in the eyes of the Government of India, this was not an ordinary case of succession to family property but an act of state and a 'politi-cal necessity', needing official sanction before the proposed adoption could take place. It was also an opportunity to put an undisputed suc-cession in place before the last surviving prince was on his deathbed. The youth of the girls was a consideration which would soon cease to be problematic, and there was no reason why the girls should not live to be mothers of numerous offspring; moreover the princes were not in particularly good health.[48] Following a legal opinion given by V. Bhashyam Iyengar, the advocate-general, recommending that the adoption was valid according to Hindu law and custom, the resident was informed to advise the Travancore *durbar* that the adoption would be recognised.[49]

Successions such as those in Idar and Travancore were not always resolved with the same ease and relative harmony. There were many cases of less amicable royal family inheritances, and British officials were on occasions able to take advantage of existing animosity to install the candidate most likely to further their goal of 'good government'.

Royal Family Disputes

The British took care to guard the interests of rightful heirs to Indian thrones whenever there was a whiff of intrigue in royal circles. Such a case occurred in Bhopal in 1891 when there was speculation that the ruling begam was attempting to break the chain of female rulers. From its establishment in 1709, the state had produced prominent female figures who were active in public and political life. Women's political influence in Bhopal was carried a stage further in 1819 when the nawab died suddenly, leaving his 18-year-old widow, Qudsia Begam, to be invested with the supreme authority of the state. Appointed regent by the British political agent until her daughter, Sikander, came of age and married, Qudsia emerged from behind the veil, hired a tutor to teach Sikander the 'necessary skills of riding and the arts of war', then proceeded to introduce wide-ranging reforms. Sikander Begam followed in this tradition, forcibly claiming the throne from her husband and proving to be a highly competent ruler. She distinguished herself, in particular, by her loyalty to the British during the Mutiny and by large-scale administrative reforms. As a result the British withdrew their proviso that the husband of the begam would become nawab, naming her only daughter, Shah Jahan Begam, as sovereign in her own right upon the death of Sikander in 1867. When Shah Jahan Begam also failed to bear a son, the dynasty of female rule in Bhopal was confirmed.[50]

However under the influence of her second husband, Sadiq Hassan, Shah Jahan was estranged from her daughter, Sultan Jahan. The political agent in Bhopal reported in 1891 that the begam was determined to set aside the succession of Sultan Jahan in favour of her half-nephew, Miah Alamgir Muhammed Khan. Rumours circulated in the *Hindu Patriot* and the *Lucknow Advocate* of the ruler's intention to disinherit her daughter. Alamgir was 'in every sense base' as his father was a child of a liaison between the begam's father and a common bazaar woman, and the Minister of Bhopal was most emphatic that the question of a change in succession should not be countenanced. Sultan Jahan was heir-apparent by right of her descent through her mother and Sikander Begam, her grandmother. The Agent to the Governor-General in Central India, R. J. Crosthwaite, agreed that action should be taken to deflect a communication from the begam to the viceroy, since she would inevitably receive 'the ignominy of a refusal'. In any case he was of the opinion that the rumours contained little substance and that a challenge to the succession was unlikely to develop.[51]

In situations where a succession was not as clear-cut as that in Bhopal, the British were not above using family disputes as an excuse to call into play the 'right' to overrule the personal wishes of the ruler and install their own choice of candidate. One such case was that of the Nawab of Bahawalpur in the Punjab, who banished his son and heir, Mobarak Khan, to a prison fort in the desert in the hope that the government would recognise Haji Khan, the adopted son of a low-caste woman whom he subsequently married.[52] In 1897 the British felt bound to interfere in the interests of Mobarak Khan as, even if the life of the heir were not endangered, it was certain that several years in Kila Dherewar Fort would render him unfit for rule. The Punjab Government requested that the young prince be sent to Aitchison College in Lahore, despite the nawab's insistence that his son was being taught Urdu, Persian and arithmetic, as well as instruction in the Quran, by a tutor. However, despite its apparent support of Mobarak Khan, the Government of India doubted his capabilities as ruler and insisted that it had no reason to depart from its usual custom of refusing to make, during the nawab's lifetime, a specific declaration as to whom it would recognise as heir on his death. The foreign secretary, W. J. Cuningham, repeated the government line that the 'principle of primogeniture determines the succession of Mohammedan states, but the successor must be fit to rule'.[53]

Such deliberate procrastination on the part of the Government of India in order to achieve the most advantageous position at the time of succession was also apparent in another Punjab state when the Mir of Khairpur requested permission in 1899 to set aside his eldest son, Imam Bukhsh, in favour of his brother, Ahmed Ali, who was of 'inferior birth'. In the eyes of the British Imam Bukhsh was of a 'weak and incapable character', while Ahmed Ali's succession was 'out of the question'. However Imam Bukhsh had three sons, all 'bright and promising boys', the eldest of whom was doing well at Aitchison College, and it was possible that the Mir might well survive until they were older.[54] Following the death of the Mir ten years later it was agreed that Imam Bukhsh should succeed to the *gadi*. However as he had been regarded by the deceased ruler as 'unfitted mentally' to take over the administration he was instructed to act in all matters under the advice of his *vizier*, referring matters to the political agent where there were irreconcilable differences.[55]

A family rift between the Maharaja of Kashmir, Pratap Singh, and his brother, Amar Singh, gave rise to a similar situation in 1906. The maharaja asked the viceroy for permission to adopt the son of his cousin, the Raja of Poonch, rather than his brother's son, Hari Singh, ostensibly on religious grounds since Hari Singh was the only male child in the family and was under an obligation to undertake the funeral rites for his own father to the exclusion of others. The maharaja pleaded that 'for a pious Hindu it is the most important religious obligation to leave a son behind for the peace and salvation of his soul, and in the Hindu *Shastras* it is considered a great sin to die childless'. However it emerged that the real reason behind the request was the ill feeling between the maharaja and his brother, Amar Singh, that had existed since their father considered supplanting the elder by the younger.[56] Sir Louis Dane, Foreign Secretary to the Government of India, was of the opinion that there was little doubt that, as demonstrated by Rajput practice, the adoption of a brother or even a brother's son, even if the only son, was perfectly valid and recognised by the *shastras*. If the maharaja had already adopted his cousin's son, as was suspected, it would be necessary to take further steps to ensure that neither of the 'unfortunate children' was killed. The best action would be to call upon the maharaja to formally adopt either Amar Singh or his son to put a stop to the uncertainty. If he refused he would be informed that no other adopted son would be recognised as heir, and that it might also be necessary to place restrictions on his own powers.[57]

Sir Francis Younghusband, Resident at Kashmir, made it clear to Pratap Singh that the Government of India would have great difficulty in sanctioning any adoption which would involve superseding Amar Singh and his son. The *sanad* of adoption granted to the maharaja was in fact only a guarantee on the part of the government that the state would not be resumed upon the failure of natural heirs. The ruler had two, his brother and his nephew, and in the interests of the state it was necessary that one of the two should succeed.[58] However Younghusband was firmly reprimanded by Sir Louis for misleading the maharaja by suggesting that his brother or nephew would succeed even if he produced a son, which at his advanced age was highly unlikely. Should a legitimate and fully recognised son be born, the question would have to be reconsidered. Indeed the actual succession would, in accordance with the general policy of the government, be settled only when the vacancy to the *gadi* occurred. The resident had advised the ruler that the orders of the government fixed the succession upon a particular member of the family during the lifetime of a prince, rather than stressing the ultimate power of the government to arrive at a decision after a ruler's death.[59]

* * *

Following the 1858 Proclamation by Queen Victoria guaranteeing the tenure of the Indian dynasties, the problem of the sovereignty of the Indian rulers was reduced but not resolved. The incongruity of Indian sovereigns as subordinate to a body such as the East India Company lessened somewhat, as they were now directly subordinate to a sovereign power. However, despite much debate, no consensus ever emerged as to the precise legal status of the rulers. Since over the years each state negotiated its own series of treaties with the British, legal scholars could find no strict uniformity of principle with respect to the princely states as a whole. Questions of succession were, like other issues traditionally settled by individual princely authority, open to a certain amount of liberal interpretation on the part of the British.

It was anticipated that, where needed, an 'adjustment of the succession' through routine government sanction of inheritance could deal with potential princely misconduct. Whenever possible a minor was selected, giving the young heir as much time as possible for the purposes of education and administrative training. As was the case in other areas of the princely life cycle, in the latter part of the nineteenth century the British goal in the Indian states was the instigation of salubrious and accountable practice both in royal private life and government. Even after accession, if a young ruler was not performing well the British could lay down stringent conditions of rule. However if the Government of India wished to limit the personal power of a prince later in his reign, the terms of many treaties raised serious obstacles to major British intervention at that stage. It was therefore of the greatest importance that in the case of an adult succeeding to a *gadi*, the candidate had to be deemed 'fit to rule' by the Government of India. This phrase could cover a wide spectrum of conditions, and government decisions were absolute.

2

EDUCATION

With the arrival of Lord William Bentinck as governor-general in 1828, the British embarked upon an intensive programme of reform in India. Building upon what had previously been little more than a vague idea that somehow British rule ought to bring 'improvement', free traders, utilitarians and evangelicals created an ideology of imperial government shaped by the ideals of liberalism. The representatives of these groups differed over the urgency of reform and the relative importance of particular measures of reform, such as law or education. Nevertheless a common goal was to free individuals from their 'bondage to priests, despots and a feudal aristocracy' in order that those individuals could become autonomous, rational beings, leading a life of conscious deliberation and choice. Individual self-reliance, character and merit were required to shape a proper society, not a hierarchy that rewarded individuals on the basis of patronage and status.[1]

However after the Mutiny there was a re-examination of the idea that it was essential to sweep away old forms of vested authority in order to achieve the educational and moral reformation which would rescue India from continued degradation. Before 1857 it was accepted that modernisation required the setting up of a British-style government but, with the disappearance of annexation as a tool of feudatory policy, the British were forced to rely upon the malleability and adaptability of Indian institutions rather than direct intervention. They now discovered virtues in the traditional aspects of the society over which they ruled, as ideas emerged of ways in which they could be turned to good use.

In his 1835 *Minute on Indian Education*, the highly influential Thomas Babington Macaulay, a junior member of the Board of Control who was seconded to the Governor-General's Council in 1834, unwittingly anticipated the policy to be adopted towards princely tutelage after the Mutiny. He asserted that the British must 'do our best to form a class who may be the interpreters between us and the millions whom we govern; a class of persons, Indian in blood and colour, but English in taste, in opinions and in intellect'.[2] Like his mentor, James Mill, Macaulay believed that princely despotism had made a substantial contribution to India's ills, and when crafting his *Minute* undoubtedly did not contemplate the adoption of the native aristocracy as suitable 'interpreters'. But after 1857 the princes were seen in a new light. In their role of 'loyal feudatories' and a link between the paramount power and the Indian peasantry it became necessary to transform them into good natural leaders. On the one hand, young rulers needed to be taught the guidelines of good government based upon European liberal principles, and on the other there was a requirement to maintain the cultural bonds between princes and their subjects. Efforts were made from 1870 onwards both by formal education, through tutors or special schools and colleges, and by the influence of political officers at court to produce a new multi-faceted breed of ruler who would act as a force for progress within his territory.

Tutorial Credentials

In large and powerful principalities such as Baroda, Hyderabad and Mysore it was deemed desirable for training programmes for young princes to be carefully supervised by British tutors. Although some candidates from the Staff Corps were chosen for the job, many tutors were selected from the Indian Civil Service. The Gaekwar of Baroda, for example, was educated by Frederick Elliott of the Bombay Civil Service, and the Maharajas of Kolhapur and Bhavnagar were put under the tuition of Stuart Fraser, also of the Bombay Civil Service, who then became tutor to the minor Maharaja of Mysore. Brian Egerton, District Superintendent of Police in Ajmer, was tutor to both the Maharaja of Bikaner and the Nizam of Hyderabad, and J. W. D. Johnstone of the Education Department of the Government of India was tutor to Scindia, Maharaja of Gwalior.

In the first half of the nineteenth century candidates for the Indian Civil Service were instructed at Haileybury College before assuming their duties in India. It has been suggested that the educational background of members of the Service was in many cases not particularly rigorous, despite the presence of luminaries such as Thomas Malthus as lecturer in history and political economy.[3] The college faculty was said to be in a difficult position in maintaining academic standards and discipline. By carrying out its duties it could come into conflict with the Court of Directors which, through its patronage, selected students. If a student failed for academic inadequacies or was dismissed for misbehaviour, the appointing director lost out as well, as 'each student represented a valuable appointment'. Moreover it was frequently the restricted possibilities of a career in Britain rather than the attractiveness of an Indian career which determined candidacy.[4]

Haileybury was closed in December 1857, owing to the introduction of a new scheme in 1854 under which members of the Civil Service were appointed by competitive examination. It was clear that selection by merit would be more efficient and more just than selection by patronage. The 1854 committee, headed by Macaulay, still wanted 'gentlemen' to run the Indian administration, but it wanted gentlemen educated at Oxford and Cambridge rather than ones randomly chosen and herded together at Haileybury. Its most influential member, Benjamin Jowett, the future Master of Balliol College, was of the opinion that the Indian Civil Service would be a fine career for 'the picked men of the universities'.[5] However, despite a promising start the scheme began to founder. The desire for graduate recruitment had persuaded the committee to recommend 23 as the minimum age of entry, after which the selected candidates were supposed to spend two years at home in legal training for their future careers. While Haileybury men might have started their Indian career at 19, a new civilian would not begin his most basic work in the field until he was

25. Since this was an advanced age to be learning apprentice skills such as linguistics, the government reduced the maximum age to 22 in 1860 and to 21 six years later. It became increasingly hard for a man to acquire a good degree before passing the Indian Civil Service exam and to attempt to do both risked failure. A substantial number of candidates did not hold degrees from Oxbridge, as was originally desired, and a surprising proportion had not attended any university, a phenomenon that became increasingly evident in later competitions. Among the total number of competitors, the proportion of Oxbridge candidates declined from a high of 62 per cent in 1858 to a low of 8.2 per cent in 1874. Many thrifty, pragmatic middle-class people questioned the merit of spending a great deal of money on their son's university education when a shorter, less expensive, course at a cramming institution proved sufficient to succeed at the examination.[6]

The success of the crammers infuriated politicians, scholars and the Haileybury men and a more radical solution to the inadequacies of the system was provided by Lord Salisbury, who became Secretary of State for India in 1874 during the premiership of Benjamin Disraeli. In Salisbury's view it was essential to put candidates back into the universities and, against the advice of the viceroy, Lord Northbrook, it was decided that the Service exam would be taken at school-leaving age, after which the successful pupils would spend two 'probationary' years at a university studying a curriculum that included the languages of their chosen Indian province. Salisbury's system was inaugurated in 1879 and lasted until 1892, when higher age limits were brought back to the relief of men such as Jowett and Monier Monier-Williams, Professor of Sanskrit at Oxford's Indian Institute, who maintained that the candidates were too immature, took little part in university life and were reluctant to exert themselves at Oxford since they had already taken the exam.[7]

Competition 'wallahs' were seldom regarded with approval by their elders in India. In 1870s, at the height of the crammers, they were seen as bookworms with little worldly knowledge. In the words of Lepel Griffin, a competitive entrant himself and later Agent to the Governor-General in Central India, 'They neither ride, nor shoot, nor dance, nor play cricket, and prefer the companionship of their books to the attraction of Indian society'.[8] Nevertheless, despite the somewhat damning assessment of the education of candidates, a number of high-performing individuals continued to be turned out on a regular basis, and it would appear that academically able men succeeded despite the shortcomings of the system. In this respect a member of the Indian Civil Service was no doubt substantially better suited to act as a tutor to a young prince than a member of the Political Service, whose attention to the physical needs of his young charge tended to be the highest priority. For political officers from the Staff Corps with a purely military background, the intellectual requirements of Addiscombe, the East India Company's military seminary, were even less demanding than those at Haileybury. Addiscombe was founded in 1809 to provide up to two years' general and technical education for boys between 14 and 18 years who had been nominated for officer cadetship in Company forces. The seminary was initially intended for students destined for engineering or artillery regiments, although it later opened to guards and infantry cadets, and academic prowess appeared to be low in the scale of priorities of both teachers and taught.[9]

However, it is possible that in the latter part of the nineteenth century tenacity was the skill of the greatest value when it came to furthering the education of the first wave of princely charges. In exposing young rulers to western ideas the challenge lay less in devising the substance of the curriculum than dealing with the hostility towards the dissemination of such ideas which was rampant in princely *durbars*. To succeed in his task it was essential for a tutor to overcome the considerable resistance existing in the palace environment.

Extraction from the Clutches of the Zenana

During Lord Mayo's viceroyalty, due to the sensitivity of the impending restoration of Mysore to native rule, much official correspondence centred upon the young adopted prince, Chamarajendra Wadiyar, in whom it was hoped to instil the qualities of good leadership. A letter from the maharaja's tutor, Colonel G. Malleson, in September 1869, emphasised the problems involved in extricating the prince from the claustrophobic atmosphere of the *zenana*, from which in state after state there stemmed relentless opposition to British control of princely education. In Mysore it was hoped that with 'prudence, firmness and kindness' sufficient influence could be exerted over the ruler to 'counteract the wretched atmosphere in which a young Native chief must live'. Criticism was made of the fact that for the maharaja 'Every whim is gratified, every wish forestalled'. It was felt essential for the boy to be taught outside the palace walls and by an independent tutor, a move vigorously opposed by the royal females who declared that to leave the palace would remove some of the young ruler's dignity. They pointed out that 'the late Maharaja was not taught, why should this one be?' and only agreed finally to the prince's tuition under the threat of being reported to the viceroy for failing to stand by the conditions imposed by the British Government.[10]

With his customary idealism Mayo saw the education of the young rulers and nobles as the cure for the secret ills of native India. The implanting of western liberal ideas would transform the states. He firmly believed that Mysore had been saved from 'much that would have given great trouble thereafter' and that British influence in guiding the prince and his family 'has worked a great cure and all intrigue and underhand work is I hope thoroughly choked'.[11] To widen his horizons, the young maharaja was to be made familiar with objects of interest in his own country and allowed 'free personal intercourse' with those from whom he might acquire information. Association with other young noblemen 'of good disposition and promising intelligence' would give the prince confidence and encouragement.[12]

One of the main reasons for propping up what in many cases was an enfeebled ruling class was the contemporary widely held view that this class still held the loyalty and adulation of the people of India. Therefore care was to be taken that western indoctrination was confined to the English language and details of government. Instruction in Indian culture and religion, insofar as 'barbarous practices' were not involved, was to continue as before. An official despatch from the secretary of state in 1871 stressed the fact that the Maharaja of Mysore would have to rule, when he came of age, over 'a Hindoo people peculiarly jealous of, and attached to, the faith of their ancestors...any measure which might alienate from him their sympathies should be carefully guarded against'. It was recognised that there was great difficulty in training an Indian prince for the future government of his state, using principles recognised by European statesmen, without 'offending the prejudices or affecting the interests of many who would fain see him reared in accordance with the old oriental model'. Therefore only a moderate success rate was anticipated in introducing European ideas via the ruler.[13] While 'truthfulness and sound morality' should be inculcated, 'no interference should be exercised with his religion in his forms of worship'. His views should be 'constantly directed to the discharge of the regal and administrative functions which his high office will one day demand'.[14]

Despite the need to continue the association of the rulers with their cultural roots, it was deemed undesirable that a native should undertake the vital role of tutor to the Maharaja of Mysore. Colonel Malleson was of the opinion that the ideal candidate should be

> a gentleman fresh from one of the English universities . . . of high character and attainments, totally unconnected with India. A greater mistake could not be committed than to appoint to that office any one directly connected with an Indian family, and still less any one now in India. No candid mind can deny that the tendency of Indian life is to bring the mind into a groove, from which, even under other climes, it rarely emerges. What is required for the Maharaja is the influence of an unfettered, unprejudiced English intellect, of a mind that has thought out problems for itself, and which takes nothing on trust.[15]

However the secretary of state, Lord Salisbury, disagreed. Writing to the viceroy, Lord Northbrook, in 1875, he declared that if there were no object other than to bestow on the young ruler 'Philosophical and Literary Knowledge' Malleson's suggestion would be feasible, but literary proficiency was not in this case the principal goal. The maharaja was soon to be invested with powers and charged with duties which would leave little time for the 'pursuits of a student life'. It was vital that he should be instructed in the principles of government and 'the warnings or encouragement furnished by the history of other Princes of his own race'. To communicate this knowledge, an officer with some familiarity with Indian administration was required and such a person could be found more easily in India than Britain. Mysore would be much in the public eye when it was returned to native rule, and the post of tutor was crucial since the 'future form and permanency of Native rule in India will be largely influenced by the career of the Prince whose education you are preparing to complete'.[16]

Since it was deemed by the British that there was no 'royal road to learning', a school with three classes was formed in the Mysore palace, modelled on the system at Winchester. The maharaja was joined by various sons of noblemen and officials of the court of about the same age. At first about 40, then later 50, came to the school, including the maharaja's two brothers. The occupants of the *zenana* continued to throw 'many obstacles' in the way of the prince's education and had to be told forcibly that further interference would result in his being removed from the palace altogether at the age of seven, when separation from his female relatives was generally considered to be highly undesirable.

The headmaster of the royal school, Jayaram Rao, was a Brahmin who remained with the maharaja until he was 15. The appointment of a native thoroughly acquainted with English was considered preferable to the selection of a British national in the post. Ootacamund was selected as the 'sanatorium' for the summer season and the maharaja, with a few of his classmates, was taken there by his tutor and guardian, J. D. Gordon (later Sir James Gordon, Chief Commissioner and Resident at Mysore), where 'free from the turmoil of palace life' his education was seen to progress considerably.[17] The government's assumption about the correct form of education was the same as the view held in Britain at the time. The public-school emphasis on games as a training in character was confidently adapted to the training of Indian princes. It was agreed that the maharaja should be taught to ride, swim, play cricket and handle firearms, and generally encouraged to participate in 'those physical and strengthening exercises which are suited to his country, position and age'.[18]

Later the maharaja's education was entrusted to W. A. Porter, a veteran educationalist who had made Kumbakonam College, 'the Cambridge of Southern India'.[19] During the latter period of his studies he received instruction in the principles of British administration, and for wider experience went on tour in the province and mixed in English society. It was the intention of the British Government to see the maharaja married to 'an educated and enlightened lady'. With this object in mind Gordon set up a girls' school within the palace for the education of the girls belonging to the royal family, together with several daughters of high Brahmin officials of the palace.[20] A report submitted to the Government of India by Gordon in 1880 declared that

> the progress made since Mr. Porter's arrival, in developing His Highness's general intelligence and giving him a proper mental training, has been marked and very satisfactory. He is now able to read and understand for himself ordinary books and newspapers and he composes fairly and writes his letters without assistance. His power of observation is keen and his judgment of persons and things remarkably sound.[21]

However the treatment of the maharaja's successor, Krishnaraja Wadiyar, reveals the extent to which ideas about princely education had changed over the second half of the nineteenth century, influenced by the emergence of the princely colleges designed for the purpose of training young rulers and aristocrats. As in his father's youth, a school was formed at the palace at Mysore for the young maharaja and boys of the same age selected from the principal families of the state, but a European tutor, J. J. Whiteley, was appointed instead of a native headmaster. The education followed the same lines as that at the major princely colleges, Mayo and Rajkumar, although the students did not reside in the school premises. A special class was formed and several of the best Hindu and Muslim students from various institutions in Mysore were invited to participate 'in order to infuse a spirit of wholesome rivalry in the mind of the Rajah'.[22]

On visiting the palace school in 1896 Mr. Cook, Principal of the Central College, Bangalore and Educational Adviser to the Government of Mysore, remarked euphorically that the 'general knowledge of the boys is superior to that of other schools' and that he 'had no idea the system was so perfect'.[23] Stuart Fraser of the Bombay Civil Service,

appointed by the Government of India as personal tutor and guardian
to the young prince,[24] reported with equal enthusiasm, 'The education
that he has been receiving is not mere cramming nor the learning of
a book-worm but is diversified, inasmuch as it embraces every art and
science which will help to make him a wise, sagacious, and highly cul-
tured ruler'.[25] Certainly with historical studies of luminaries as diverse
as Clive, Warren Hastings, the Marquis of Wellesley and, somewhat
surprisingly, Haider Ali and Tipu Sultan,[26] the maharaja had a colourful range of political views from which to choose. Moreover, in addition to his class studies, Krishnaraja Wadiyar devoted two hours a day
to special subjects such as international law and Indian political law,
the principles of legislation, the history of the land-revenue system,
civil and criminal justice in Mysore, forestry, famine relief, excise and
assessed taxes.[27]

Nevertheless Whiteley expressed a certain unease as far as the
young maharaja's moral environment was concerned and the difficulties involved in his exposure to the less-desirable aspects of religious
ritual and *durbars*. It was impossible to change religious ceremonies
and the only available course of action would be to let his mother,
the maharani, know how necessary it was for such ceremonies to be
conducted in a manner as 'innocuous' as possible. *Nautches* (court
dances) could not be stopped, but could be made 'more formal and
less suggestive', however this would be a particularly delicate matter for any Mysore official to tackle. In addition Whiteley saw the
need for Krishnaraja Wadiyar to be given separate living and sleeping
apartments in the palace to which the tutor would have access at all
hours, since the latter was constantly met by '*zenana* difficulty' when
he ought to be able to go in and out of the young ruler's rooms at will,
except when prevented from doing so by caste and religious ceremonies
such as eating and praying. The young ruler should pay no social visits, except to relations, and no guests should be able to associate with
the maharaja without the permission of the tutor as the representative
of the Government of India. In Whiteley's view, the maharani should
be made fully aware of the importance of the 'innocence of youth', and
its significance in British eyes.[28] Nevertheless the maharaja's existence
was by no means dull, and outside the palace he participated in a

surprisingly eclectic mix of social appointments. While at Bangalore from 1895 to mid-1896 his schedule included visits to the races and a polo tournament, the afternoon 'At Home' at the Residency, a vegetable show and a visit from the Papal Delegate.[29]

As in Mysore, official efforts were made in Hyderabad to distance the young ruler from the 'unwholesome' atmosphere of palace quarters. Captain John Clerk, equerry to the Duke of Edinburgh, was employed as guardian and tutor to the young nizam, Mahbub Ali Khan, in 1874, however the appointment was hardly productive. Sir Richard Meade,[30] Resident at Hyderabad, reported in 1876 that the access to the tutor was so restricted that 'it was impossible for him to educate in the narrowest sense, much less exert any moral influence over his charge'.[31] Moreover Meade referred to medical reports declaring that the nizam was 'disgracefully fed and clothed, and the sanitary condition of his rooms dreadful'. He was exposed to 'dissipated proceedings in the *zenana*' and the procurement of liquor via certain 'delinquents'.[32] The viceroy, Lord Lytton, was in no doubt that the object of the diwan, Salar Jung I, was to reduce the nizam to a 'cipher', in order that the power of the state might remain concentrated in his own hands:

> for this purpose he keeps the boy secluded, almost a prisoner in the palace, where, I am told, he is waited upon by 25 young women trained to debauch him. Salar Jung visits him daily, but everyone else seems to be zealously excluded from his presence, and he is rarely allowed to leave the palace. Thus withdrawn from healthful external influences, it cannot be said that the development of his mind or body have fair play, nor that the objects on which the Government of India laid so much stress in constituting the Regency are being loyally carried out.[33]

In 1894 the resident suggested to Mahbub Ali Khan that, like Clerk, an English gentleman should be appointed to superintend the education of his own son, the sahibzada Mir Ali Khan, in his case from the age of eight or nine. The superintendent would not take a share in the teaching but would oversee the entire tutorial and household staff. The

year would be divided into three or four terms with a suitable proportion of vacation, and the pupil could live during the term time in
the same house as his superintendent. All vacations would be spent at
home, but during the term it would be best to restrict the visits to the
palace to special occasions.[34] Such an arrangement, it was hoped, would
break the ever-present 'continuity of *zenana* influence', and at the same
time prevent the boy from becoming 'over-Europeanised' and alienated from his own people. Ideally five or six young native gentlemen
of appropriate age and rank would be educated with the nizam's son
and subject to the same rules and discipline. For the first few years the
staff would be native Muslims, but at least one of the masters would be
selected from the Education Department for his knowledge of English
and Urdu, and for his special ability to teach. The aim was to turn the
sahibzada into an 'educated Mohammedan of the highest type', yet one
able also to read, write and speak English to a high standard. After two
to three years the boy could be placed under an English tutor.[35] The
course of studies was to be approved by the nizam and not altered without his sanction, however it was stressed that 'Ample time should be
left for recreation and for outdoor games and exercises'.[36]

There was reluctance on the part of the nizam to agree wholeheartedly to such rigid demands. The resident reported six months later
that the ruler had assigned a separate house to his son within the
precincts of the palace, in which he was supposed to pass the day. At
night he returned to the *zenana*, as it was contended that its inhabitants would not agree to 'more complete separation'. The nizam had
appointed four elderly nobles, each of whom was to have charge of the
boy in turn and be responsible for his conduct. In the opinion of the
resident 'Nothing but harm can ... come of this arrangement. Elderly
men are not suitable companions for boys of nine and I should imagine
that this unfortunate lad will be perplexed by the varying counsels
and prohibitions which these worthies are likely to impose on him'.
Nothing as yet had been done to find a teacher. The minister, Nawab
Vikar-al-Umra, generally agreed with the views of the resident and felt
that little would be achieved until the boy had an English governor to
look after him: 'No native will ever stand up against palace influences.
The governor ought not only to be European, he ought also to be a

government servant especially selected whose personal character, age and experience would carry weight'.[37]

In 1898 the viceroy, Lord Elgin, wrote that the nizam was 'entirely neglecting' his son, a 'poor boy who is growing up in the worst surroundings' surrounded by 'scoundrels who have the Nizam's ear, to keep his son a poor ignorant creature that they may use him in his turn'. There might still be a hope of saving him if a British tutor or guardian were introduced into the palace, but it was clearly impossible to ask a British national to accept conditions such as those proposed by the nizam, as he must have a position 'which the Palace crew cannot pretend to control'.[38] The Government of India was in a difficult position as it was not responsible for the sahibzada in the way that it had been responsible for his father, who was a minor orphan when he succeeded to his inheritance.

However in 1898 the nizam agreed to give Brian Egerton, previously the tutor to the Maharaja of Bikaner, 'a fair trial' by appointing him on probation for two years. The nizam set out the following conditions:

> He shall be considered strictly as a private servant of my household, and as such he shall be subject to the restrictions which custom and my own habit have necessarily imposed on that service. He shall in no way meddle with the political and administrative affairs of my State. Nor should he, without my permission, visit or receive any official or nobleman whoever he may be. Breach of such conditions will entail immediate dismissal at my discretion.[39]

As far as the Government of India was concerned, the requirements were that the candidate should be 'a gentleman of the highest class. One who would keep entirely aloof from faction, be incapable of intrigue, able to assert control over teachers and the household, and at the same time keep in view imperial interests'.[40]

Under Egerton, and living away from the palace, the sahibzada was seen by British officials to flourish with a 'freedom hitherto unknown'. Egerton was said to be 'most patient and long suffering' and the boy, although 'dull and very backward', was of a good disposition and anxious to learn. It was believed that the nizam had been personally anxious to separate his son from palace life some years before but had experienced great difficulty in 'overcoming the prejudices of his inordinately extensive *zenana*'.[41] However in 1903 it was apparent that the royal women and palace officials still wielded a considerable influence as far as the progress of the sahibzada was concerned. After consultation with the principal nobles the nizam announced that his son was too old to go to Mayo College. Marriage had become 'an imperative necessity in order to safeguard him from mental and moral temptations peculiar to his present age' and rather than venturing further afield, he would benefit from visiting different parts of his own country and becoming acquainted with the administration.[42]

The *zenana* was not in all cases the main hindrance to the establishment of a salubrious atmosphere in which a princely education could be effectively accomplished. Pratap Singh, discussed in the chapter on succession in his role as Maharaja of Idar, was for a long time in charge of his nephew, the young heir to the Jodhpur *gadi*, but in 1895 in the interests of both it was suggested that he should have a British officer to assist him as companion and tutor to the boy. Pratap Singh had failed by allowing the maharaja to be in the constant and almost exclusive society of people who were not deemed suitable companions for the future ruler of a state. The late maharaja had objected to this state of affairs and it had become both 'irksome and distasteful to the young Maharaja'. Under such circumstances the presence of a qualified British tutor would enable the ruler to acquire more general knowledge and enlarge his 'mental vision', and if he were to live in separate accommodation with the officer he would be severed from his present social environment.[43]

Nevertheless the Government of India considered that, in view of the satisfactory way in which the administration of Jodhpur had been conducted during the minority, there should be as few changes as were 'compatible with good government'. The viceroy preferred that the maharaja should remain under the care of Pratap Singh, aided by the resident, rather than under a young British officer appointed as guardian or tutor. Pratap Singh would no doubt find opportunities to instruct the ruler in state administration, and he should be told that the viceroy was especially anxious that the maharaja should avoid dubious company and have his attention directed towards more serious duties.[44] The resident, A. Martindale, reported in 1898 that to give him an insight into the working of courts, the ruler was personally trying judicial cases and submitting his reports to the residency. To train him in economy and accounts he had been allowed to supervise and control branches of the administration within budget limits, and he was also used to attending meetings of the State Council.[45]

The removal of a young prince from the influence of unscrupulous court personnel was also a goal in the state of Jind in the Punjab. In 1897 a despatch declared that 'His Highness's personal character is so entirely unformed that it would be imprudent to entrust him with ruling powers in the near future'.[46] Sir Louis Dane, later Lieutenant-Governor of the Punjab, observed that if the treatment of minor rulers were left entirely to state authorities, the princes concerned would at 18 be 'turned out on old native lines with some sense of dignity, some regard for tradition and, for the old State families, some interest in their State, and some prospect of carrying on in the old grooves the processes of administration'. However the 'march of ideas' even in the states had been so rapid that it was almost impossible to equip the rulers with the 'necessary qualities for keeping straight'. Self-interest was so strong and intrigue so prevalent among hereditary officials that they were the worst people to educate the princes.

Dane appreciated that in Jind there was no family with a sufficiently 'wholesome atmosphere' under whose head the young ruler, Ranbir Singh, could be disciplined and trained by tutors. Since a prince was unlikely to find a 'disinterested and capable guardian', the government should make him its ward. There was always a danger in separating a minor prince from his family and the influences of the court to such a degree that he was alienated from the state and disinclined to accept his responsibilities. Therefore the government should be careful to impress upon a potential tutor that the ruler should be kept in touch with hereditary officials and the people of the state, and should remain receptive to their ideas.[47] In response to a request from the rulers of the other Phulkian states, Patiala and Nabha,[48] that the education of the Jind ruler be placed in the hands of three officials, one from each state, Dane was adamant that such interference was not warranted.[49] Moreover the proposal was entirely opposed to one of the fundamental principles of the policy of the paramount power, namely that no native state be permitted to interfere in the internal affairs of another. A list of the tasks which the three officials intended to undertake in training the prince hardly suggested that he would be reared according to western ideas:

> Their duties will be to look to his diet, the protection of his health, and his companions, to teach him the laws of religion and state matters, to arrange for the appointment of Aid de Camps [sic] and household servants jointly, to effect economy in his personal expenses, and to keep the two Chiefs informed of all important matters so that they may make proper arrangements in consultation with the State Council.[50]

As Dane pointed out to the English tutor, Captain F. E. Bradshaw, who was appointed to superintend the young ruler's education, his job would not be easy. The Prince of Jind was almost 18 and 'in dealing with a Native Chief of such an age the exercise of both tact and temper on your part is essential, and you will doubtless endeavour to influence him more by example and precept than by actual exercise of authority in the last resort'. It was felt unlikely that much could be accomplished by 'mere book learning', but the prince was to be encouraged to keep up his studies and the selection of reading matter would form an important part of the tutor's duties. The instruction of the prince in the duties of state administration was in itself a somewhat delicate matter, as the tutor had to superintend such instruction without being able to intervene himself in the administration, channelling all orders through the Regency Council. However, the tutor was to have complete control over the person and surroundings of the ruler and the expenditure of his privy purse, as soon as the amount of this had been determined in consultation with the council and sanctioned by government.[51]

Westernisation

The influence of British tutors did not always achieve a desirable result in the eyes of the paramount power. Sayaji Rao Gaekwar of Baroda, successor to the deposed Malhar Rao,[52] was particularly keen to keep his autonomy unfettered by the British. The roots of Sayaji Rao's antagonism can be traced to the ruler's desire, shaped by the unorthodox teaching of his tutor, Frederick Elliott, to run his state on 'original lines'.[53] The period of Elliott's influence lasted from 1881 to 1895 and was a time of continuing reform in the state.[54] To all intents and purposes Sayaji Rao developed into a humane, cultivated and conscientious prince. His day began at six in the morning with prayers, after which he spent a few hours reading authors such as Bentham, de Tocqueville, John Stuart Mill and Shakespeare.[55] However despite the dissemination of suitable liberal texts Elliott was by no means popular in British Government circles due to his espousal of Baroda interests over those of Britain, and in 1895 he was forced to revert to British service. British officials identified the fruits of Elliott's influence in arguments put forward forcibly by the gaekwar to combat supposed British infringements of his liberty, as displayed in a report of an interview in 1898 in which the ruler declared, 'I am only quoting the words of Mill ... when I call the Government of India a despotic Government. It is without doubt a despotic Government, some may call it a despotic despotism, but it is nevertheless despotic'.[56]

Having been versed by his tutor in the benefits of exposure to western ideas, the gaekwar objected in particular to the ruling of the viceroy, Lord Curzon, that Indian princes wishing to travel to Europe must give notice to the Government of India, so that an official verdict could be given on the necessity or advisability of such a trip. He complained that the notice had now become 'a communication in the nature of an application for permission' to leave India and affected his 'position and dignity'. In the opinion of successive viceroys the gaekwar showed great dereliction of duty in his absenteeism from Baroda. The ruler was away from his state for periods aggregating seven-and-a-half years between 1886 and 1908 and, in the view of the Baroda resident, had failed to recognise the 'injury' such absences caused the

administration and the 'discontent and dissatisfaction ... engendered
in the minds of the people'.[57]

At the Foreign Office, Sir Henry Durand in 1894 recognised the

> danger in educating Native Chiefs too much according to our own
> views, they become too fond of English amusements, and lose
> all pride and interest in their States. They thus lose their raison
> d'etre and become useless as part of the Indian political system.
> We want ruling Chiefs, in touch with their people, not absentee
> landlords who race and drink. They are worse than useless.[58]

The difficulty in reconciling western and oriental ideas when it came
to princely rule was well demonstrated in the state of Pudukkottai.
Nicholas Dirks considers that the British success in weaning the minor
raja, Martanda Bhairava Tondaiman, away from the 'seething intrigue
of the *zenana* and state' eventually resulted in the ruler's premature
retirement and total withdrawal from state affairs.[59] When Martanda,
adopted grandson of Raja Ramachandra, succeeded to the *gadi* in 1886
there was a certain amount of British relief that the young heir had
been spared the insalubrious aspects of palace life due to his youth
and adoption from outside the main family. The British Government
resolved to pay particular attention to the education of the raja,
appointing Frank Crossley in 1887 as his English tutor with explicit
instructions to ensure the inculcation of British ideas and values.

The western-educated diwan of Pudukkottai, A. Sashiah Sastri,[60]
expressed grave fears concerning the young ruler's education when
Martanda was removed from Pudukkottai to a bungalow near the
British cantonment in Trichinopoly to be educated by Crossley and
instructed in social skills by the political agent, R. H. Farmer.[61] By
1890 the attention to body over mind was a daily fact of the raja's routine, described by Sastri in a letter to the Maharaja of Travancore: 'He
nominally goes through a few lessons in English, Sanskrit, and drawing in the hot hours of the day and spends all the morning and all the
evening in driving, tennis, golf, shooting in the jungles, playing chess,
playing the banjo and the violin and billiards'.[62] In his yearly reports
on the progress of his royal charge, Crossley mentions repeatedly the

importance the political agent placed on scheduling the raja with 'less time to the cultivation of the intellect and more to the body', nevertheless noting that his 'increasing obesity gives grounds for serious apprehension as regards his health'.[63] Travel was an important component of his education, and paramount importance was attached to exposing the young raja to wider vistas and perspectives so that he would not become engulfed in the 'Byzantine preoccupations of court life'.[64] He was taken on grand tours of northern India and Europe to accomplish this objective.

The progress of the eager and able student pleased Crossley to such an extent that the British viewed Martanda's accession to the throne in 1894 with 'a mixture of complacency and optimism', although it was soon apparent that the qualities so assiduously instilled in the ruler were to make his rule 'highly troublesome'.[65] It was noted that the raja was 'always knocking about amusing himself and but seldom troubles Pudukkottai with his presence . . . Mr. Crossley has, I fear, done him no good of late, and instead of pressing him to buckle down to the task of governing has encouraged him to do quite the reverse'.[66] In August 1897 a letter from the Madras Government declared that 'the Raja is more like a coloured European gentleman, with entirely European tastes, than a Native Prince', and as a ruler he had made no real effort to gain insight into the administration, the wants of his people or the expenditure of state funds.[67] Between his installation in November 1894 and the writing of this letter the raja spent a total of eight weeks in the state, returning principally for festivals and shooting expeditions, apparently encouraged in this somewhat untaxing lifestyle by Crossley.[68]

In the Rajput state of Bikaner the dissemination of western ideas had an equally significant effect upon the young ruler, with a somewhat more successful outcome. The majority of royal Rajput families preferred to employ a Brahmin as the predominant educative authority in the palace. Such a teacher would be imported from Rajasthan, Gujarat or Kashmir to teach their sons Sanskrit texts such as the laws of Manu, and epics such as the *Mahabharata* and the *Ramayana*.[69] Despite British pressure, there was great reluctance on the part of some royal Rajput families to employ an English tutor to impart administrative knowledge at the expense of a religious education.

Maharaja Ganga Singh's first tutor at the Bikaner court was Pandit Ram Chandra Dube, a Kashmiri *pandit* who was with the maharaja through his childhood and adolescence. He was not quoted often in the maharaja's later correspondence and did not leave his mark in the records of the regency period, although he remained Ganga Singh's tutor even after the Regency Council decided in 1889 to send the maharaja to Mayo College to complete his education. The diwan and vice-president of the Regency Council, Sodhi Hukm Singh, a Sikh who was constantly conspiring in the *zenana* and who headed the most important faction at court, saw the return of Ganga Singh from Mayo College in 1894 as a threat to his influence. The diwan concurred with the view of other members of the council that the young ruler should go to Mount Abu[70] to learn Persian and Urdu, before visiting other parts of India and England under the guardianship of a competent and trustworthy officer, ostensibly 'to keep him away from bad temptations'.[71]

However the agent to the governor general in Rajputana, Colonel Trevor, informed the council that Brian Egerton, the 'scion of an old English family of high standing in Cheshire' who 'combined sympathy and tact with firmness and a wholesome believe [sic] in discipline',[72] should be appointed as a guardian. Normally *durbars* rather than the Government of India hired professional tutors for their sons, however Egerton's record had impressed Curzon to such an extent that the viceroy deliberately selected him to further British influence in the Bikaner minority administration. Egerton's background and his conservative outlook were common features of political officers in native states. His previous assignments in Rajputana as District Superintendent of Police in Ajmer, where he wrote the report on the 1891 census, followed by a position as Boundary Settlement Officer in Udaipur from 1892 to 1895, suggest that he had 'the disposition of an inflexible bureaucrat rather than of a humanist'.[73] Ganga Singh remembered Egerton's arrival in Bikaner in the hot season when the young maharaja was living in part of the recently completed old palace 'minus electric light, minus electric fans ... and minus water pipes'.

Colonel Tom ffrench-Mullen, a senior British officer, was of the opinion that it was impossible for a European to stay there in temperatures of 110 degrees, but Egerton declared that 'his place was with his ward and he insisted on residing in the Fort'.[74]

An ordinary day's routine for the young ruler of Bikaner consisted of riding or shooting before breakfast, studying during the morning and afternoon, and playing polo and roller skating in the evening. On holidays the routine included visits to the royal residence at Gajner, a pleasure palace and a favourite shooting retreat of the Maharajas of Bikaner. Visits to other parts of the state were frequent, including interviews with nobles and landowners, and religious and state ceremonies were strictly performed after some years of laxity under the regency.[75] The pupil received a grounding in Hindu law before he applied himself to state administration. Thereafter his training consisted of the explanation of various files and papers by senior officials of each department of state, following which he wrote up his own decisions on cases, making notes on the evidence on record. Land-settlement classification and an examination of correspondence between former ministers, the maharaja and the residency also formed part of his administrative education, and biographies and letters of 'great men' were read to learn the history of Bikaner and of India.[76] Christopher Bayly suggests that residents and tutors in states assumed 'the position of close personal adviser which had been occupied by uncles or royal mothers in the independent courts',[77] and Ganga Singh often repeated that the 'after life [sic]' of a minor prince depended mostly on the right choice of guardian. He deemed himself very fortunate to have had a much more rigorous grounding than most other young rulers in finance, revenue, customs and excise, and other departments of administration.[78]

The diligent efforts on the part of the British to ensure that a young male ruler achieved as much administrative wisdom as possible were not, to her regret, available to the only female ruler of India. In Bhopal Sultan Jahan Begam received her early education at the hands of court officials of the day. Mohammed Jamal-ud-din, the first minister of the state, taught the princess Arabic and Persian and the private secretary,

Munshi Husein Khan, taught her English. After she reached the age of five a regular timetable was prescribed, including the study of the Quran, handwriting, arithmetic, Pashtu and fencing. Whenever the political agent, or any other British official, came to Bhopal, he would be asked to examine Sultan Jahan in English by her grandmother, Sikander Begam, a great believer in the merits of education.[79]

However Sikander Begam's daughter, Shah Jahan Begam, altered the arrangements for Sultan Jahan's education after her grandmother's death, and the girl's usual nine or so hours of study dwindled to four a day. In her mother's opinion it was more important that she should acquire experience in domestic and official duties than 'progress in scholarly knowledge'. Having read the entire Quran before she was 11 she was now made to study it a second time, and English and Persian were her only other lessons; however she was also made to read and write orders upon various official papers, which were sent to her daily by her mother.[80]

Years later, at the start of her own rule, Sultan Jahan realised that these were papers on which orders had already been passed and which were connected with matters of no interest or importance, giving her neither experience nor information. After her marriage she was to recognise the shortcomings of her own education and lack of administrative work, declaring that 'The training of a young chief can never be adequate if it is confined to the study of books and to such experience as he can gain from intercourse with his teachers'.[81] Nevertheless for a Muslim princess at the end of the nineteenth century, the breadth of Sultan Jahan's education does appear to have been extraordinary. At the start of the twentieth century, having discussed the question of princely education with Lord Curzon, Sultan Jahan seriously considered sending her youngest son, Hamidullah Khan, to Mayo College in Ajmer. However to use the education of her son as an example to others she decided instead to establish a special school for the *jagirdar* class, which he would attend following a short period under the tutelage of an Oxford graduate, C. H. Payne. The Alexandra Nobles School, designed by Sir Swinton Jacob at an estimated cost of Rs. 153,241, was opened in Bhopal in 1903.[82]

Broadening Princely Horizons

Not surprisingly, given the example of blatant neglect of state affairs displayed by rulers such as Martanda Tondaiman of Pudukkottai, young princes were not encouraged to leave India to complete their education. A proposal in 1876 by Lieutenant Colonel C. F. Minchin, political agent in the Punjab state of Bahawalpur, that the young nawab should come to Britain to study with three other boys was greeted by the secretary of state with some misgivings: 'the Nawab will have completed his fifteenth year, and it seems to me questionable whether, after attaining that age, a native of India is likely to derive advantage from a two years' residence at a public school or with a Tutor in England'.[83] When aristocratic Indians did aspire to educational qualifications in Britain, problems tended to arise. Sahib-Zadah Wahid-ud-Din, a member of one of Mysore's leading families, accumulated large debts while studying for the Bar but was treated sympathetically by the India Council as the case represented 'the first genuine experiment' and required 'exceptional clemency'.[84] There could also be ulterior motives in educating the scions of Indian ruling families abroad. It was believed that the Nawab of Rampur[85] in central India kept his younger brother, the Sahibzada Nasir Ali Khan, in an English school for reasons of 'jealousy or fear'. The nawab appeared to be under the impression that if his brother returned to Rampur before a lawful heir was born, he might become a 'centre of intrigue and danger'.[86] However, in 1899, the Government of India took the view that there was already sufficient intrigue and danger in Rampur for it to be desirable for the sahibzada to remain in England to complete his education, having passed his Moderations at Oxford before reading for the Bar.[87]

Towards the end of the nineteenth century there was greater princely enthusiasm for a British education, arousing further disapproval among government officials.[88] The secretary of state, Henry Fowler, wrote to the viceroy, Lord Elgin, in 1894, that 'it was possible to overdo the English education of young Chiefs'. The sons of two or three princes were at Eton and being brought up 'in all respects like English boys ... how this may affect their influence in their own States is a question of some difficulty'.[89] When the Gaekwar of Baroda intended his sons to go to Eton and Balliol, Lord Curzon objected strongly since he was convinced that at a British public school and university an Indian might develop some contempt for his own people. The viceroy was proved correct when the eldest son of the gaekwar, Fateh Singh Rao, had to be removed from Oxford due to 'idleness and misconduct' and upon his return to India 'developed great extravagance'. Curzon observed that 'A youth, either at Eton or Oxford, acquires ideas and tastes which are incompatible with subsequent residence in a Native State, or with sympathy for the people over whom he may be called to rule'.[90] This was not a purely British point of view. The Maharani Suniti Devi of Cooch Behar, whose sons were at Eton, also recognised the shortcomings of a British education. The young princes returned to India speaking French and Greek, but not Sanskrit, Urdu or Bengali, and no longer fluent in the local dialect of Cooch Behar. Moreover Suniti Devi decried the lack of any practical education for future maharajas, stressing that to rule well they needed a vocational understanding of legal, accounting, engineering and agricultural subjects more than a classical education.[91]

However, despite the appeal of a famous establishment such as Eton, in the last decades of the nineteenth century British efforts to set up Indian colleges, modelled on the very English public schools[92] to which some Indian rulers aspired, failed dismally to capture princely imagination and to prove a great enough incentive to break centuries of educational and cultural habits. For many royal families in the first years of transition from traditional kingship to modern ruler, the concept of such an extreme form of westernised education came too soon and was too alien in nature.

The First Phase of Princely Colleges

In his study of the effect of the English public-school system upon the British Empire, J. A. Mangan sees the creation of colleges for Indian royalty and nobility as a 'tangible symbol of both political expedience and moral conviction'. The British hoped to win over at least some of the influential traditional minority and 'so succour a band of political evangelists sympathetic to the gubernatorial standards of the imperial race'.[93] The idea for establishing such schools sprang from Captain F. K. M. Walter, the Political Agent in Bharatpur, who in his 1869–70 annual report declared that

> If we desire to raise the chiefs of India to the standard which they must attain in order to keep pace with the ever advancing spirit of the age, if we wish to make clear to them that our only object is to perpetuate their dynasties and to make them worthy feudatories of the crown of England, we must place within their reach, greater facilities for bestowing on their sons a better education than they can possibly now attain. Then and not till then can we hope to see the native princes of India occupying the position they ought to hold as the promoters of peace, prosperity and progress among their own people and hearty supporters of British authority.[94]

To achieve this aim, Walter urged 'the establishment of an "Eton in India", a college on an extensive scale ... with a complete staff of thoroughly educated English gentlemen, not mere book-worms but men fond of field sports and outdoor exercise, and the elite of the Native gentlemen belonging to the Education Department'.[95] Walter's ideas were formally adopted by the viceroy, Lord Mayo, who at a *durbar* in Ajmer in 1870 asked for the cooperation of princes and nobles in Rajputana: 'If we wished you to remain weak, we would say, "Be poor, and ignorant, and disorderly". It is because we want you to be strong that we desire to see you rich, instructed and well governed'.[96] Mayo believed that for the sake of civilisation the *durbars* should not be allowed to sink into disrepute, and under his viceroyalty schools such as Mayo College for Rajputana and Rajkumar College for Kathiawar in western India were founded. These were followed by Daly College for central India and Aitchison College for the Punjab.

The four main princely colleges were subject to the general control of the Government of India and each was controlled by a council or committee responsible for general administration, made up of distinguished British and Indian members. For example, the Mayo College council included among its members the viceroy, the Agent to the

Governor-General in Rajputana, the Commissioner of Ajmer, 17 rulers of Rajputana and political officers to the states involved.[97] The colleges were by no means open to all; even a boy of high birth would not be admitted unless he or his father was a *durbari* and entitled to assist at *durbars* convoked to meet a viceroy. To aid the cause of poor *durbari* nobles and 'prevent the decadence of the native aristocracy' a considerable number of scholarships were created, which were assigned according to the merits of the fathers of candidates.[98]

While the colleges were founded on the initiative of the British, they were financed initially by large contributions to endowment funds from the native rulers themselves and to a lesser degree by government support. As numbers of pupils increased, Indian royalty and nobility gave generously to provide extra classrooms. The proposal for Mayo College, confined initially to the sons of rulers in Rajputana, was received with enthusiasm by the local princes, who promised contributions amounting to Rs. 594,500 to an endowment fund. In addition to these grants, the rulers of Jaipur, Jodhpur, Udaipur, Bikaner, Alwar and Jhalawar gave large sums for the construction of boarding houses for pupils from their respective states. The Government of India undertook to provide seven *lakhs* of rupees: three for monthly payments towards the working expenses of the college and four to be spent on buildings, houses and sports facilities.[99] Fees made up the bulk of annual revenue in all colleges except for Mayo, where the munificence of the rulers' endowment fund was sufficient to run the establishment. Fees were paid by the individual state to which the young ruler belonged or by the estate of his family and were generally determined according to means by the political officer concerned. The cost of educating individual pupils was by no means standardised, as in the public schools of England, and could vary considerably.[100]

The question of an appropriate architectural style for Mayo College was not easily resolved. In the end seven separate designs, submitted by four different architects to three viceroys, were required before construction began. A classical design was Lord Mayo's original preference and in the summer of 1871 he asked the executive engineer, J. Gordon, to prepare a plan for a 'plain but handsome Hall, with class rooms surrounding a pillared verandah'. The princes, when consulted belatedly in 1872, also gave their support to the 'Grecian' model, however it was finally decided to use an Indic design.[101] The college was, after all, meant for the use of the rulers of Rajputana who, although now incorporated as feudatories within the British imperial system, still embodied some of India's oldest ruling dynasties and formed the link with India's past to which the British wished to gain access. It was important that these men were able 'to mark out visibly in their architecture their position as leaders of such a "traditional" order'. It was unthinkable that the 'Indian Eton' set down in the Rajasthan desert, despite its playing fields and boarding houses, should take the shape of a Grecian temple.[102]

The architect of the college, Major Charles Mant of the Bombay Engineers, used a style termed Indo-Saracenic, which had been developed as a result of the debate over the relative suitability of various styles for British building in India. This debate involved not only criteria such as climate and cost but also political considerations. It was insisted on the one hand that the style chosen, whether classical or Gothic, must be western; that the mission of empire was civilising and westernising in matters of law and education, and that British architecture should reflect the same values. On the other hand it was argued that the role of empire was paternalistic and it was desirable to see the adoption of Indian styles, or the evolution of a style incorporating Indian features. The phrase Indo-Saracenic was originally adopted to describe India's Islamic architecture, generally characterised by a blend of Indian and Islamic design ideas.[103]

The Building News, illustrating the design for Mayo College, announced that Mant had 'boldly taken the indigenous ancient style' and yet had produced a construction that was both 'suitable and essentially modern'.[104] The interior layout of the college, with its lecture halls and teaching rooms, represented the modern world the British were attempting to bring to the princes. However Indian symbolic forms too were prominently displayed. The main lecture hall, for example, decorated throughout with richly carved panelling, had in its ceiling two large flat lights of coloured glass: one 'a conventional representation of the sun, and the other one of the moon, the mystical sources from which the chief Rajpoot Dynasties claim to have sprung'.[105] In the view of Lord Curzon, the young rulers were similarly 'to combine the merits of East and West in a single blend'. Trained and educated in western ways, but ruling their states 'upon Native lines', they were to be treated 'not as relics, but as rulers: not as puppets, but as living factors in the administration'.[106] Mayo College, where an elaborate Indo-Saracenic façade enclosed rooms in which young princes were to study British history and geography, perhaps most vividly represented Britain's inconsistent vision of princely India.

The college opened on 1 October 1875. Mangal Singh, the Maharaja of Alwar, was the first and initially the only pupil. Since no accommodation was at that stage available in the college grounds, the maharaja lived in a house outside the grounds and commuted to his daily studies on an elephant. Seven boys soon followed him from Jaipur; six from Jodhpur, including the maharaja's youngest brother; six government wards; two sons of *thakurs* from the Ajmer College; and Zalim Singh, Maharaja of Jhalawar. Other pupils were expected from Udaipur, Bikaner and Tonk. The age of the boys ranged from 7 to 17, but most pupils were between 9 and 13. In the first year of the college there was a British staff of three: the headmaster, the principal and a writing and arithmetic master. In addition an Indian staff of three was employed: an Urdu and Persian tutor, a Hindi and Sanskrit tutor and a junior English and vernacular master.

Major Oliver St. John, principal of the college, wrote in 1876 that 'as yet the nobles of Rajputana generally had shown no spontaneous inclination to send their sons to be educated and for some at least, constant pressure will have to be exerted on parents through the *Durbars* of the States'.[107] However by the time of the annual report for 1876–7 the number of pupils had increased to 40. Major St. John declared that the

> moral and physical improvement throughout the College has been more remarkable than the mental. Little taste, if not decided disinclination, was shown at first to all but comparatively sedentary games, and even to riding … in study the boys are inclined to be idle, and are at first generally insubordinate;

but I have, I am glad to say, as yet found it unnecessary to inflict any corporal or other severe punishment.[108]

Such attention to moral rectitude was also apparent at the opening of Rajkumar College, when Colonel Anderson, the Political Agent in Kathiawar, voiced the feelings of those present at the opening ceremony when he exhorted the teaching staff to mould 'a manly set of noble youths ... burning with emulation to outstrip each other in the glorious task of elevating humanity'. Like Mayo, Rajkumar was to become an 'eastern Eton' which would stamp its mark on every pupil. However when the first term started in 1871 there was little to suggest that the college would ever achieve this ideal. Among the dozen or so *kumars* who comprised the initial enrolment there were several reluctant members who soon deserted the classroom for the more comfortable surroundings of the *zenana*, while those who remained, such as the princes of Bhavnagar and Junagadh, were always accompanied to their lessons, according to *The Pioneer* newspaper, by 'bands of armed retainers, strange, wild-looking creatures who might have come out of the middle ages'.[109] The headmaster, Chester Macnaghten, a Cambridge graduate, felt that his task at Rajkumar was not to turn out erudite scholars, but to mould the character of his pupils so that they would emerge as efficient and benevolent rulers. High on his list of priorities was the ability to accept advice:

> Another question specially applicable for you who are here to be under my training is – do I do my duty towards my superiors, to those who are placed in authority over me? Am I obedient to them, and respectful? Do I do as well as I possibly can all that they tell me to do, all that they gave [sic] me to learn?[110]

It is conceivable that the authoritarian tone adopted by Macnaghten revealed the ultimate goal of the establishment, which was to create 'a generation of rulers who would automatically look to their political agents for advice and invariably do the bidding of government'.[111]

In the internal organisation of the schools, the British clung faithfully to the 'familiar educational blueprint' which served the upper classes in England. The Mayo timetable was virtually indistinguishable from its English counterpart, however in the early years a shortage of European staff resulted in a different house system. Houses were supervised not by British housemasters but by *musahibs* or *motamids*, native staff who were rarely teachers but responsible for matters such as tidiness and general behaviour.[112] At Mayo there were ten houses, organised to accommodate boys from the states which had endowed the individual buildings.[113] At Rajkumar the wings of the main building formed two houses, and boys took rooms as they became available. Arrangements at Daly were similar, with Rajputs and Muslims mixed together in four houses. At Aitchison, on the other hand, there were three houses, for Muslims, Hindus and Sikhs respectively.[114]

The annual report for Mayo College for 1875–6 makes it clear that the system of separate boarding houses 'although doubtless a necessary deference to Rajput prejudice' had many disadvantages when it came to discipline and the promotion of friendly relations among the boys of different states. It was felt that it was difficult to instil 'habits of cleanliness and decorum combined with a proper feeling of self reliance' into boys surrounded by a 'set of dirty and obsequious servants' during the entire time that they were absent from study. In accordance with the original proposals for the school, boarding houses were maintained by the states which built them and boarding-house staff were state, not college, employees, over whom the college had only partial control. Under the rules boys were allowed three private servants, however the rule seems to have been interpreted liberally from the start and many boys retained more than the prescribed number.[115] Individual arrangements had to be made for some pupils: the Maharaja of Kotah arrived at Mayo with 200 followers, for whom a special village was built, and the Maharaja of Alwar had a stable of over 20 polo ponies and 4 carriage horses.[116]

Academic and Sporting Prowess

As at Eton, private tutors were a feature of the schools; however their role, influence and numbers varied from college to college. These tutors served as an instrument for British rule, in all cases had to be approved by the government and were frequently selected by political officers. Occasionally, when a pupil's status merited it, they were British nationals. Although Indian language and culture maintained a strong presence, English as a subject was 'a vital element of the curriculum' in all colleges, and successive viceroys stressed its importance in princely government. Speaking to the students at Mayo College in 1883 the viceroy, Lord Dufferin, insisted that

> English is the official language of the Supreme Government under which you live, and of the books which deal with the public affairs, the domestic administration and the general interests of your country, and it will be of continual use – indeed I may say of absolute necessity – to you in the positions which you may be called upon to fill. The keen-witted inhabitants of many other parts of India have fully appreciated this fact, and all their energies have consequently been devoted to the acquisition of English.[117]

Before 1890 the boys of Mayo College were prepared first for the entrance examination of Calcutta University and later for the matriculation examination of Allahabad University. The subjects studied were English, English and Indian history, physical and general geography, arithmetic, algebra, Euclid and mensuration, Sanskrit and Persian, and Hindi and Urdu. E. Giles, Education Inspector of the Bombay Northern Division, in a report on Mayo, pointed out that this course was very long, difficult and uninteresting, and of little use compared to other courses that might to advantage be chosen. As a foundation to a scholastic career it was satisfactory, but as an education in itself it left much to be desired. The instruction that a young ruler obtained at Mayo College was, in nine cases out of ten, all the education he would receive for the rest of his life. Therefore, at Giles's suggestion, the course was changed, the university textbooks abandoned and a special curriculum drawn up for the college.

In spite of efforts to make the range of subjects more attractive, academic standards at the princely colleges continued to fall as a result of professional complacency on the part of the staff and laziness on the part both of masters and pupils. The teaching of English was not as thorough as it might have been and general studies suffered from a lack of goals.[118] Giles bluntly laid out further reasons for poor intellectual standards in 1890 in a report on Mayo College. The inspector found 'a tendency towards idleness and indifference due to a lack of any necessity to learn, pupils' prolonged absences from college, a disinclination to return at the end of holidays and antagonism towards the school within the boys' homes'.[119] However he was greatly impressed by the 'admirable training in discipline, truth and manliness', which sent the boys out as 'honest and straightforward gentlemen, who may become worthy rulers of their own people, and the loyal and enlightened subjects of the Empire'.[120] One area which was proving most successful was character training for leadership and, as at an English public school, the games field was the site for this achievement.

The ideal of manliness was pursued in the colleges by generations of schoolmasters imported from Britain for the purpose. The epitome of such a master was Chester Macnaghten, a 'pioneer of the public school education of the feudatory chiefs'. Macnaghten came from a family with a long history of service in India. After an English education culminating in a Master's at Trinity College, Cambridge, he returned to the subcontinent in 1867 where he became tutor to the Maharaja of Darbhanga, the great Bengali *zamindar*, before joining Rajkumar College. As headmaster he attached the 'utmost value to games as a training in character'.[121] In his view they developed 'energy, promptitude, judgement, watchfulness, courage, generous emulation, appreciation of the merits of others and the highest standards of truthfulness and duty'.[122] A typical prize-giving address emphasised the need to combine the moral and physical with the mental:

we have aimed at the training of a liberal character, the sort of training, *mutatis mutandis*, which characterises English Public Schools. We have wished, of course, that our boys may be scholars, but we wish that they may be much more than mere scholars, that their bodily faculties may be developed as well as those of their minds, that they may be practical men of the world, knowing the right and daring to do it, retaining, amid the influence of the western ideas, the chivalry of their Rajput ancestry.[123]

The emphasis upon manliness in the ethos of the princely colleges is perhaps somewhat surprising in the light of the fact that two of the colleges were founded to serve the boys of the Punjab and Rajputana, both classified by the British as breeding grounds for the 'warrior races' of India, as opposed to Bengal, deemed to be the home of the 'effeminate breed' of Indian. The people of the Punjab and Rajputana, whether defined by race, climate or personality, most resembled the British self-image. However Indian tradition and the somewhat hedonistic lifestyle of the nobility ensured that the fairly Spartan games-orientated public-school existence was viewed by many upper-class Indians, even in the Punjab and Rajputana, as most unpalatable. Such distaste was not confined to the operation of the princely colleges. There was also little enthusiasm on the part of rulers for alternative educational establishments for their sons.

Durbar Antagonism

Throughout the latter part of the nineteenth century there was evidence of much resistance emanating from *durbars* against any form of princely education which removed a young ruler from the palace environment, although matters gradually improved. The Local Education Committee return for Delhi College in 1845 reported an encouraging

> diminution in the existing prejudices on the part of the Native Aristocracy, against our system of Public Education. Two youths of noble families, one a son of the Nawab of Jhujur, and the other a son of Rajah Sohun Loll, late prime minister to the King of Delhi, had been sent to the college and it was expected that more of the same grade would follow.[124]

Education reports throughout Delhi College's history continued to show that, in spite of the presence of some leading Muslim scholars on the staff and occasional examples of lavish Muslim patronage, the founders' original intention of attracting the sons of the displaced Muslim elites to the classrooms had never really been fulfilled. Although some of the alumni from the pre-1857 classes won high reputations in scholarly circles in the second half of the century, most of the Muslim students were neither from *ashraf* backgrounds nor did they make much impact in their subsequent careers. The enrolment of the relation of a nawab was certainly an occasion for comment, as for instance when the son of Nawab Faiz Muhammed Khan of Jhajjar chose to study at the college. This was rare, since the Muslim aristocracy preferred private tuition for their sons. The sons of *ulama* families were also usually taught privately, albeit in some cases by Delhi College lecturers in their own time, or 'drawn in preference to the many renowned traditional *madrasas* of the city'.[125]

A clue to the unpopularity of Indian high schools was given in the *General Review of Benares College* for 1844–5, where:

> A special class has been instituted to those people whose parents, being persons of wealth and rank, wish them to be kept separate from the general mass of the students. For this privilege, a monthly payment of five rupees, or such other sum as the Committee may direct, is demanded. The feeling which induces Natives of respectability to dislike their children mixing familiarly with those of a much inferior grade, is not thought to be unreasonable. Some feeling of the kind probably exists in every country. But there is much inconvenience necessarily attendant upon a special class, which requires special accommodation and separate instruction.[126]

The problems of mixing social classes was also evident in Agra College, criticised in 1846 by C. C. Fink, Superintendent of Indigenous Schools, for the fact that schools such as the college, which offered free instruction, injured not only the indigenous schools by drawing away scholars who could pay for their education, but the college itself by making it accessible to the lower orders of the community, deterring 'respectable' people from sending their children there.[127] However it is clear that the question of consorting with social undesirables was not a factor that taxed most princely families. For many *durbars* the mere departure of a young ruler from his state was perceived to have potentially disastrous consequences. In the view of Herbert Sherring, headmaster of Mayo College at the end of the nineteenth century, antagonism towards the princely colleges arose because the public-school education of a future ruler tended to mean state officials' loss of influence and power. Within a state, the

> most influential men hope to increase their own influence in proportion as their chief's capacity is lessened; and to such persons the idea of an educated ruler means prevention of illicit gains instead of aggrandisement. The wish and desire and the aim and object of the evilly disposed men of power and status in any state are to retard the education of their master, and in this they are ably seconded by court sycophants who lose no opportunity of placing temptations to entice their leader astray.[128]

A tutor was often employed on the advice of some favourite *durbaris* who were well aware of the advantage of procuring a man who would be under their control and would not interfere with their plans for securing their own advancement. As he had little authority the service of a man of 'intrinsic worth and independence of character' was not likely to be obtained. The whole idea of educating princely youths was seen by some noble families as inconsistent with their rank and position. Rajkumars were born 'to wield the sword, to command others, to rule and to live in clover on the properties of their ancestors'.[129]

In the opinion of Chester Macnaghten there was also the significant resistance of the *zenana* which 'very often in the acts of Native Courts possesses a visible authority which its invisible presence does not prepare us to accept'.[130] Such authority was evident in a lengthy correspondence in the 1890s concerning the Dowager Maharani of Indore who, against the wishes of Maharaja Shivaji Rao Holkar, vociferously opposed the education of his two nephews at Daly College. Holkar, in a letter to W. J. Cuningham, foreign secretary, revealed an impressively modern attitude in denouncing his stepmother's interference in what he considered to be a matter of great importance:

> You will agree with me that my nephews and illegitimate brother have been simply wasting their valuable time, which,

in my opinion, should be devoted to education only. The con-
sequent result is that they are surrounded by all sorts of evil
influences and are becoming mischievous and troublesome ...
What I would suggest is that they should be sent under proper
guardianship either to Poona, Jabalpur or Allahabad High
School, or to the Mayo College at Ajmere, and that I would
remit to them their allowances through the Residency authorities ... otherwise the blame of neglecting their education will
be placed on me.[131]

However although R. J. Crosthwaite, Agent to the Governor-General
in Central India, was prepared to threaten the dowager with an unfa-
vourable report to the Government of India, the viceroy himself was
'reluctant to offer advice on such a delicate matter'. Intervention in
court politics, even to further princely education, was not to be under-
taken lightly.[132]
Despite the rosy picture painted by Holkar of discipline and dedi-
cation to work at the princely colleges, in 1891 Giles made the point
that one of the negative aspects of Mayo College was that the students
were freed from the 'stimulus of poverty and the necessity of employing
education as a means of livelihood'. The inspector maintained that if at
Eton a large number of boys did as little work as possible, it was hardly
surprising that at Mayo there was a tendency towards idleness or indifference, most marked among those students who joined the college at
an age when their 'habits of life have become to some extent settled'.[133]
To some extent justifying *durbar* antagonism the private secretary to the
viceroy, Sir Walter Lawrence, wrote that two Rajput boys who left Mayo
College in 1894 had informed him 'that the boys drank and had intercourse with prostitutes' and 'ran a risk of becoming profligates'. Captain
A. F. Pinhey, Resident at Udaipur, also complained about the facility
to obtain liquor, an inadequate knowledge of English and bullying
between older and younger boys.[134] Satadru Sen makes the point that
the 'established anti-intellectual culture' of the colleges and their deliberate rejection of benchmarks such as final examinations and degrees
had left it unclear whether academic failure was a failure at all. At the
same time, since these were undeniably academic institutions with an

explicit mission to impart a 'liberal education', intellectual shortcomings could not be ignored.[135]

However in the opinion of Narullah Khan, an old boy of Rajkumar College and a Cambridge graduate, British efforts at princely education had gone far in overcoming difficulties which at first seemed 'insurmountable'. Such difficulties included the reluctance of rulers to allow their sons to associate even with young men of their own rank and position; the 'paternal affection' existing at court, which was such a deterrent to separation and engendered fears that the youths might become victims 'to the machinations of designing persons'; and a false idea of their own dignity, which led rulers to look down upon each other even though they were of equal or nearly equal rank.[136]

Yet while some Indian rulers proved to be enthusiastic supporters of the colleges, many were indifferent or apathetic. By the end of the nineteenth century, after some 20 years, the schools could only muster about 190 pupils in total.[137] Both the low numbers and the status of entrants produced disappointment. In 1897 it was noted with regret that at Mayo 'As regards rank and numbers, the chief drawback is that no heir or ruling chief from the three first class states of Udaipur, Jodhpur or Jaipur has attended the College, nor has any prince or *thakut* [sic] been entered from the States of Bundi or Dungaput'.[138] In 1901 Sir Walter expressed the opinion that the low number of pupils suggested 'the grand conception' of Lord Mayo had not yet 'commended itself to the Rajputs in spite of their loyalty to the English and their admiration of English customs'.[139] Mayo College had been created, in part, to bring Rajputs into the public affairs of their states. However the college was offering its education not only to princes but also to the great barons' sons who had neither the need nor the inclination for *durbar* employment, who scorned such employment as 'subservience to a chief who was only the first among his equal clan coparceners', and who were in fact not employable by their *durbars* because the maharajas feared to bring them too close to their *gadis*.[140]

Why were the 'ruling chiefs' prepared to contribute with such generosity to the building and running of the princely colleges when they were patently unprepared to send their offspring to such establishments? The significance of a display of largesse among Indian princes may well have played a major part in stimulating their generosity, despite the fact that for the great majority an adherence to the tradition and safety of education within palace walls was well entrenched and unlikely to change before the twentieth century. In linking themselves to objects of public concern such as schools, albeit schools for such an elite clientele, rulers could be seen to be meeting the needs of broad-based social and political welfare, as well as focusing attention on the giver. Ram Singh, Maharaja of Jaipur, had under his patronage Maharaja's College, which after the Mutiny became the premier institution in Rajputana for the recruitment and training of a modern professional and administrative class, and in 1861 he founded the Nobles College in Jaipur, anticipating by more than a decade the major British effort to educate the Rajput nobility.[141] Other educational beneficiaries of princely plenty were the Khalsa College of Amritsar, of which Hira Singh, Maharaja of Nabha, and Rajinder Singh, Maharaja of Patiala, were both patrons at the end of the nineteenth century.[142] Subscriptions to such educational establishments, as well as those to the princely colleges, were well publicised and inevitably enhanced the status of the individual ruler. As is emphasised in the chapter 'Servant of the Empire' the royal gift was basic to statecraft in pre-colonial kingdoms, and princes frequently supported both traditional and modern projects in an effort to maintain an aura of largesse.

For those royal and noble families who were prepared to send their sons to the princely colleges there was undoubtedly a certain amount of prestige involved. The volume of *Chiefs and Leading Families in Rajputana* of 1894 identifies at least 26 young rulers and members of the nobility as having attended Mayo College. Individual biographies compiled by C. S. Bayley, the Political Agent in Bikaner, suggested that for some members of the ruling class such an education was a prized commodity worth displaying.[143] However there is little to suggest that it made a significant difference to the students' later roles in life. Remarkably few *thakurs* applied themselves to duties over and above managing their estates, although Thakur Mangal Singh of Pokaran, having passed the university entrance examination, became a member of the Maharaja of Jodhpur's Council[144] and the son of Thakur Chatar Sal of Fathpur was employed in the state police.[145] Three of the *jagirdars* elected to the Jagir Council of Alwar in 1907 – Daulat Singh of Khora, Phul Singh of Para and Sawai Singh of Chimraolim – were graduates of the college, and leading the bureaucratic opposition to the same council was the judicial minister, Durjan Singh of Jaoli, also an alumnus of Mayo.[146] For some old boys, however, the benefits of a British education bore no fruit: Zalim Singh, Maharaja of Jhalawar, had his ruling powers withdrawn in 1887 'having failed to adminis-ter his government in accordance with the principles laid down for his guidance' and his administration was entrusted to a British officer, as had been the case during his minority.[147]

Curzon's Cure

By 1902 Lord Curzon was complaining that only 12 out of the 32 'rul-ing chiefs' of Kathiawar had been educated at Rajkumar College.[148] Moreover most of the rulers of the Punjab failed to send their sons to Aitchison College, and Daly College never attracted the princes and nobility of the larger central states such as Gwalior, Bhopal and Dewas.[149] V. A. S. Stow, headmaster of Mayo College in the 1940s, commented that there had always been a fluctuation in numbers. The presence of an heir apparent at the college tended to result in an influx of other boys from that particular state, and when the heir left the oth-ers followed him. Alternatively, some fairly trivial incident could lead to a withdrawal of support from an individual state.[150]

However to a great extent the ruling classes had shown that they wished to cling to their own culture and were far from keen to give their children a British education. Ganga Singh, Maharaja of Bikaner, complained that the long periods of absence at school contributed to an estrangement from his people and his responsi-bilities as a ruler, while the Council of Regency in the state enjoyed too much freedom in its decisions. Ganga Singh did not send his son, Sadul Singh, to Mayo and also discouraged his nephew, Karni Singh, from going there.[151] As a regular financial contributor to the college he encouraged other princes to carry more weight in deci-sions concerning education, and his comment that 'science must be compulsory' suggested that his negative experience at Mayo could be due to what he perceived as scant attention to the new demands of princely rule.[152] By 1900 complaints of the standards in the colleges were circulated widely. The Gaekwar of Baroda criticised the English public-school model in the journal *East and West* in January 1902, and his criticisms were reproduced in *The Voice of India* and *The Kathiawar Times*. As a result Curzon was under no illusion as to the rulers' dissatisfaction with the 'high cost and general irrelevance' of the education provided.[153]

The viceroy called a conference in Calcutta in 1902 to discuss the reform of the constitution and curricula of the colleges.[154] The conference lasted for four days and was attended by principal political officers, representatives of the native rulers and heads of existing colleges. In his opening speech Curzon laid out what were in his opinion the three main cases for the low number of pupils in the colleges. First, there was the deeply embedded conservatism of the states, enforcing the tradition that young rulers or nobles should be trained among their own people and supported on the one hand by the strength of the *zenana*, which was alarmed at the idea of 'emancipated individuality', and on the other by the court, which was conscious of the loss of prerogative and authority which would result if the 'young recruits from the west start to stir up the sluggish Eastern pools'. Secondly, there was the fact that college education was too costly, and many rulers had been affected by famines and other adversities. If families found that it was considerably cheaper to educate their sons by private tutors within the home, it would not be unnatural for them to adopt that course of action. Thirdly, it was doubtful whether the rulers or nobles were entirely satisfied with the class and quality of the education. Too much appeared to be spent on 'bricks and mortar' and too little on tuition. The viceroy demanded of the college committees:

How can the best pupils be expected without the best teachers and how can the best teachers be forthcoming unless you offer them adequate prospects and pay? Where are the Public Schoolsmen, and where are the University graduates, European and Indian, upon your staffs and what is their number?[155]

The relatively low academic standards of the princely colleges were undoubtedly dictated to some extent by the educational backgrounds of those who taught in them. Although the first headmaster of Rajkumar College, Chester Macnaghten, had a Cambridge degree, his original staff consisted of five Indian teachers and no Europeans, a situation which had obvious disadvantages when it came to instruction in English subjects. The first three principals of Mayo College – Major St. John, Major Powlett and Colonel Loch – were all military officers seconded from the Political Department and were as such probably less fit to attend to the scholarship of their charges than officers of the Indian Civil Service who had been subject to a more rigorous education. Colonel Loch himself admitted that the quality of teaching was poor; both he and the headmaster, Herbert Sherring, were neither public-school men nor university graduates: 'Twenty-three years ago I was appointed to the Mayo College as Principal ... with, I fear, no other qualifications than a love of discipline and an affection for natives engendered from a service of thirteen years in my old regiment, the 19th Bengal Lancers'.[156]

As a result of Curzon's reorganisation of Mayo College in 1903 provision was made for a teaching staff of twelve: four British teachers and eight Indians. The British staff, while remaining members of the Indian Educational Service, were to form a separate branch of the service to be known as the Chiefs' Colleges Cadre, especially recruited for such colleges and serving under the Political Department. A university degree appears to have been an essential requirement for the branch. Two assistant masters were recruited from Britain: F. J. Portman, a graduate of Oxford[157] and S. F. Madden, a graduate of Cambridge. The early death of Madden resulted in the appointment of another Oxford graduate, C. H. H. Twiss, who was at the time teaching at Aligarh College.[158] The more impressive academic input no doubt contributed to the fact that by 1912 the numbers at the colleges had risen to a total of 413.[159]

Unsurprisingly, by dealing exclusively with royal and aristocratic families there was little demand for the princely colleges to offer schooling for bureaucratic and professional employment. During a ruler's minority a temporary administration was frequently set up, based on the larger bureaucratic machinery of British India, ensuring that there was no great need for a prince to be deeply involved in the administrative affairs of his state. When Jai Singh, Maharaja of Alwar, returned from Mayo College in 1897, his perceived view of a westernised Rajput ruler conflicted with the independent role which the rationalised bureaucracy had made for themselves in the Alwar Government. The Alwar state servants were reluctant to accept a reassertion of the maharaja's power, in either modern or traditional terms, and retained enough influence to oppose him in his efforts.[160]

While Sir Charles Wood, Secretary of State for India, had hoped that through education the 'better class' of natives would not only be trained in 'noblesse oblige' but also fitted for employment 'in our services'[161] (and presumably states' services), the British officers who made Mayo College's policy were decidedly uninterested in preparing the sons of impecunious and obscure Rajput cadet families and the younger boys of ordinary *jagirdars* for gainful employment. In 1876 the viceroy created a few posts in various government offices to be filled by 'young men of rank and education', but the government would not allow the princely colleges to prepare their students for university matriculation.[162] Until it would, they could only 'limp along' trying vainly to transform the sons of a handful of princes and nobles who were not greatly interested in attending at all and 'still less in being transformed into a nobility with serious obligations to anything but their families and their families' estates'.[163] Mayo College came finally to resemble an Indian Eton and to function like one only during the first decades of the twentieth century, when the British Government gave way to the princes' request to allow the college to become a university preparatory school for Rajputs who wanted careers for their sons.[164]

However Curzon did provide a scheme, the Imperial Cadet Corps, for the military employment of a limited number of sons of princely or aristocratic families following their education at Mayo and other princely colleges. Cadets, aged between 17 and 20, would pass through a two-year course and be from time to time in personal attendance upon the viceroy on ceremonial and other occasions. For the successful candidates there would be a third year of training, and the rank of a British officer in staff or other extra regimental military employment would be conferred upon them. In the mould of the princely colleges, Curzon designed the Cadet Corps as an institution for political purposes to attach the higher ranks of Indian society to the British Government by closer ties, in order that they could act as a bridge between the paramount power and states' peoples and to prevent their defection into the emerging Indian meritocracy. The function of the corps was to discipline and educate rather than to train the young scions of princely families in a career of arms. As a result the scheme met with much disagreement from the Rajput princes who desired the award of 'real' commissions, enabling successful candidates to serve on terms of equal regimental rank and duty with the Indian Army's British officers.[165] The First World War proved to be a watershed, and in 1917 nine former imperial cadets were awarded the first king's commissions granted to Indians.[166]

* * *

The British probably performed as well as they could when it came to individual princely education at the end of the nineteenth century. In some cases it was remarkable, bearing in mind the highly conservative tradition-bound nature of Indian *durbars* and the considerable power wielded by the *zenana*, how easily the Government of India was able to convey to royal families the desirability of palace schools based on English models and of British tutors imparting ideas of a radically different nature to those of native tutors formerly employed in the same role. However for the first generation of young princes to be exposed to such an education the conservative nature of royal Indian life was often a saving grace. In the few cases where western views were too emphatically imparted by British tutors and too readily accepted by their pupils, the young rulers tended to be stranded in a no man's land in which they fitted neither into a western nor an oriental template. Sayaji Rao, the Gaekwar of Baroda, used his English education to adopt an independent, modernising stance within his state which proved unacceptable to the wary paramount power.

In the case of the princely colleges, the British approach was in many ways hugely arrogant in supposing that, however warmly they may have admired some aspects of British society, Indian princes and noblemen would wish to emulate an English education. The character-building elements of the public school with boys in mixed houses, a Spartan style of living and an emphasis on sport must have engendered an inevitable reluctance to leave a somewhat sybaritic lifestyle, particularly if there was encouragement from the *zenana* and *durbar* officials to eschew any exposure to western ideas. Moreover to the first generation of young rulers, used to a rigid religion-based tutelage at home, the indigestible mixture of English subjects must have seemed a challenging and unappetising prospect. However for the members of the Indian ruling classes who did attend the princely colleges, the true failure of the system lay in the fact that there were virtually no opportunities to use the somewhat inadequate grounding they had received. The sons of nobles were patently unfit to pursue a professional or bureaucratic career and by the start of the twentieth century only a handful of princes wielded sufficient power to be able to participate fully in the administration of their states and to demonstrate that their education in British hands had been a worthwhile exercise.

Commenting on the benefits of an English education, as a product of Rajkumar College, Narullah Khan declared that there was

evidence that the critical faculty has been developed amongst an Oriental people, owing to the material and moral advancement which society is undergoing under the enlightened British administration ... To recommend and support a policy which will effect reforms, diffuse education and enlightened ideas, encourage culture and abolish old customs which are unsuitable to the wants and needs of the present is therefore a duty especially incumbent upon educated and thinking men.[167]

In his view 'anarchy was the rule rather than the exception and the people groaned under misgovernment' before British supremacy had been established.[168] However if by the end of the nineteenth century 'anarchy' in the states had to some extent been overcome, it was due less to the influence of the western education 'diffused' to traditional rulers than to the education in British India of a more humble breed of bureaucrats who were able speedily and effectively to mastermind the administration of a state.

3

MARRIAGE AND ROYAL WOMEN

To the Victorians the state of moral degeneration of India's women was visibly represented by the *zenana* and the veil.[1] Confined to a life of languid idleness in closed rooms, hidden from view, India's women were seen by Victorians as suffused with 'an unhealthy sexuality and a disabling passivity'.[2] In his study of the 'imperial imagination' Lewis D. Wurgaft suggests that, more than any other Indian institution, the locked doors of the *zenana* symbolised the barrier between British society and the unsettling mysteries of native life. On a practical level the British in the nineteenth century were particularly concerned with bringing the Indian woman out of the darkness and into the light. Wurgaft maintains that one part of the impulse behind this need for reform was genuinely humanitarian. Another part of it helped to rationalise the strain of liberal thought behind the conviction that 'social rather than political reform was necessary for genuine progress' and that only Britain could guide India to that end. However there was a third element in the commitment to reform: the need to bring Indian sexuality into a 'more open and accessible sphere, where it could be controlled and tailored to imperial requirements'.[3]

Palaces were considered to be riddled with mystery and intrigue, often permeated with sex and excess, and rulers were frequently pictured surrounded by servants egging them on to uncontrolled sensuality or even debauchery. Travelling as a journalist in the states of Rajputana, Rudyard Kipling was constantly oppressed by the configurations of the native palaces. In the palace of Amber he found 'crampt and darkened rooms, the narrow smoothwalled passages with recesses where a man might wait for his enemy unseen, the maze of ascending and descending stairs leading nowither, the ever present screen of marble tracery that may hide or reveal so much', suggesting that 'it must be impossible for one reared in an Eastern palace to think straightly or speak freely'.[4]

In the late nineteenth century British architects found rational motives for bringing about a change in the architecture of princely palaces. Sir Lepel Griffin, Agent to the Governor-General in Central India, wrote that in the past a palace had been required to offer 'protection against attack from without and privacy to a very large female population within'. The first of these requirements no longer existed and the second was rapidly losing its force, as chiefs 'become content with one wife and do not need the 100 rooms and hazy labyrinths of an Oriental *zenana*'. For those princes, Sir Lepel continued,

> whose minds have been enlightened by English training, the old, and it may be, picturesque designs of native palaces are odious. They cannot breathe in the confined rooms and narrow passages which were good enough for their fathers. They demand well-ventilated rooms, light and air, wide staircases and imposing halls. Such conveniences find no place in the conventional designs of native architecture.[5]

It was suggested that once incorporated into the new order of the Raj, with his values and expectations appropriately transformed, an Indian ruler would inevitably find an old insalubrious palace unsuited to his new moral transparency and, like him, the female members of his household would be exposed to the 'light and air' of which they were deprived in the *zenana*. To this end British officials worked rigorously to eradicate the more unwholesome sexual aspects of palace life. However the Victorian view of female suppression in India was not borne out without exception. There is evidence to suggest that, far from displaying a 'disabling passivity', a small number of royal women, often ironically by acting as a conduit for British liberal ideology, were capable of wielding a degree of power in affairs of state which was remarkable not only by Indian but also by British norms of the time.

Early British Impact on Marriage Practice

The British system of indirect rule affected all aspects of royal practice, influencing both the motives behind and the contracting of royal marriages. One of the first casualties of British intervention was the practice of polygyny, which declined as a result of general British policy towards the Indian states rather than a deliberate British moral crusade.

Rajputana provides an interesting model of polygyny, in that the practice assumed particular importance in the region due to the military and political problems that the Rajput chiefs faced in the creation, expansion and consolidation of their territories and the social structure they evolved to meet the situation. The major Rajput clans came from outside Rajasthan and conquered lands from other ruling groups such as the Bhils. Subsequently they fought continuously against each other for the further expansion of their territories. The Rajput chiefs adhered to a social system based on kinship and clan, which served to keep them united for purposes of military strength. The recruitment base was narrowed down to the individual clan, and within this restricted field the supply of manpower was only possible if there were an adequate number of male offspring. The Rajputs also used marriage to form alliances with other clans to expand their area of influence and military strength. The marriages of Rajput chiefs were not arrangements between individuals but between two houses, and political relationships were forged through matrimonial agreements.[6]

Although the Mughals established their rule over the Rajput rulers through informal arrangements and matrimonial relations, this did not bring about any fundamental alteration in the political system, other than loosening the clan bonds. With the coming of the British, Rajput rule underwent important changes. In concluding precisely written treaties during the first decades of the nineteenth century the British took upon themselves the responsibility of safeguarding the territory of the Rajput princes, under which the rulers agreed to act in subordination to the British Government. In her study of Rajput courts Varsha Joshi makes it clear that polygyny lost its appeal as political marriages lost their use, since 'The clan army no longer had a role. The concept of having more male progeny to increase fighting strength had lost its relevance'. Moreover under British rule the Rajput *jagirdars* were particularly sensitive to the fact that a large number of children would result in the fragmentation of *jagirs*, as there was now no possibility of territorial expansion.[7]

Under Lord Bentinck zealous British reform resulted in further intervention in Indian royal marriage practice with the enactment of the abolition of *sati*[8] in 1829, which had a particular impact on royal widows. *Sati* resulted from the political and economic circumstances of the polygnous marriage system and the hierarchical structure of the *zenana*.[9] On the death of a chief, the mother of the son who succeeded to the *gadi* enjoyed higher status and privileges over the other ranis. In the case of a ruler being a minor she was designated queen regent, and in that capacity all the powers of administration were vested in her. The life of a widowed rani whose son was not heir was dramatically degraded and, like other Hindu widows, many restrictions in dress, food and physical movement were imposed upon her.[10] The instances of self-immolation were relatively rare after the first decades of the nineteenth century, partly due to the decrease of polygyny and partly due to British use of sheer constraint where warranted. When Maun Singh, Maharaja of Jodhpur, died in 1848 one rani, four concubines and one female slave committed *sati*. However his successor, Maharaja Takht Singh, left on his death in 1873 about 28 legal and 15 illegal wives as well as an 'immense number' of slave girls, yet, as a result of British orders to lock and guard the doors of the *zenana*, not a single woman attempted self-immolation.[11]

Choice of Bride

As the nineteenth century progressed emphasis was placed by the British less on reform than on the desirability of regulating royal marriages and brokering sound political matches motivated by, in

British eyes, good judgment rather than the Machiavellian intrigues of individual *durbars*. There was hope that through the introduction of western ideas on, for example, monogamy, the lax moral standards which existed in many Indian palaces could be considerably tightened. The Government of India made it clear that it expected to be well informed about forthcoming royal alliances. When the Nawab of Rampur declared that it was a curtailment of his rights to divulge details of his various marriages, British officials saw it as a 'curious perversion' on his part, since it was understood that the Government of India needed such information in order to deal with problems of succession.[12] Indeed the matter of succession emerged as a item of considerable importance in the case of the Nawab of Rampur. Much official correspondence was generated by the question of whether or not the nawab was a Shiite and his son by an informal marriage to a concubine therefore able to qualify as a legitimate heir.[13]

Similarly, when it was discovered that the proposed wedding of Madho Rao Scindia, Maharaja of Gwalior, to a girl from a Tanjore family had been negotiated in secret by the president of the Regency Council and the regent maharani, the Agent to the Governor-General in Central India expressed great displeasure since the Government of India had a responsibility in the matter of all important marriage negotiations and needed information on family, age and other details of the parties concerned.[14] It appeared that the marriage plans had been deliberately hidden from the Government of India with the 'real object' of getting the maharaja out of his guardian's hands as soon as possible.[15] Scindia was 13 years old and the girl 11, and although the ceremony was to take place within the next month or so there was no intention of allowing the young ruler to live with his bride for some years. The president of the Council of Regency, Bapu Sahib Jadu, had suggested that she lived in one of the palaces in the meantime, however the resident, Major David Barr,[16] was of the opinion that she should return to her parents. Had she been of a good family, the marriage would have taken place at her father's house, but 'being of small account' she was 'to be consigned like a bale of goods, to the keeping of the Maharani'.[17] There was a strong probability that she would reach puberty in two years when Hindu religion and custom would require the maharaja to live with her, after which all further efforts to educate the boy would be futile.[18]

In fact the Tanjore bride was subsequently found to be 12 or more years old and therefore agreed by all to be unsuitable. It was suggested that the Government of India should take advantage of the situation by informing the maharani regent that in the interests of Scindia's education, training and general welfare, the ruler's future bride should be at least five years younger than him.[19] A somewhat unsuitable consort for a chief of such an 'exalted position' was eventually found in Satara, having exhausted the princely families of Baroda, Kolhapur, Nagpur, Tanjore and others, however the viceroy was disinclined to forbid the match as 'direct interference in such a matter should, if possible, be avoided'.[20]

The words 'direct interference' were open to interpretation. Political officers on the whole appeared to need little encouragement to enter into the cut and thrust of marriage arrangements between states and the business of marriage could prove to be a mutual accommodation between the British and their princely clients, having the potential to increase the status of the ruler concerned and to portray the imperial power as a sympathetic facilitator. Aye Ikegame in her study of Mysore marriages suggests that Indian princes, although 'ostensibly reliant' on the network of British officers and the viceroy for the approval of their marriages, did not submissively follow residents' advice. Rather 'they used the network when necessary, taking from the imperial structure only what suited their requirements'.[21]

An example of princely use of the 'network' occurred in 1896, when British political officers were involved in intense diplomatic negotiations to marry one of the Mysore princesses to the Maharao of Kotah, aged 22, who was looking for a wife over 13 with 5 *lakhs* of dowry to cover the wedding expenses. Colonel Loch, Principal of Mayo College (who was by his own admission better fitted for personnel work than academia), telegrammed to the Resident at Mysore that in his opinion the young man possessed an 'honest and absolutely faithfull desposition [sic] gentle bright sympathetic and most thoughtful health excellent has no signs whatever of any hereditary disease his personal views are I know entirely in favour of monogamy'.[22] However the Agent to the Governor-General in Rajputana reported that there was no chance of such an alliance succeeding at this stage, due to the conservatism of ruling families in Rajputana and prejudice over matters of caste and other social questions.[23] This proved to be the case and the maharaja's three sisters eventually married Ursus, members of a lesser branch of the Mysore royal family.[24]

The vexed question of finding an appropriate royal partner for their brother was illustrated by a report sent to the viceroy, Lord Elgin, from the Resident at Mysore, Donald Robertson, on the negotiations in 1897 for the Maharaja of Mysore's marriage:

> At one time there seemed some chance of an alliance with Baroda. The Maharani favoured the idea, and I was given to understand that the Gaekwar would have acquiesced. An insuperable difficulty arose, however, in the tender age of the girl. She is only five years old and it would hardly have been prudent to bind the young Maharaja here to celibacy for seven or eight years more.[25] A marriage with Baroda would have extinguished, for all time, the chances of a matrimonial alliance with a good Ruling Family in Rajputana, but, as Your Excellency is aware, the prospects of such a match are exceedingly remote. The Diwan next tried Cutch. The Rao is, I believe, a good Rajput and everything promised favourably. A deputation was indeed to start thence for Mysore, when it was discovered that the Mysore and Cutch families both claim to belong to the same gotra, or sect, of Kshattryas. Marriages within the same gotra are prohibited ... the objection as regards Cutch applies, unfortunately, with equal force to the other Bombay States, which are branches of that House. There are, however, two or three more eligible Chiefships left in Bombay, an alliance with one of whom may serve as a stepping stone eventually to something better in Rajputana, and these the Diwan is now exploiting.[26]

A confidential memorandum from the Diwan of Mysore in July 1898 listed the requirements for those *in loco parentis* making a selection of possible brides for the maharaja. Top of the list were the purity of Kshatriya blood, the personal health and appearance of the bride, the respectability and status of the family and the character, temper and disposition of the candidate.[27] The maharani regent was well aware of the great benefit which would accrue to her children and the Mysore royal family of marriage alliances with Rajput families in the north of India, despite the inevitable unpopularity that such matches would produce in the local community.[28] Regardless of the failure of the maharaja's sisters to find Rajput husbands, a delegation was despatched from Mysore to Rajkot, consisting of a high-ranking member of the council, the maharani's brother, the civil surgeon in Bangalore and a palace official, to seek the 'good advice' of the Bombay Government and in particular that of the Political Agent in Kathiawar, Colonel J. M. Hunter, since such a marriage would offer 'considerable temptations to unscrupulous adventurers'.[29]

In 1899, with British political officers acting assiduously as marriage brokers in 'the process of exhausting all desirable and possible selections', the maharaja under pressure agreed to a match with the elder daughter of the Rana of Vana, a Rajput 'connected with other ruling Chiefs' in Kathiawar. The girl was eleven, four years younger than her husband-to-be, and apparently desirable in appearance, physical condition and temperament. It was suspected that the family was not of a sufficiently high political status for a matrimonial union with Mysore, but British officials saw the objection as relatively minor in importance while the advantages were 'weighty and obvious'. It was a new departure for the Mysore royal family to seek a bride in the north, and it was unusual for a Rajput Kshatriya ruler to forsake his 'conservative traditions' in contracting alliances. For some years Mysore had been 'practically isolated' as far as marriage was concerned and the claims of the royal family to be Kshatriya at all were held to be 'mythical rather than historical', therefore it was a privilege to be able to marry into a Kshatriya family with as high a status as Vana. Eventually marriages between Mysore and important Rajput states might be negotiated on level terms, but at this stage the proposed match in which a comparatively obscure *thakur* allied himself with one of the wealthiest houses in India was considered a 'satisfactory advance'.[30] After the wedding the young bride would live with and be trained by her mother-in-law at Mysore. The maharani's 'good sense and right feeling' could be confidently relied upon for a judicious and timely decision on the matter of the consummation of the marriage, and it was proposed 'to defer the commencement of marital relations for about three years'.[31]

The maharani's fears over local disapproval of the alliance with Vana were well founded. A letter to the viceroy from the editor of the Bangalore *Evening Mail* dramatically illustrated the complications which could ensue from all but the most clear-cut of royal marriages and questioned the authority of the maharaja in relinquishing the traditional practice of a local marriage. It declared that the decision to bring in a foreign bride was 'attended with many evils'. It was asked whether 'domestic felicity' could be maintained if such a princess were introduced into the palace. The princes of Mysore were 'pure vegetarians' and the Rajputs 'generally flesh-eaters' and drinkers of alcohol 'who have no hesitation even to mix with the Mahomedans'. In the palace there were many priests, sycophants and dependants, who were always trying to 'work out some intrigue', and the introduction of people of 'dramatically opposite views and practices' would, it was claimed, ruin the harmonious atmosphere. Relations between mother-in-law and daughter-in-law would be 'peculiar' and there would be no common language in which to converse. Doubtless the wife would exert her power over her husband and through her influence his 'present practices and habits' might be changed, causing annoyance to his subjects since a prince should live 'not for himself but for his people'. The editor demanded to know how suitable matches for the offspring of such a marriage were to be made, and whether the 'degradation' of a change of caste would be necessary. Neither Rajput princes nor Mysore Ursu families would consider alliances with the children. The social organisation of India was 'very complicated and very rigid' and the Mysore royal family would be forced to look for bridegrooms and brides from other communities, leading to 'further complications and disturbances in the palace'.[32]

Western Influence on Royal Marriages

Complications arising from British intervention were not confined to marriage brokering. The introduction to a British education and cultural differences also had a substantial impact on some rulers in changing the

traditional approach to marriage. There was evidence that at the turn of
the nineteenth century Ganga Singh, Maharaja of Bikaner, was strongly
influenced by the ideas of his British tutor, Brian Egerton, whose adherence to austerity and discipline may have been at odds with the somewhat loose custom of betrothal. After Ganga Singh succeeded to the *gadi*
the Regency Council attempted to betroth him to the daughter of Fateh
Singh, Maharana of Udaipur. In 1897 when marriage negotiations were
taking place, the Bikaner ruler expressed his determination not to marry
the Udaipur princess, alleging that the betrothal ceremony to her had
not been formally completed but in fact because he felt that the ultra-
conservative maharana would be a troublesome father-in-law and the girl
was too young and not sufficiently good-looking.[33] The maharana wrote
to the Agent to the Governor-General in Rajputana, R. J. Crosthwaite,
emphasising that the betrothal was valid. In a letter to the viceroy, Lord
Elgin, Crosthwaite made the maharana's feelings plain:

> [he] tells me that, if the marriage is broken off, there will no
> longer be friendship between the States, and he and Bikanir
> will have a bad name throughout the whole of Hindustan. The
> result, he will probably say, of English education and an English
> tutor, is that young Chiefs learn to break their engagements ...
> if the Maharaja breaks the engagement, he will be considered
> to have acted contrary to the Rajput code of honour. He will
> undoubtedly inflict an injury on the Oodeypore lady. She has
> been reserved for him, and it will be difficult now to find a suit-
> able match for her. It is to be regretted that the Maharaja hav-
> ing been brought up by an English tutor should commence life
> by acting in a manner which the Chiefs will probably consider
> dishonourable. We must, however, expect that the Western wine
> will break the old Hindu bottles.[34]

The viceroy, although sharing some anxiety over the breach of harmony between two states, could not hide his satisfaction in noting that
the policy of giving young rulers 'some insight into the ideas of morality and social habits' which were considered 'essential points of modern
civilisation' had been somewhat successful. He admitted that 'as we

have educated the young Maharaja in an English fashion, we must not be surprised if he finds it difficult to conform to Hindu custom'. The Rajput custom of betrothal was inconsistent with the progress that the Government of India had tried to encourage, and it could not be maintained except under a system of polygyny that was no longer welcome to young rulers. In substance Elgin agreed with Crosthwaite: 'As you say, "the Western wine must break the old Hindu bottles" and while we must take care that it is not our hands that deal the blow, I see no reason in a case like this to regret the smash'.[35]

Nevertheless the decision not to marry the daughter of the maharana was hardly a wise move in Rajput society. Ganga Singh could be seen to be committing a breach of faith and acting dishonourably towards the most prestigious Rajput ruler. At only 17 it is possible that the maharaja thought that in challenging the Hindu custom that betrothal could not be severed he was adopting a modern stance and the British would commend his action.[36] The British certainly did not discourage him, and bearing in mind the amount of influence exercised by Egerton over the young ruler it is possible that the tutor was to some extent responsible for Ganga Singh's surprising refusal. However later in life the maharaja was to display a decidedly less-disciplined attitude to marriage practice in general and, dashing British hopes that he would eschew polygyny, Ganga Singh married three times in order to obtain male heirs.[37]

Despite the potency of 'Western wine' and its perceived benefits, exposure to western ideas did not always have a successful outcome. As Barbara Ramusack has pointed out, both British and Indians condemned miscegenation, and British society in India viewed white women who were sexually attracted to Indian men, and thus subverting the colonial hierarchy, as 'overtly betraying the imperial mission and covertly undermining claims of British masculinity and Indian male effeminacy'.[38] The complications of an Indian prince marrying a European woman were well demonstrated by the marriage of Ranbir Singh, Raja of Jind, in 1900 to Olive, said to be the daughter of P. A. von Tassel, a balloonist and parachutist 'of Dutch or German origin'. After the wedding von Tassel received a sum of Rs. 35,000 from the raja, the bulk of which was to be deposited in an English bank for the bride but which appeared to be rapidly disappearing in the hands of her parents. The Government of India much deplored the misjudgement of the raja in contracting such a match, as he had recently changed from a 'mere idler and pleasure-seeker' to 'a man addicted to business habits with something of a real regard for his duties towards his people'. It was regretted that the political officer, Lieutenant A. Irvine, had been unable to stop the match, however after the raja's investiture Irvine had been instructed by the Lieutenant-Governor of the Punjab, Sir Mackworth Young, to teach the young heir to stand alone and to seek advice only when absolutely necessary. Recognising that his action might not meet with British approval, the raja had resorted to the 'utmost secrecy and rushed the ceremony at the dead of night'.[39]

Problems were also generated by the marriage proposed in 1905 by the Nawab of Rampur's brother, the Sahibzada Nasir Ali Khan,[40] although in this case due to the fact that the groom was impecunious. The nawab for dubious reasons wished his brother to settle down in England after he finished his education there, offering him an allowance of £1,000 a year on the condition that he remained out of India until the nawab requested his return and stayed loyal to his brother, avoiding any 'intrigue' with other subjects of Rampur. Nasir Ali Khan was free to marry and to take up an offer he had received to enter the Middle Temple and qualify as a barrister. Matters were complicated by the fact that he was enamoured of a Miss Ethel Hopkins, daughter of a London art dealer, who was well educated with 'considerable personal attractions' and the prospect of an inheritance of £100,000. E. M. Hopkins, her father, objected to any formal engagement unless the nawab settled on his brother an income sufficient to maintain a wife. Moreover he drew up a set of extraordinarily demanding marriage stipulations: Nasir Ali Khan was to become a naturalised British subject, he was to renounce forever all rights and claims to the succession of Rampur, his children were to be brought up in his mother's religion and, finally, he was to settle in approved British trust securities a sum sufficient to produce an annual income of £3,000.

British officials noted that the position of the sahibzada was a 'peculiar one'. He had received a British education, all his 'tastes and proclivities' were British, and he wished to marry an English girl who was said to be clever and attractive. Every obstacle had been placed in the way of his return to India, and if he were to remain in England he could do much worse than to marry Miss Hopkins. It was noteworthy that he was the first Indian native of high birth to take a high degree at Oxford or Cambridge, and his record at school and college had been blameless.[41] Extremely grudgingly the nawab was eventually persuaded by the Government of India to offer his brother a guaranteed income of £1,020 a year, plus £820 a year to his widow and children for their lifetime, and the sahibzada was strongly recommended to accept the offer as it was felt that better terms would not be forthcoming.[42]

Due to his enforced existence in England and his wish to take an English bride, the Muslim Sahibzada of Rampur's alliance was a particularly unusual case. However royal Muslim marriage arrangements in India by no means followed a hard and fast formula. The two cases of Hyderabad and Bhopal illustrate the extent to which such arrangements could differ.

Royal Muslim Marriages in Hyderabad and Bhopal

At a meeting in Hyderabad in 1882 between the resident, W. B. Jones, and the minister, Salar Jung I, the living quarters for a possible wife for the nizam, Mahbub Ali Khan, were discussed in an effort to dissuade the ruler from participating in some of the more unsavoury sexual practices of the royal household. In the opinion of British officials in the state, the wife should remain in the Purani Haveli, the official residence of the nizam, and no females other than those permitted to attend upon her should have access to the palace. Salar Jung expressed the strongest disapproval, declaring that the control necessary to keep other females from entering the palace would be a 'violent innovation contrary to the customs of the *zenana*' and derogatory to His Highness's wife. He further asserted that it would be contrary to all custom and usage to keep His Highness's wife apart from the general *zenana*; that if his wife were in the Purana Haveli the nizam would 'necessarily' be in and out of the *zenana* in any case, and this could not be prevented; and, finally, that the restraint proposed to be placed on the nizam would be displeasing to the ruler. The minister stated that marriage would make no difference to the nizam's opportunities for intercourse with women in attendance on his wife, and would fail to check his desire to avail himself of such opportunities.[43]

The resident suspected that Salar Jung was afraid to consent to any arrangement which would be particularly distasteful to the nizam's mother and to the *zenana* in general. Captain Clerk, the nizam's tutor, later reported that the young ruler had decided to perform a *nikah* cere-mony.[44] To Clerk it seemed that in British terms this ceremony was 'worth but little, our marriage customs being so different to those of the *zenana* and our point of view so different to the Mahomedan'. Yet if the ruler were anxious to contract a marriage he should be allowed to do so, provided his grandmother and mother approved of the girl. It would be inconsistent for those immediately concerned with his training to make an objection to the ruler's doing what was 'lawful and right by Mahomedan law', while allowing his licentious behaviour to continue. The only restriction that might be made would be to limit his so-called 'visits to his mother' to 'what, strictly speaking, they ought to be'. As far as the issue of a *nikah* wife was concerned, the first-born male, whether legitimate or illegitimate according to European 'notions' of the status of the mother, would be recognised as having the first claim to succeed to the *gadi* according to the custom of the state.[45]

Over 20 years later moral standards in the Hyderabad palace were said still to be 'exceedingly lax' and the power of the *zenana* unbroken. Sir David Barr, Resident at Hyderabad, expressed much concern over the unmarried state of the sahibzada, the eldest son and heir of the nizam. It was suspected that the nizam had in fact never been involved in a marriage ceremony and had no recognised wife, only an 'enormous number' of concubines who constituted the *zenana*. In Sir David's view, having experienced 'the evils – not to say discomfort – of an establish-ment of this nature', the nizam should save his son from such a miser-able fate by allotting him one wife with whom he could lead a happy and respectable life, 'such as has not been known in the Hyderabad palaces for many years'. It was not the custom for British women to 'interview' any of the women of the *zenana* when visiting the palace, but supposedly the nizam's mother was the virtual head of the household and, although not of high birth herself, she exercised considerable control over her son. Sir David was of the opinion that the *zenana* was the worst aspect of the Hyderabad palace: 'The number of women maintained at the cost of His Highness is I believe nearer 10,000 than 5,000; they live under very unsanitary conditions – and their manners and customs, according to common report, are altogether shocking and disreputable'.[46]

In Bhopal, the second-largest Muslim state, the approach to royal marriage was infinitely more circumspect than that existing in Hyderabad. In selecting a husband for Sultan Jahan Begam, noble birth and a frugal disposition were the first considerations which her grandmother, Sikander Begam, required, 'though a handsome appearance and the habits and manners of a gentleman were by no means unessential'. It was agreed that a few of the most eligible boys should be presented to Sikander, and if one of the candidates met with her approval he was to go to Bhopal where arrangements for his training would be made. After sufficient time to form a 'just estimate of his habits and temperament', a final decision would be given. The begam alighted upon a representative of one of the noblest and most ancient families of Jalalabad, Ahmad Ali Khan, who at the age of seven was taken to Bhopal where he was constantly with his prospective bride, both in study and play, until the age of 18. By that stage it was agreed that his behaviour 'left nothing to be desired' and his progress in his studies was 'more than satisfactory'. However the final decision to marry in 1874 did not rest with the royal family. It was apparent that in the case of Bhopal the traditional power of a ruler to choose his or her spouse now required British sanction. A *kharita* had to be sent to the viceroy for his approval, without which the marriage could not be concluded.[47]

A marriage contract was drawn up which not only curtailed the rights of the groom but also gave a remarkable degree of control to a Muslim wife. The marriage would be annulled if Ahmad Ali converted from Sunni to Shia Islam. He was to fulfil 'all the duties of a husband' and not interfere in any way with his wife's *jagir* or other personal property. Failure to abide by these terms would give her the right to bring about a separation. The groom agreed not to take a second wife (permissible under Muslim law) without the 'express permission and approval of Sultan Jahan', and to have nothing to do with the marriages of any of his wife's children, male or female, leaving such matters to her and her mother. He promised to treat the nobles, *jagirdars* and officials of state with respect and not to retain in his service any person to whom the ruler or her ministers might take exception, or who was reputed to be ill-disposed towards the state or the British Government. None of his relatives or friends was to intervene in affairs of state. Finally he authorised his mother-in-law, Shah Jahan, to decree a separation in the event of a 'serious disagreement' between his wife and himself, a separation that would be binding and not questionable in a court of law. For Sultan Jahan the marriage contract contained conditions which would also enable her to end the marriage in case of disagreement, interference or sheer incompatibility. This document received the signature of the political agent to give it British approval.[48]

Although Sultan Jahan herself admitted later that many of the clauses could not be legally enforced,[49] the marriage contract displayed the uniqueness of Bhopal as an Indian, and in particular a Muslim, state in allowing a ruling female such exceptional powers over her husband and independence in her affairs. However other royal women in India during the period, although not rulers in their own right, also succeeded in wielding a considerable amount of power, often by subscribing to British ideas on matters such as education and government and thereby gaining British support for their personal position within the state administration. The increasing influence of the press and access to British legal advisers was also able to further the cause of female members of royal families.

Raising Female Status

A truly public profile was inconceivable for all but a handful of royal females, such as the Begams of Bhopal. However, as far as raising their status was concerned, royal Indian women were to find one of their greatest champions in Lord Lytton. Aware of the social advantages assured to the viceroy as the first representative of the Crown within

India, Lytton saw no reason to continue to defer to Indian custom as far as women were concerned, whether such custom applied to princely or plebeian circles. In a letter to the Queen's Private Secretary, Major General Ponsonby, the viceroy declared that, while using the Imperial Assemblage of 1877 to do away with the 'worn out and inconvenient system' of exchanging presents, it appeared that the occasion was 'singularly fit and favourable' for introducing the European manner of displaying women in public. Lytton admitted that the idea was revolutionary in India, 'the strict seclusion, not to say suppression of the female sex is so prevalent throughout the East, that the appearance in public of any Englishwoman, of the least rank or position, would shock native prejudices, and lower her in the eyes of the natives'.

However the viceroy was persuaded by 'previous personal intercourse with the better class of natives in India' that this was an anachronistic official tradition. Why should the British

> conform our own social life and customs to the low standard of those whose masters we are by reason of our superior social enlightenment. In any case, the particular prejudice which this un-English custom was intended to satisfy appears to me to be one which it is not only beneath our dignity and self-respect to adopt and incorporate into our own manners and customs, but also contrary to the acknowledged principles of our policy, and the best interests of our Government, to encourage and perpetuate on the part of the natives themselves. We have put down *suttee* with the strong hand and have done much to improve the position of Hindu widows and Mahomedan wives. We are establishing *zenana* schools throughout India and exhorting the better class of natives to educate their women and humanise female life in their homes. Is it consistent with such a policy to stultify our precepts by our practice? ... To me the adoption of such a course seemed singularly inappropriate to the solemn proclamation of the title of a female sovereign to the Empire of all India.[50]

Accordingly at the assemblage, Lytton determined that his wife should accompany him on his state entry into Delhi and was most satisfied to see that, in the light of the British position of social supremacy, such an assault on Indian accepted practice had no adverse effects. The viceroy declared that 'So far from shocking the Native Princes, it has, to all appearances, greatly flattered and pleased them. Each of those who were present at the Viceroy's subsequent receptions spontaneously asked to be presented to Lady Lytton and all of them showed her the most deferential and courteous attention ... as respectfully and cordially as the most polished Englishman could have done'.[51]

The disregard for traditional Indian ideas of female subjugation was reinforced by Lytton's request to the queen in 1877 for the initiation of a special order for women within the Indian empire.[52] Such an order would be 'extremely useful and advantageous', not only in raising 'in the estimation of husband and male relatives the present depressed social condition of the female portion of Your Majesty's native subjects', but also in helping 'to introduce the personal influence of the Empress of India into the *Zenanas* of Native Courts, which are at present shut to British influence, and where the other influences now predominating are often as mischievous as they are powerful'. The viceroy recommended the Maharani Jumnabai, adoptive mother of the young Gaekwar of Baroda, as an ideal candidate, reporting that she was in need of British support:

> the object of many influential native officials being to destroy the influence of Her Highness over her son by surrounding him with all those temptations which generally make the royal *Zenanas* of this country the more deplorable schools for male or female character. All this she has nobly and successfully resisted.[53]

Maharani Jumnabai was just one of a number of powerful female regents during the period.

Regents

Prior to Lytton's recommendation the Maharani Jumnabai had indeed shown a particular aptitude for administrative detail and a desire to instil methods of accountability within her state. She demanded a significant role in the administration during the minority of her son, Sayaji Rao III, and a scheme was devised by the resident for the minister, T. Madhava Rao,[54] to spend a day a fortnight with her to discuss a short report on the state. The minister was to arrange for members of the Gaekwar family in the palace to seek her advice with regard to their various needs. He was also to frame budgets for the palace and for 25 *karkhanas*, on the principle that within the budget arrangement the maharani was to have complete authority in managing the *karkhanas* apart from being obliged to submit six monthly accounts. In framing the budgets the maharani was to be freely consulted, and if there were a difference of opinion between the maharani and the minister the matter was to be referred to the agent to the governor-general.[55]

The royal women of Mysore also demonstrated an extraordinary enthusiasm for improvement in matters of state. In 1877 a *kharita* from the senior maharanis to the viceroy, Lord Lytton, raised with great clarity a number of subjects including the education of the young maharaja, in an effort to achieve the 'enlightened principles of justice' which were 'so characteristic a feature of British rule'. This was particularly significant in light of the fact that Mysore was to be restored to native rule in 1881. The maharanis requested an English gentleman from an English university to be appointed as tutor to the young ruler, and a 'high officer of ability and standing' to act as guardian and to train him in the 'principles of good government'. Moreover as he was 15 they wished to see him married in accordance with the Mysore 'religious code'. They expressed the need for the 'machinery of Government' to be simplified, since the current administration did not compare favourably with its predecessor and the Mysore people were 'not a whit more prosperous'. Public Works and other departments were not working well and radical change was required. The current famine was being badly mismanaged and the remissions of assessments 'too grudgingly and sparingly made', while thousands of Mysoreans had died as a result of leaving the state to find food and employment. The royal women, in a surprisingly perceptive paragraph, recognised that there was a need for the imposition of a 'house tax' on the nobility. The middle classes of the community and Muslim descendants of aristocratic families lived in virtual destitution as they drew very small salaries; more could be employed in the palace, with an allowance continuing to their heirs after their death. Finally, the maharanis suggested that the office of town magistrate and president of the municipality be filled only by a European officer of experience, since the present incumbent was disliked by both Muslims and Hindus due to his overbearing conduct.[56]

Suggesting that a female grasp of political matters was an ongoing feature of the Mysore court, the widow of Chamarajendra Wadiyar, the Maharaja of Mysore whose education the senior maharanis were discussing in their *kharita*, displayed similarly assertive qualities. In December 1894 the resident, Colonel Henderson, wrote that he was of the opinion that it would be unwise for the Maharani Vanivilas Sannidhana, to be appointed regent, since she was

a lady of domestic tastes who has not concerned herself with events beyond the range of her family and the palace walls. The palace is, as it ever was, a hot bed of petty and mischievous intrigues, and a lady living in seclusion might with the best intentions be moved by evil influences to exert her authority in a wrong direction.[57]

It would be advisable to 'leave Her Highness the control and management of all affairs connected with the palace and of the expenditure of the Civil List, subject to certain restrictions, and I am inclined to think that she would not wish for more'. However, by January, Henderson was aware that he had underestimated the maharani's potential. He was informed by her brother that she had expressed strong feelings against the diwan's autocratic behaviour. Moreover

she had felt very much the practical seclusion of her own countrymen from palace and power, and considered that a Council should be more representative than the present one, and should wield more influence. She was averse to the Brahmin element being too strong in the public service, and especially the Madras Brahmin element.[58]

The maharani declared her opposition to any British move to appoint the diwan as regent on the grounds that it would be more suitable for her to fill the position. The resident admitted, 'I have come to the conclusion that the Maharani is a woman of decided opinion and of considerable strength of character, and that any one who supposes she is going to prove a puppet is likely to find out his mistake'. It appeared that she was 'a lady of education and intelligence not likely to be much influenced by bad advisers' and it would be very difficult 'not to give due weight to her representations'.[59]

An account of a meeting between the resident and the maharani, 'without the intervention of the *purdah*', reinforced the picture of a forceful female character. The resident pointed out to her the 'manifest difficulties' of carrying out the duties of regent while living in 'oriental seclusion'. He also stressed that in a constitutional state responsible officials carried out all administrative work under certain laws and regulations, and that opportunities for the exercise of direct authority were rare. The maharani replied in English that she was always perfectly willing to give audiences to her advisers, she had received a good education in both English and her own language, and was willing to devote time and trouble to the cases before her. She understood that in a state where the government organised the system of administration it was not necessary to interfere in the details. Wherever action was necessary on her part she would ask for and follow the advice of the resident, whose supervision she hoped would be closer than before. The maharani suggested that the minority council should not be purely consultative as at present, but with executive functions apportioned among the members and important matters referred to the entire assembly. She was particularly adamant that members should not be appointed by the diwan, but by herself as regent or by the Government of India. Mysoreans were not represented sufficiently in public service or in the council and she wished her countrymen's interests to be 'cared for' in these areas.[60]

Despite her obvious admiration for a more open British style of rule, the maharani expressed great reluctance to relinquish any form of control over her son, Krishnaraja, to British officials and resented in particular the arrangements for separate rooms for him at Bangalore and Mysore.

When the door leading to the *zenana* from these rooms was locked by the young prince's British guardian, there was much discontent from the 'Palace party'.[61] The maharani installed a telephone wire from her own bedroom to the Summer Palace to maintain contact with her son, despite the fact that there was already telephonic communication day and night, and also appointed her own official to supervise the preparation of the maharaja's meals. However the ruler's guardian, Stuart Fraser, refused to tolerate the presence at the Summer Palace of an Old Palace official who was not subordinate to him but who nevertheless gave orders to his servants and demanded that the maharani recognise the limitations of her powers as regent in matters connected with the prince, since it was the Government of India which exercised the guardianship.[62]

It was agreed that it would be difficult to remove the maharaja, aged 11, from the care of his mother, but there were 'corrupting influences about the Palace' over which the maharani had little control, despite the fact that in many ways she was an 'educated and sensible woman'.[63] In 1896 there were signs that the maharani was still attempting to interfere with the terms set out for the young ruler's residence at the three palaces in Mysore, Bangalore and Ootacamund, announcing her intention while at Bangalore to proceed to Mysore for a religious ceremony, taking him with her. The resident, Colonel Robertson, was forced to point out how unsettling this was for the maharaja and how carefully his programme of studies should be followed. He admitted that 'this little lady, extremely nice though she be, when roused is exceedingly determined and overawes her relations and dependents'.[64]

The differences of opinion appear eventually to have been satisfactorily overcome. At the end of the regency the diwan in Mysore reported that

> in arrangements made for the education of the Maharaja, in management of Palace affairs as well as in concerns of State, Her Highness has shown a great capacity to grasp the bearings of the questions that have come before her ... Her Highness is almost a unique instance in the history of Mysore of a lady of her position responding successfully to an emergency and establishing

by her breadth of mind, natural sagacity and high sense of duty a reputation which cannot but reflect on her sex.[65]

It was recommended that the maharani should continue to receive a 19-gun salute with accompanying honours.[66] By this stage the maharaja to all intents and purposes had assumed power within the palace. Stuart Fraser noted that as the ruler became more mature his mother possessed 'little power to move him when he has made up his mind'. A case in point was a unilateral decision to postpone his nuptials until after his installation, a matter in which normally 'custom would make the voice of a Hindu mother supreme'.[67]

Female Protagonists

With access to British advisors and the new opportunities offered by the availability of the press at the end of the nineteenth century, some royal females were able to defend themselves against male relatives or ministers of state to an impressive degree, if not always with maximum success. In the 1890s the Indore ranis carried on a lengthy and highly acrimonious battle with the maharaja, Shivaji Rao Holkar. The maharaja bemoaned the fact that it 'may appear at first that my stepmothers, women as they are, cannot do anything against me, who am the ruler of the State possessed of full powers', whereas they 'bribe my personal servants and attendants and the police peons on watch duty at my palace with a view to annoy and irritate'. He gave orders to the treasurer to stop paying his stepmothers' allowances until they, first, stopped fighting him over the Khasgi estate in Bombay, of which they retained possession; secondly, sent his nephews to a boarding school such as Daly College; and thirdly, dismissed their lawyer, Mr. Rochfort Davis, and other similarly employed persons.

In Holkar's view there was 'serious misconduct' on the part of the Dowager Maharani Radabhai. On the death of the ruler's mother, acting on the advice of the Agent to the Governor-General in Central India, Francis Henvey, Holkar had given orders for the Khasgi Department to be taken over by his *durbar* and for the current land agent, Madhav Rao Gogte, to be dismissed as unsatisfactory. However the Dowager

Maharani Varanasi Bai who, in the maharaja's opinion, had 'no right to interfere in any way in the administration of the Khasgi or any other department of my State' directed the agent to bar access to Holkar's nominee and to take orders only from her, as she considered herself to be the heiress and ruler of the Khasgi Department. Holkar stated that he could, on application to a civil court of law, have Gogte turned out and his own nominee installed in his place, 'but I shrink from proceeding against a member of my own family in an open Court of Law, and virtually the suit would be against the Maharani Radabhai'.[68]

One of Maharani Radabhai's advisers, Rochfort Davis, was a pensioner of the British Government who wrote defamatory articles against Holkar in the *Eastern Herald*. As Henvey pointed out in 1890, such articles 'revived and exacerbated' the fury of royal Indore family quarrels. If the maharaja were a private individual he could prosecute the newspaper, but a ruler of his rank could not according to 'native usages' appear in the Cantonment Magistrate's Court and subject himself to the ordeal of cross-examination. However if he remained silent, the maharaja feared that the accusations against him would be repeated in every corner of India. Henvey recognised the unfairness of the position of the ruler:

> Whatever may be thought of an unlicensed freedom of the press in British India, a cantonment of British troops, or a Residency situated in foreign territory and in the midst of powerful, suspicious and sensitive Chiefs, should not be used as a place of refuge, from which coarse and defamatory attacks may be securely levelled against Her Majesty's feudatories.[69]

The anti-Holkar publicity initiated by female members of the royal family was held to be both 'mischievous and politically dangerous'.[70]

Both the Dowager Maharani Radabhai and Junior Maharani Parwatibai had received large monthly allowances from the state treasury which were partly used for the payment of men such as Rochfort Davis, whose 'injurious articles' induced the dowager maharani to give him money for his services. The cash payments which Holkar proposed suspending were, the ruler emphasised, unrelated to expenses for living, that is houses, food, clothes, servants, carriages, attendants and guards, which were 'provided free by the State in the most liberal style'.[71] In 1891 the Agent to the Governor-General in Central India, R. J. Crosthwaite, responded to a memorial from the dowager maharani by declaring that he was unable to interfere on her behalf since she was continuing to retain the Khasgi estate in defiance of Holkar. Moreover she refused to meet the ruler's wishes regarding the education of his nephews, whom she retained with their mother in her custody, apparently in the hope that the elder boy would succeed to the *gadi*. Under the Treaty of Mandisore the British Government had declared that it had no concern with any of the maharaja's children, relations, dependents, subjects or servants, over whom the maharaja had absolute control.[72]

A memorial of 1899 written to the viceroy by Maharani Varanasi Bai, incensed at the lack of British justice in failing to reinforce the property rights of royal women such as herself, shows no signs of female reticence. It dwells at length on the fact that, as the Maharani of Indore, she was the trustee of vast estates held

> on behalf of future Maharanis ... The Khasgi estate is in the nature of a *jagir* in the Indore State and the possessor has inherent rights like any other *jagirdar*, chieftain or landlord which cannot be tampered with. The ruling Rani exercises supreme revenue and judicial powers, subject to an appeal to the Maharaja in respect of serious offences alone. The Rani holds *Durbars* for the transaction of business. There is a separate throne, a separate seal, a separate establishment; separate *nazars* are presented to her on solemn and festive occasions; and the Rani at the time of her accession is placed on the throne and receives a salute in the same way as the Prince does ... Further the Khasgi has a treasury of its own. It has independent jurisdiction both in matters civil and criminal.[73]

The maharani pointed out that in the history of the Khasgi estate over 150 years no possessor had been removed. Twice attempts had been made by the reigning prince and on both occasions proved unsuccessful as a result of the interference of the British Government. It was hoped that, as her position as Maharani of Indore precluded her from appealing to a court of law,[74] the viceroy would now afford her the same protection as that given to her female predecessors so that she could attend to 'the maintenance of the dignity of the senior maharani, and the performance of charitable and religious acts'.[75] However she failed to receive such a guarantee of protection from the viceroy, since relations between Holkar and the Government of India were by the end of the century so strained that it was felt that it would hardly be advancing the cause of the maharani to interfere in royal financial transactions.

Rani Janaki Subbamma Bai, second wife of Ramachandra, Raja of Pudukkottai, also benefited from the newly found accessibility of British advisers. From 1878 to 1886 while Ramachandra was still alive, the diwan of the state, A. Sashiah Sastri, began measures to end corruption among palace servants, to reorganise some overstaffed departments and to put the palace buildings in good repair. After Sastri assumed the regency of Pudukkottai during the minority of the young heir, Martanda, the diwan's interference in every detail of palace life was 'overt', given clear encouragement from the British. However, as Joanne Punzo Waghorne points out in her study of the Pudukkottai royal family, the rani after 1886 'left nothing undone' in order to bring about Sastri's departure from the state, hiring a British lawyer to put forward her case to save her remaining authority in the palace. Her argument was preserved by Sastri in his own printed response to her formal letter to the political agent, which he entitled 'Memorandum Drawn up by the Dewan Regent Stating Categorically the Result of Correspondence between him and the Political Agent and Orders of the Government on Various Subjects alluded to and Allegations Made by the Junior Ranee Sahib'.[76]

The rani's 'mystifying and confounding' defence, conducted through her lawyer, raised issues which seemed as trivial as Sastri claimed. An argument over the use of a playground for the minor raja roused the rani to assert her right to freedom of religion. The senior princess's wrath was incurred because Sastri wanted to move her temporarily out of her old apartments in order 'to make them sanitary'. The rest of the ill will arose from the women's unwillingness to give up the company of 'a band of notorious villains', which included a group of unsavoury playmates caught openly playing cards with the raja's brothers, and the supposedly dangerous dancing girls who were found 'in constant company with the Princess'. It appeared that 'the beleaguered Dewan had only persisted in his duty, much against the petty stubbornness of the palace ladies'.[77]

However the expulsion of the 'dancing girls' was an act which fundamentally affected the existence of the princess, as these girls, the *devadasis*, served crucial functions for the palace women. At the end of the nineteenth century, the Tondaiman royal females were still expected to keep *purdah*. The *devadasis*, who were free from such restrictions, accompanied them on all their visits outside the palace and held up cloth screens to protect them from the public eye as they moved from their palanquins. The education of the palace women depended on the *devadasis* who taught the essential arts of song and dance. Deprived of their company, the senior princess would literally be captive in the palace and prohibited from fulfilling many of her ritual obligations.[78]

Sastri argued that many of the rani's objections to his rules of cleanliness in the palace, and to his mandates for the places where the minor raja should play and which apartments her daughter should occupy were based on 'superstition'. But the rani countered Sastri in a long letter to the political agent:

> To meet me with the plea that my objections are untenable because they are superstitious is a dangerous answer in the mouths of the representatives of the British government. It is but so much of a slip from the domain of sentiment to the domain of religion. Yet could you expect obedience from me or approval from the government if you were to turn a deaf ear to my objections against the proselytizing of my son on the ground that the adherence to my own creed was a foolish form of superstition?[79]

In dealing with this particular issue the rani was arguing convincingly that Sastri's reforms fell into the category of the interference into Hindu religious affairs prohibited by the Queen's Proclamation of 1858. However her letter of complaint resulted in an interview with the Governor of Madras which, instead of being a hearing of her grievances, backfired into a stern lecture on her behaviour. As the diwan reiterated in his official answer to her complaint, the rani's 'character' was already well known to the British. Reports of past political agents portrayed her as the 20-year power behind the throne in Pudukkottai. She and 'her relations' and 'two or three Brahmans, her special favourites' supposedly inveigled the raja out of the state seal and 'took control of the judicial process'. In addition 'her Brahman Parasites' weakened the power of the former diwan's office. Sastri pointed to the 'disgrace and ruin she has been to the character of her late husband, and to the State'.[80]

The obsessive ambition displayed by the Rani of Pudukkottai was by no means unique. In 1890 the viceroy, Lord Lansdowne, scathingly observed of the Maharani of Rewah in Rajputana that she was representative of a breed of grasping royal widows:

> In all cases where a very young ruler succeeds to a Native State, the widows of his predecessor give an infinite amount of trouble. Their object is of course to get hold of the boy and to bring him up under conditions which in a few years will convert him into an imbecile and leave the power in their hands. Our object is to prevent such a state of things arising.[81]

Cynically the viceroy agreed with the maharani's regret that owing to the 'abolition of *suttee*', she and other widows of the late maharaja 'were prevented from removing themselves from this troublesome world immediately after their consort had left it'.[82]

However not all royal mothers were so eager to wrest power from their offspring and were able to use British advice, on occasions turning to the Government of India itself, to ensure that their children were not usurped by other, possibly less desirable, candidates to the throne. Following the death of her husband, the Maharani of Dumraon expressed her unwillingness to adopt a son in order not to disinherit her daughter, the Maharani of Rewah[83] and her possible offspring.

It was noted by Sir Charles Paul, advising the Council of India, that the late maharaja had been well aware of the chance of the power of adoption not being exercised after his death and had deliberately left the matter entirely to the wish and option of his wife. Legally she was not bound to adopt, moreover it was impossible to hold the view that she was incompetent to manage the property in question until her daughter inherited it. The late maharaja had spoken of his wife in his will as 'possessed of great intelligence and capacity for business', moreover when interviewed officially she had given satisfactory answers and could read and write 'freely'. In the eyes of Sir Charles to be female was not a disqualification for owning an estate: 'As *Purdanashin* ladies do not go out into the world but manage through Managers', this particular role was well suited to those women capable of running a successful business.[84]

The Begams of Bhopal

When it came to demonstrating their capability, the profile of royal women was highest in the state of Bhopal. Yet, ironically, despite the traditionally martial stance of female rulers in Bhopal, during the latter half of the nineteenth century the ruling begam, Shah Jahan, was to provide a good example of 'disabling passivity'. Moreover under the sway of her second husband her unwillingness to cooperate with political officers undoubtedly decreased her political authority. Like her mother, Sikander, Shah Jahan Begam was honoured by the British in the late nineteenth century for her loyalty to the paramount power. However government files revealed internal problems in Bhopal from 1881, when high officials in the Foreign Department were informed of the compilation of 'seditious' works on *jihad*, or religious war, by Sadiq Hassan, Shah Jahan Begam's second husband and a prominent supporter of the Wahabi movement. Named after the Arab evangelist, Abdul Wahab, the movement focused upon the puritan values of Islam, drawn from the Quran and Sunnah, and in the eyes of the British engendered religious fanaticism.

The 1857 Mutiny, although it originated in the army and found supporters among Hindus and Muslim alike throughout northern

India, was widely viewed as a product of enduring Muslim animosity towards the British. Into the 1860s this aura of suspicion remained a powerful force, shaping the British perception of the empire's Muslim subjects.[85] Constantly on the alert for outbreaks of violence, the British saw in the Wahabi movement the gathering together of the more extreme elements of 'the tribes of Islam' to 'wage holy war against the *Faringhi*'.[86] However this view was gradually re-evaluated, mainly as a result of the publication in 1871 of William Wilson Hunter's *The Indian Mussalmans* which questioned whether 'these British subjects' were 'bound by their religion to rebel against the Queen'.[87] The central object of the work was to urge upon the Government a less hostile policy towards Muslims and to distinguish between the 'fanatical masses' and 'the landed and clerical interests'.[88] In fact despite the British fear of pan-Islamic activities (particularly in the wake of the Madhist revolt in 1881 in the Sudan) Islamic movements, even that of the Wahabis, very rarely presented a significant threat to the British.[89]

Although Colonel Henry Daly, Agent to the Governor-General in Central India, initially dismissed fears of Bhopali disloyalty, the situation came to a peak under his successor, Sir Lepel Griffin, when the nawab-consort persisted in disseminating his publications, and works in Arabic, Persian and Urdu appeared in major centres of Arabic scholarship such as Egypt, Constantinople and Mecca. Late in 1885, the Government of India publicly stripped Sadiq Hassan of his titles, salutes and rank.[90] Such an extreme reaction may not have been justified. Francis Robinson points out that Sadiq Hassan was no charlatan but a leading Muslim fundamentalist reformer who wrote over 200 books and has been studied in depth.[91] Moreover Claudia Preckel notes that the model of a reformed and modernised Islamic state, which was created with his advice, survived his deposition. Throughout Bhopal in the nineteenth century there was 'a strong development of Islamic religious and cultural reform'. This Islamic revival could have been regarded with disapproval by the British authorities, however its inclusion of 'huge architectural projects, educational and literary efforts and economic as well as administrative reforms' resulted in a growing admiration for the female rulers of the state both within Indian and British circles.[92]

After her husband's deposition, although Sir Lepel was often blunt and rude to the begam in private[93] he continued to show respect for her in public meetings, placing all the blame for corruption and intrigue in the state on the nawab-consort.[94] However a lengthy article in *The Times* of 27 December 1886 revealed sordid details regarding the begam's second marriage. The article declared that the begams, in the mould of female rulers such as the Czarina Catherine, had never been famous for their 'domestic virtues' and that Sadiq Hassan had been a 'too successful lover'.[95] The Foreign Department issued apologies, yet in all of the correspondence surrounding this incident the charges against Shah Jahan were never actually contradicted. Instead, officers remarked on the 'want of prudence and generosity' involved in publishing in an international newspaper the 'fact' of a reigning princess having been 'seduced by a clerk'.[96]

To British officials in India Shah Jahan, far from emulating the Czarina Catherine, fitted neatly into the role of the 'degraded' Oriental woman existing in submissive subordination to her husband. A government memorandum of 1886 pointed out that since her second marriage the begam, who previously appeared in public and took a personal and active share in the administration, 'has retired behind the *purdah*, and has become a mere cypher in the hands of her husband'.[97] Sir Lepel dismissed the ruler as 'a weak misguided woman, completely under the influence of her husband, [who] had permitted her State and her subjects to become the prey of an adventurer'. Nothing short of banishing Sadiq Hassan from the state would provide an effective remedy for the existing maladministration of Bhopal. As long as her husband was allowed to remain, the begam would be entirely unable to shake off his authority and govern on her own account through responsible ministers. In Sir Lepel's view:

> It is impossible to exaggerate the ascendancy which he [Sadiq Hassan] has acquired over the Begam. All her attendants and relations attribute it to charms which he has given her, and which she wears in her hair and there is, indeed, something almost miraculous in her steadfast adherence to a man whose forgeries, perjuries and tyranny are thoroughly known to her.

She cannot plead ignorance and she is as fertile as her husband in inventing lies to screen offences and crimes of his, which she is unable to deny.[98]

The inaccessibility of the begam was much to be regretted, 'she and her mother having been accustomed to come in public unveiled and dispose of State business face to face with their Ministers'. Moreover her female visitors had been discouraged from coming to the palace with the result that she was 'virtually a prisoner'. All information on state affairs 'she has heard with the ears of the Nawab and seen with his eyes alone'.[99] Sir Lepel suggested that if the ruler were to come out of *purdah* many of the difficulties of administration would be removed. The begam, hinting that the image of a 'mere cypher' may have been wrongly ascribed to her by British officials, replied somewhat acerbically that the agent to the governor-general appeared to imagine that her ideas and opinions were written on her face, standing firm in her refusal to come out of *purdah* as it was 'contrary to her creed'.[100]

With the removal of Sadiq Hassan from the administration, and his death in 1889, Shah Jahan to some extent reasserted her political position. The political agent in Bhopal, Colonel W. Kincaid, congratulated her on her personal conduct of various areas of the administration. The ruler was prepared to sit in court daily during certain hours 'ready to hear all reports and listen to complaints' to ensure that justice was carried out, and to issue speedy orders for enquiries into cases against the police. Moreover she had given an order for the jails to be inspected twice a month and was in the process of dividing the authorities in control of jails and police.[101] Nevertheless the acting minister, Colonel C. Ward, now had full power in all departments, subject to the begam's orders given by her personally, in the hope that 'Constitutional Government will … take the place of a crushing and omnipotent tyranny'.[102]

Demanding more control in affairs of state, in a spirited *kharita* to the viceroy in 1888 Shah Jahan complained forcibly that her authority had undergone 'great diminution' and that the state had become a 'laughing stock to its enemies'. The appointment of an empowered minister and the substitution of a new system of administration for the old customs of the state had reduced the position of begam to an 'imaginary picture'. She complained that no cases, except those connected with *jagirs*, were referred to her and demanded 'full powers to conduct the State as formerly'. Such powers included the ability to engage a minister to her liking on a salary reflecting the small revenues of the state; to introduce measures for improving and bettering the condition of subjects, officials and *jagirdars*; to punish officials by fine or dismissal; to appoint and promote officials; to call for reports from officials for negligence or irregularity; and to settle all cases according to the established usage of the state.[103]

Colonel Ward stressed that, despite her protestations, the begam still possessed great authority: 'there is not one single case of any importance in which she has not been consulted by me, either revenue or civil. As for money matters, she is supreme – even my office bill goes to her monthly for sanction and payment'.[104] Ward also credited Shah Jahan with a certain amount of acuity in dealing with administrative reforms and, in particular, the problems facing the state in the collection of settlement revenue. The begam regretted the excessive burden of taxation on her subjects and demanded that the minister fix an assessment that was more realistic.[105] However the Agent to the Governor-General in Central India, R. J. Crosthwaite, was not equally euphoric over her conduct of the administration when it was suggested that she should receive a further two guns to her personal salute. He was of the opinion that 'As a lady she has many difficulties to contend against, and the ability and discretion with which she governs are worthy of admiration. But in the actual condition of the State there is nothing in the administration which calls for special praise'.[106]

Sultan Jahan Begam, Shah Jahan's daughter, from whom the ruler was estranged for much of her reign,[107] observed of her mother that, 'like the majority of her sex, she was wilful and obstinate'. She could rarely be induced to change her opinion, or to deviate from a course of action she had once determined to follow.[108] Yet Shah Jahan was by no means without her successes. It was not until her reign that Urdu literature flourished in Bhopal. The begam was particularly fond of poetry and offered substantial state pensions to the men of learning who gathered at her court, also acting as patron to a circle of female poets. The most remarkable of Shah Jahan Begam's writings was *Tahzib un-Niswan*, a 475-page manual for women first published in 1889. It was written in a simple style, which made it accessible to most Urdu-speaking females, and as a result it was extremely popular and was reprinted several times. Considered the first women's encyclopaedia in India, the volume covered a wide variety of topics relating to women's work in the household and their status in Islam. It attempted to give women some control over their own lives by teaching them about pregnancy, child-rearing and hygiene, as well as marriage, divorce and other ceremonies within Islam.[109] Throughout, Shah Jahan emphasised the need for females to save themselves and their families from helpless dependence.[110] However it is apparent that the book was intended for privileged women, who had servants and who were able to afford the seclusion of *purdah*.

Shah Jahan's most visible programme as ruler consisted of extensive undertakings in urban planning and architecture.[111] The most dramatic building towering over the city of Bhopal was the Tajul Masajid. Seen at the time as the largest mosque in Asia, it positioned Shah Jahan Begam as a highly visible protector of Islam. One particular feature was a dedicated area for women, a highly unusual design element in South Asian mosques, favouring the involvement of females in public congregational prayer instead of prayers in their homes. In 1887 she provided the funds for the construction in Woking in Surrey of what would be Britain's first purpose-built mosque as part of an Oriental Institute intended to foster sympathy for 'the East'.[112] Shah Jahan also recognised the need for a hospital specifically designed for the needs of *purdah* women, and 'The Lady Lansdowne Hospital for Women' was opened in Bhopal in 1892.[113] In the view of Barbara Metcalf the begam remains 'a complex, intriguing figure: an observant Muslim woman who was a ruler; a reformer who fits … uneasily into any simple category of progress or regress'.[114]

During the last years of Shah Jahan's reign, under the minister of state, Munshi Imtiyaz Ali Khan, the administration of Bhopal deteriorated to an alarming degree. A corrupt system of revenue collection resulted in a fall in the state population from 900,000 to 600,000 due to death or emigration, and courts of justice degenerated into arenas

for 'bribery competitions'.[115] Munshi Imtiyaz Ali's successor, Maulavi
Abdul Jabbar Khan, was old, inexperienced in revenue administration
and unable to tackle the corrupt practices which he had inherited in
all departments. After Shah Jahan's death Sultan Jahan determined to
train herself in administrative detail. In many ways she revealed herself to be as 'wilful' as her mother. In the light of ministerial behaviour
during Shah Jahan's reign, she believed firmly that it was impossible
for a minister to be 'in sympathy with the people and their interests
to the same extent as the natural ruler of the State'.[116] For a year and
a half the begam ruled the state unaided, then, unable to cope, com-
promised by appointing two ministers and dividing the work between
them. At the start of her reign in 1901 she made a personal tour of
the various districts of the state to deal with settlement arrangements,
noting that,

> The affairs of every *mahal* that I visited stood in urgent need
> of reform and of the personal attention of the ruler. Four thou-
> sand six hundred and ninety-nine petitions were presented to me
> during this tour ... amongst these there were very few which
> were not deserving of attention, and on which orders were not
> passed.[117]

In her inspection to determine and grant leases it was impossible to
get through the work of a single *mahal* in less than eight days: 'My
own work occupied me eighteen hours daily ... sometimes until past
midnight, I was occupied with correspondence on various State matters, and in devising and directing measures for the suppression of
plague'.[118]

Apart from a revision of the settlement procedures, one of Sultan
Jahan's first reforms consisted of the appointment of a legislative
council; moreover she heard, personally, every appeal that was made
against the decisions of the ministers' courts. In 1903 she displayed
considerable courage and determination in undertaking a hazardous
pilgrimage to Mecca, in the course of which Bedouins fired upon the
royal party.[119] The newly installed ruler also opened the Madrasa Tabia
Asifia, specialising in the teaching of Unani[120] medicine, in 1903 and,

against much opposition influenced by '*purdah* considerations', opened in the same year the Madrasa Suleiman, the first school for the education of girls in Bhopal.[121] After visiting Europe in 1911, Sultan Jahan's educational and social campaign for women's emancipation moved to a wider stage and she became the founding President of the All-India Muslim Ladies Conference in 1914. The conference supported girls' education and raising the age of marriage but discouraged the abandonment of *purdah*.

Ten years later the begam attended the All-India Women's Conference on Educational Reform. By then, at the age of 70, her stance on *purdah* had mellowed. At the conference, well aware of the need to make life easier for her gender, rich or poor, she advocated 'a lessening of *purdah* restrictions, greater focus of work on under-privileged women and a style of education less geared to domestic matters'.[122] After the death of Shah Jahan, Sultan Jahan, in describing her mother's life, recognised the problems faced by all the begams of Bhopal – and indeed faced by other royal Indian women in positions of power at that time: 'When we realise the difficulties of the position she was called upon to fill, remembering at the same time the limitations by which in Eastern society ladies of noble birth are surrounded, we cannot but be amazed that her success was so great and her mistakes so few'.[123]

* * *

The British regulation of Indian princely marriages was not simply part of the imperial exercise to create a more ordered, tidy society in the states. It had several specific aims. First, by demanding that the details of proposed marriages were reported to the Government of India it was possible to eliminate the substantial wheeling and dealing of *durbars* in contracting alliances. Such monitoring on the part of British officials tended to include a thorough inspection of the physical and mental attributes of the parties concerned, thereby preventing weaknesses occurring in the line of descent. Secondly, marriage was seen by the more devious members of the court as a means by which the young heir could escape the clutches of British tutors or guardians. The British determination to ensure that a bride was sufficiently younger than her royal husband to allow him to live independently until an age when he had completed his education put paid to this ruse. Thirdly, there were obvious advantages, particularly in major states, to a suitable political match.

Cooperation between royal families and the paramount power in concluding marriages could prove to be of mutual benefit. The families involved were able to use the British network of contacts to their advantage, and to be seen to support princely activity helped to legitimise the British position. However resentment was caused by the British attempt to supplant the allegedly more licentious practices of the *zenana* by the introduction of monogamous royal marriage, an effort which was still proving somewhat fruitless by the start of the twentieth century. Official condemnation of princely marriages with European women, with the potential for far-reaching problems, also failed to be entirely successful in deterring rulers from entering into such arrangements. Nevertheless, despite the fact that they were without a mandate from the Government of India to enforce western norms, limited interference by political officers was enough to remove total independence in marriage matters from many *durbars* and to alter traditional practice to some extent.

Whereas within a state the status of a prince could be considerably diminished as a result of British efforts to change traditional rule at the end of the nineteenth century, the women of his family stood to gain much by adopting and implementing British ideas, particularly in the areas of princely education and administration. It must be stressed that those who took advantage of such an opportunity were few and far between. In the vast majority of princely *durbars* in the latter part of the nineteenth century, the highly resistant and conservative weight of the *zenana* constantly thwarted British efforts at improvement. However those royal women who proved themselves 'useful' in the process of British indirect rule were able, remarkably, to assume a female role in affairs of state which, with the exception of the monarch herself, was inconceivable at that time in Britain.

With access to the press and British legal advisors, if not the law courts of British India, royal women also became capable of defending their position. Just as princely honour was being undermined by British intervention in palace life, it could also be undermined by a challenge in public from a female relative. However, far from arousing admiration for the spirit and determination of the female protagonist, such behaviour tended to confirm 'the Orientalist stereotype of *zenana* women as idle intriguers who, ignorant of substantial affairs of the world, preoccupied themselves with making trouble for others'.[124] 'Idle intriguers' or not, by the start of the twentieth century the power structure of the *zenana* began to change shape in that the introduction of western ideas in some *durbars* opened up state administration and exposed the conduct of the palace, and the women's quarters could no longer act as effectively as a source of invisible, but at times almost despotic, power.

4

RULER OF THE STATE

MALADMINISTRATION AND MISRULE

The first section of this chapter on the adult Indian ruler concentrates upon the challenge faced by senior British officials of eradicating misrule of Indian states while at the same time moderating the much-despised intervention of political officers, who seized every opportunity to preach reform and improvement to the rulers and *durbaris* with whom they came in contact. Reform within the states was undoubtedly required, since British policy after 1858 appeared to have achieved little in moulding the princes into responsible servants of the Crown. In fact it was argued that it had made the *durbars* more belligerent and unyielding in their conservatism.

The Official Post-Mutiny Approach to Intervention

Renowned in British Indian circles as a force for improvement, the viceroy, Lord Mayo, was equally conscientious in his approach to the states and possessed a powerful vision of the direction in which they should be led. Until his assassination in 1872 he threw himself into the work of his political portfolio with an enthusiasm reminiscent of Dalhousie. Mayo was the first governor-general to undertake a comprehensive tour of the princely states, and he found the experience disturbing. He informed the secretary of state, the Duke of Argyll,

That in Joudhpore, Ulwar and Odeypore and several of the small
states a state of chronic anarchy prevails – that corruption and
intrigue is as rife in several courts as it was in the days of the
Emperors, that female infanticide and many of the other old evils
prevail to an enormous extent – that to begin what must be the
work of many, many years, an Entire Change of Policy must be
adopted, the present mixture of *Laissez-Faire* and niggling interference must be abandoned and the Chiefs must be told what
they will not be allowed to do.[1]

Mayo was convinced that if the princes were to act as 'loyal feudatories',
a policy must be found 'to exalt the dignity, strengthen the authority and increase the personal respectability of these ancient families'.
Britain should 'obtain real and lasting influence by showing them that
that which they value above everything, i.e. the support of the British
Government ... is only to be gained by the exercise of justice, by the
certain punishment of crime and the encouragement of those who support our recommendations'.[2]

The task was not an easy one, since the majority of rulers hardly
constituted promising material. Mayo referred scathingly to 'these
men who are children in some respects but treacherous and savage in
others'.[3] Moreover relations with the states were extremely ill-defined:

We act on the principle of non-interference but we must constantly interfere. We allow them to keep armies for the defence
of their States but we cannot permit them to go to war – we
encourage them to establish courts of justice but we cannot
hear of their trying Europeans – we recognise them as separate
Sovereigns but we daily issue orders to them which are implicitly
obeyed – we depose them ... when the Ruler commits or sanctions a grievous crime – or create an administration for them as
in the Ulwur case when the Chief misgoverns and harries his
subjects – with some we place political agents, with others we
do not – with some as with Jeypore, Bhopal and Puttialla we
are on terms of intimacy and friendship, with others as with
Dholepore we scarcely ever address them except to find fault

with some gross neglect of Duty ... [we] are governed by the Circumstances of the Time and the Character of the Ruler.[4]

Mayo did not believe that the princes had a natural entitlement to imperial protection. As a part of the new hierarchy which was to emerge as a result of the Queen's Proclamation he was adamant that the Indian rulers should earn British support. Speaking to the assembled Rajput princes at Jaipur in October 1870 he outlined his view:

> If we respect your rights and privileges, you must also respect the rights and regard the privileges of those who are placed beneath your care. If we support you in your power, we expect in return good government. We demand that everywhere throughout the length and breadth of Rajpootana justice and order should prevail; that every man's property should be secure; that the traveller should come and go in safety; that the cultivator should enjoy the fruits of his labour and the trader the fruits of his commerce; that you should make roads, encourage education, and provide for the relief of the sick.[5]

However there was little evidence of the adoption of a consistent policy emanating from the highest levels of the Government of India to bring about the 'good government' to which Mayo aspired. Examples of a desire to avoid a too-harsh imposition of British rule appear frequently during the viceroyalties of both Mayo and his successor, Lord Northbrook. In 1871 the official reaction to disputes between the Maharaja of Bikaner and his nobles declared that 'Her Majesty's Government are averse from a direct and authoritative interference in the affairs of the State, regarding such interference as being, except in extreme cases, inexpedient, especially when, in the case of Bikaneer, it is not provided for in our Treaty with the Chief'.[6] The Maharaja of Marwar's decision the following year to appoint a council to deal with grievances of his nobles was commended by the secretary of state, who approved the 'intimation to the Maharaja that we have no desire to interfere in the Government and that our interest in the state is confined to its being prosperous and well governed'.[7]

A similar line was adopted when dealing with Tukoji Rao Holkar, Maharaja of Indore, who was allegedly confiscating the holdings of those nobles beneath him whose guarantees did not exist in the recently republished Treaty of Indore: 'it must be borne in mind that in the absence of an express guarantee, we have no right to interfere between Holkar and his feudatories'.[8] The case of Indore illustrated the paradoxical situation in which a ruler was able to exploit his subjects in the safe knowledge that the threat of British intervention prevented internal uprisings within a state. Referring to Holkar, Sir Lepel Griffin, Agent to the Governor-General in Central India, wrote to the viceroy, Lord Ripon, in 1881, 'These chiefs are proud of their extortions, and boast that the British Government would never dare to take what they can from the people; forgetting that it is no love for them which keeps their subjects quiet, but the great shadow of the British Government which is ever seen sheltering the Raja's throne'.[9]

Even in cases which would have aroused the fury of social reformers earlier in the century, if a ruler was not directly implicated in misdeeds within his state no particularly stringent action was taken by the Government of India. When dealing with the failure of the Rewah *durbar* in 1870 to investigate two cases of *sati* and punish those involved, it was merely suggested that surprise and displeasure be conveyed to the prince, which 'may lead to increased vigilance in the repression of the crime... in other Chiefs'.[10] Ian Copland refers to the all-out effort to reform the states in the image of the west in the period,[11] but at a high official level this effort was in many cases tempered by a desire to persuade miscreant rulers to change their ways rather than to force them into action. In attempting to eradicate the kidnapping of children in the Madras and Bombay presidencies, advice was given by the India Office to the effect that native rulers should not be forced into supporting British efforts at reform:

> the obvious duty of each political officer [is] to urge on the Chief to whose *Durbar* he is accredited that the summary repression of this infamous practice is due, not so much to the demands of the British Government, as to those of common humanity and that, on this ground, Her Majesty's Government fully rely on his cordial cooperation in a matter so closely affecting the welfare of his subjects.[12]

In his study of Alwar, Edward Haynes makes it clear that, unless it was essential, the Home Government was anxious to avoid radical intervention in the states in the early 1870s. The conflict between the ruler, Sheodan Singh, and the powerful body of *jagirdars* who during his minority had held power had reached a state of virtual civil war as the prince turned to small landlords and minor administrators for support. Haynes states that his removal was urged by officials both in India and Britain, 'but the political and psychological realities did not permit such a drastic break with tradition. In many ways, the Victorian British acted out their view of monarchy which placed great stress on the irrevocable right of a Prince of the Blood to royal office despite personal failings'.[13] An article from the *Delhi Gazette* of February 1871 reported that, following India Office policy, the debasement of the Alwar prince had not been deemed appropriate. His position had been 'scrupulously respected', although at the same time he had been effectively deprived of the means of doing further harm. He might still be involved in intrigue but it would be 'a waste of time and trouble' as long as a competent political officer remained in charge.[14]

During the 1870s it was unlikely in any case that particularly effective intervention in states' affairs would have been possible.[15] When Mayo took over the viceroyalty Indian finances had shown a deficit for the past three years, and resources were hardly available to fund the employment of a sufficiently large force of political officers to deal with all erring rulers. Moreover, as the following section makes clear, intervention by political agents was often seen as far from constructive by both Calcutta and London.

The Blight of the Political Officer

In their zeal to improve matters the rise to prominence of political officers in the 1870s was highly significant. The vast majority of the Indian Political Service shared the optimistic view of Lord Mayo and his chief political adviser, the Calvinistic Sir Charles Aitchison, that with proper guidance the princes could be induced to mend their ways. Few politicals qualified as intellectuals in the narrow sense of the term, but they tended to be, especially the younger men, imbued with a strong sense of purpose. Most came from middle-class British families and, although there is little evidence that many were ideologically fired by the undiluted force of utilitarianism and evangelicalism which had galvanised the reformers of the first half of the century,[16] they shared the devotion to progress which formed an essential part of the Victorian middle-class creed. However they were not only zealous but also impatient and, like Mayo, wished to see the states develop in their own lifetime. Many were confident of convincing the Indian rulers of the virtues of reform and improvement by rational argument and force of personality, however few possessed the required skill or charisma. In practice, therefore, at the grass-roots level of British Government in the states the *mission civilisatrice* became a pretext for various degrees of coercion.[17]

As a response to the constant intrusion into states' affairs official condemnation of the Political Service flowed both in government despatches and viceregal correspondence throughout the latter part of the nineteenth century. The India Office made it clear that British political officers would 'most surely earn the approbation of the Government which they serve by abstaining from all obtrusive and vexatious interference with details, while showing themselves ready to aid with their advice the chiefs and rulers to whom they are accredited'.[18] With the exception of Curzon's viceroyalty, the majority of political officers were given little official encouragement beyond a prince's minority period to indulge in anything but the most minimal intervention in state government, such as maintaining the equilibrium between the different parties involved.

The loudest and most vigorous criticism of the new wave of political officers came from the Council of India. During the Duke of Argyll's term as secretary of state (1868–74) hardly a despatch went out which did not contain either general or specific criticism of political style. Two of the most able and experienced members of the council, Sir Erskine Perry and Sir George Clerk, voiced their views clearly in notes attached to a despatch of 1873 on the succession of the grandson of the Maharaj Rana of Dholpur. According to Perry, if the small states who gained independence at the break up of Maratha power were not supported by the officers of the paramount power, they would be absorbed by the larger princes, such as Patiala and Scindia.

He cautioned however that 'Our presence however prevents this sort of natural crystallization going on, which is the tendency of native (perhaps of all) society. We keep things in "status quo" but at the same time we destroy all energy and capacity for self-government'.[19] Clerk agreed that 'Faction is fomented, responsibility paralyzed and the self respect of Rulers destroyed in this puerile meddling and muddling in the affairs of certain ever loyal States, willing in all emergencies to serve us with their entire resources'.[20]

In response to such criticism, sympathy was given to a plea by the Maharaja of Bharatpur to be relieved of the continual presence of a political agent at his court, on the grounds that the agent tended 'to diminish his self-reliance and to cramp his personal exertions'. The India Office advised the Government of India that

> Her Majesty's Government would be loth to encourage among Native Chiefs any possible feeling that, whilst the evil results of the system in force are attributed to the Native ruler, the good is assigned to the interposition, more or less directly exercised, of the British officer, that they have responsibility without independence and that they are placed in a false position with respect to both the British Government and their own subjects.[21]

On the grounds of the 'highly satisfactory account' of the prince, agreement for the removal of the agent was accordingly given.[22]

Similar British consideration was shown by Argyll over the appointment of a resident to the court of Kashmir, a measure fiercely opposed by the maharaja on the grounds that his treaty exempted him from such supervision. The secretary of state admitted that 'it is the very fact of dependence which makes the arrangement distasteful to Native Princes in India. In the case of really independent nations, there is no danger of the representatives of other States interfering or being troublesome; whereas our Residents, in virtue of our Suzerain powers, are very apt to be perpetually interfering and practically make the Princes feel that their "Raj" is over'.[23] Correspondence between Ranbir Singh, Maharaja of Kashmir, and the Afghan leader, Sher Ali, which was intercepted in 1879, revealed the extent to which the Indian ruler detested British interference. It was reported that the maharaja had written letters to the effect that

> the practical difference between the British and the Russian Raj, assuming one or other to be our master, is that, under the Russian Raj, we shall at least be spared the intrusion of the Resident Political Officer. The Russians put garrisons where such garrisons will give them the military and political control of their subject Asiatic provinces, and to the native rulers of those provinces this involves only a matter of tribute, the amount of which, if left to their own devices, they can always wring out of their subjects. The British, on the other hand, come upon us with certain preconceived and semi-religious ideas (which, like all religious ideas, are not susceptible of open discussion) about administrative proprieties, and the duties of rulers towards their subjects, etc; which ideas are not only uncongenial, but absolutely incomprehensible to us... The presence of a political officer lifts our 'purda'; and the moment our 'purda' is lifted, goodbye to our local independence. If we do not act in precise conformity with the foreign notions prevalent amongst what is, so far as we can judge, the lowest class of a distant western community, necessarily ignorant of the practical conditions of our Eastern life, the political officer immediately reports the fact to his Raj; and his Raj then comes down upon us with a heavy hand, in the name of 'humanity' or 'civilisation', or some other such absurdity undreamed of in our philosophy. Under the Russian Raj, we should no doubt still be feudatories, but feudatories free at least to wallop our own packages with our own sticks in our own way, and rid of that intolerable nuisance – 'the British Political Officer'.[24]

Northbrook's successor, Lord Lytton, was in entire agreement with the maharaja as far as the intervention of heavy-handed political officers was concerned:

> I have long thought that the British Resident at Native Courts is on the whole a political mistake. I am certain that he is regarded

by those Courts as an intolerable nuisance, and that, instead of facilitating our relations with them, or increasing our influence over them, he is either a chronic source of irritation to them, or else, for all practical purposes, their agent and advocate in every matter of dispute with the British Government.[25]

However although the viceroy prided himself on the 'great dominant purpose of the British Raj to improve and civilise wherever it extends its power', whereas the Russian Raj 'craves power in every direction, without any reference to the power of doing good', he was unable to produce a formula which would move the states forward to an ideal standard of 'political perfection and social prosperity' without some form of British presence. With limited resources to furnish every ruler with a political officer of substance, there seemed to be no practical alternative between 'crushing' a ruler or leaving him alone.[26]

Throughout his viceroyalty, Lytton remained convinced that the general system of residents had not been successful: 'certainly our best relations are with the Punjab states, at whose Courts we have no Residents', and criticism had been made that no case could be cited of any 'really important' reform in a native administration directly due to the influence or agency of a resident since all such reforms had been carried out by the direct intervention of the Government of India during minorities, or under similar conditions. But the viceroy did admit that the reason why it was possible to withdraw political officers from some native courts was that 'the relations between those Courts and the Suzerain Power have long ago been reduced to their right permanent position by the local action and influence of the Resident'. The work of Sir Richard Meade in Hyderabad was one example of a highly competent political officer in the demanding position of dealing with a 'feudatory authority whose personal aims we know to be incompatible with our political interests'.[27]

As a matter of long-term policy, Lytton favoured the system originally suggested by Lord Mayo of reducing the number of political officers and grouping native states under 'collective relations to one superior political authority' with few officers resident at their respective courts. This measure would 'strengthen our political control over the feudatory Courts, and greatly improve our relations with them'.[28] A proposed amalgamation of the Central Indian and Rajputana agencies could create savings of Rs. 218,920 per year. It would not be necessary to delegate greater powers to one agent to the governor-general than were already possessed by two. Moreover when railway communications were complete, one agent could see more of every chief than two had been able to do previously and could 'easily manage to visit every State in the two Agencies, at least once a year, if required, even taking his camp with him', since 'there is not a State which could not be reached within two days from the nearest railway station'.[29]

However, despite proposals intended to streamline the organisation of the Political Department, continuing evidence emerged of complaints over the amount of British intervention in the states at both a high and low official level. In 1885 the secretary of state, Lord Randolph Churchill, declared that

A much more generous and pleasing policy might be pursued by the Foreign Office at Calcutta towards many of the Native Princes. My impression, when I left India, was that relations between many of the Native Princes and the Foreign Office showed a constant nagging petty interference by the latter with the former in all affairs, small and great, and that this was working great mischief.[30]

Churchill's successor, Lord Hamilton, agreed with this view. Writing to the viceroy, Lord Curzon, in 1899 he expressed the opinion that it would be worthwhile to 'cultivate kinder relations' with the Gaekwar of Baroda, 'a man of ability ... [who] governs his territories well'. The secretary of state added, 'Few, if any, of our great Feudatories love the Paramount Power, and I am not at all sure that in several cases this antipathy is not largely due to tactlessness, mistakes and undue interference on the part of the various Foreign Offices and Political Residents'.[31] In the case of Sir Lepel Griffin, Agent to the Governor-General in Central India, such criticism was quite possibly justified. When Sir Lepel was accused by the Begam of Bhopal of using 'imperative terms' while addressing her,[32] a senior British official failed to rush to his defence, noting that 'Local officers in these matters are not always safe guides. They allow themselves to be influenced by local prejudices and they are apt to fancy that any opposition to their wishes is a crime against the State'.[33]

When it was reported that the Nizam of Hyderabad 'bitterly resented' a proposed examination of his personal finances, and, rather than undergo such an indignity, was prepared to give the Government of India a guarantee that he would limit his expenditure to 55 *lakhs* from the public treasury, Curzon saw the proposal as not unreasonable: 'I am certain that these Princes are to be got at by a little personal courtesy, and that what is represented as disloyalty to Government is often no more that the irritation produced by a long course of friction with a not very tactful British representative'.[34] On the other hand, in Curzon's view, turning a blind eye to princely activity was hardly the answer to good management of the states. On a visit to Chumba, a minor Himalayan state which 'wisely or unwisely, we leave almost entirely to itself', Curzon noted that no political officer or resident was *in situ*, and the young raja was visited only once or twice a year by the Lahore Commissioner. As a result he had degenerated into a 'timid and useless inebriate ... For want of a little schooling he has gone hopelessly to pieces'.[35]

Curzon had little praise in general for the Punjab system of managing states, which 'leaves them utterly alone until they have turned into fuddle-headed jockeys, like Patiala, or into hopeless debauchees, like the late Bhawalpur ... Every day that I am here, I am more impressed with the futility of managing Native States through Local Governments, who have neither the tradition, the training, nor the men for the job'.[36] Of the twelve 'gun' rulers of the Punjab, the viceroy identified no fewer than seven who 'afford a spectacle that cannot be studied with complacency'. Local administrations possessing no Political Service had failed to provide support to young rulers who had 'enjoyed the advantages of tuition at the best European hands'.[37] The Raja of Jind was allotted a military member of the Punjab Commission to act as his tutor and guardian.[38] However, as discussed in the chapter on royal marriage, the raja subsequently secretly married the daughter of 'a professional aeronaut of low character', which to Curzon illustrated

'how imperfect the authority and control of the Local Government
must be', supporting his view that 'wherever possible, these young
Chiefs, at the most ductile period of their lives, should be put in [the]
charge of Political Officers, not picked haphazard from the ranks of
the Army, or from the Civil Commission, but selected from the trained
Political Department'.[39]

Writing to the secretary of state in 1900 during a tour of Cochin
and Travancore, Curzon repeated his criticism of the monopoly of
local governments over princely states in their control. He declared
the system 'utterly vicious and rotten'. Practically it would be difficult for the Foreign Department to manage either the states of
Madras, because of their distance from headquarters, or the states of
Bombay, because their administration would 'add so immensely to
our own labours'. Yet there was great danger in leaving the local governments to supervise states and rulers 'whom they now consistently
mismanage, and who, under this plan, drift away altogether from the
Imperial system'.[40] According to the viceroy, the inevitable weakness
of the local organisation lay in the fact that residents had no political
training before they were sent to a state: 'Everything depends on the
idiosyncracies [sic] of the individual; but there is no system, no tradition, no body of rules; and a tactless Political Officer, with a weak
or obstinate Native *Durbar*, can very soon bring the whole edifice to
the ground'.[41] Such officers were in stark contrast to those men who
reported directly to Curzon:

> From my Agents to the Governor-General I receive incessant and
> minute reports. I know everything that goes on in the Courts of
> the Chief under their charge ... [but] take the case of the Local
> Governments. During the 2½ years in which I have been in India,
> I have had only one reference from the Madras Government with
> regard to Cochin and Travancore. With the exception of the
> boundary dispute, I have never had any reference from Bombay
> about Cutch. Till famine arose, and they required loans from us,
> I never heard a word about the Kathiawar States ... The Local
> Governments, in their treatment of their Native States, pursue

a policy of absolute independence, and never refer anything to the Government of India except in the last resort.[42]

However the Political Committee in England was adamant that the control of states under local governments should remain under their governors rather than be transferred to Calcutta. The committee contended that were such control transferred to the Political Department of the Government of India, departmental officials would find it impossible to supervise the increase in work. Moreover there would be the greatest difficulty in finding men outside the areas where the states were situated who had an adequate regional knowledge of race, customs, traditions and systems of administration and taxation. The secretary of state did recognise that local governments lacked departments or high officials adequately trained to scrutinise the work of political agents in order to ensure continuity or energy within the service. It was suggested that a compromise might be found whereby the Government of India should have a voice in the selection of agents. They should be taken from the local service and there should be a division of issues to be referred for orders: those relating to revenue matters and local habits to be referred to local governments, and those political in a broad sense to be referred to the central government.[43]

Princely Misrule

Princes were often bound by treaty to rule according to British advice, making the post of British resident at an Indian court one of considerable responsibility. However since residents were often divided in the priorities of, on the one hand, the progress of their royal charge and raising the moral tone of the royal household, and, on the other, the demands of setting up an efficient system of government, it was not surprising that many princes resorted to favoured members of the palace entourage and parallel administrations which they could control. Much misrule and princely excess were the products of the challenging situation in which a prince was placed, and the dichotomy he faced in attempting to reconcile western and oriental expectations. For a political officer a similar tension was created by the clash of

a western upbringing with an alien Indian culture, and the degree
to which he was influenced by the widely held Victorian construct
of India as 'backward and uncivilised', associating the subcontinent
with such depravities as oriental corruption, female incarceration and
tyrranical rule.

Although, other than during Curzon's regime, it was officially seen
as desirable to reduce interference to a minimum, serious abuses of
power within princely administrations could not be tolerated. As links
in the chain of British rule, the Indian princes were not allowed to
appear as symbols of depravity, although during the latter part of the
nineteenth century there was little evidence of a defined Government
of India policy to deal with major or minor princely shortcomings.
Of great significance was the ripple effect that disciplinary behaviour could have upon other rulers, and the consideration given to such
an effect appeared to vary from viceroy to viceroy. An enquiry into a
relatively isolated area of misrule could have a negative impact on the
reputation and political utility of the princely order as a whole, and
there was a fear that the removal of a ruler from power might unleash
instability and disorder in the state concerned and neighbouring areas
of princely and British India.[44]

However, despite the negative consequences of inflicting a highly
visible punishment upon a prince, disciplinary action was required in
certain cases. Following an attack upon an individual by armed men
in the employment of Raghuraj Singh, Maharaja of Rewah, which constituted not only a serious outrage but a breach of his treaty with the
British Government, the ruler was fined Rs. 10,000, which it was held
'will no doubt serve to note the liability of a Chief, in his position, to
punishment when avenging, in outrageous form, an insult'. In 1875 the
maharaja made the state over to the care of a political agent 'until debts
were discharged, and a fair system of administration established'. The
state revenue had dwindled from thirty-five *lakhs* to eight and a half
lakhs, and the ruler had squandered vast sums in gifts to *jagirdars* and
priests.[45] The Nawab of Janjira, who killed two gaolers by flogging,
having previously displayed his unfitness to rule by other misdeeds,
was deprived of criminal jurisdiction and allotted a political agent at
his own expense.[46] Given the opportunity, the Bombay Government

would have inflicted a similar punishment on the Rana of Porbandar for the torture and murder of an Arab who entered the *zenana* of his late son. The Government of India opposed such strong measures, but under pressure from Bombay agreed to demote the prince to the third class of Kathiawar rulers.[47]

In cases of excessive misrule Britain was forced to take more serious action. If the princes were now to be representatives of the Crown, a certain standard of civilised behaviour was required on their part and, if such a standard were not met, it would be necessary to remove them from power. The Home Government duly approved the deposition of the Maharaja of Patna in Bihar in January 1871, as a result of cases of 'scalping and human sacrifice'.[48] Forceful, if less drastic, punishment was meted out to Dungar Singh, Maharaja of Bikaner, in 1884. In marked contrast to the rule of his somewhat enlightened son, the maharaja had shown a 'persistent disregard' for the advice of the Government of India. In January a despatch declared that if

> owing to chronic misrule a Native State has fallen into a condition of disorder so complete that the authority of the Chief can be maintained only by the employment of British troops, it appears to us that the Government of India is ... bound to take adequate steps for the reform of the administration and the redress of the grievances from which the people of the State are suffering.[49]

A political officer was to be appointed and the upkeep of the agency was to be borne by the maharaja, as well as the cost of a British military expedition sent to end a dispute between the ruler and some of his *thakurs*.[50]

On the whole, the more powerful the state the more severe was British treatment of misrule. British leniency in a major, much-exposed test case would be seen to create a dangerous precedent. Moreover, whereas in minor states there were limited British resources to control the administration and it was necessary to gain the cooperation of local rulers, in the largest of the princely dominions British manpower and financial support were much more readily available. Malhar Rao of Baroda was without doubt the most important prince to be deposed in the second half of the nineteenth century. Baroda was opened up for the first time to British influence, and the princes at large reminded forcefully of the strength of the paramount power.[51]

The report of the Second Baroda Commission, published at the beginning of April 1875, proved totally inconclusive. Sir Richard Meade and his two English colleagues serving on the commission found the gaekwar guilty of attempting to poison the Baroda resident, Colonel Robert Phayre, with drink laced with arsenic and diamond dust. The three Indian members, consisting of the Maharajas of Jaipur and Gwalior and Sir Dinkar Rao, former diwan of Gwalior, held him to be innocent. The supreme government was faced with a grave problem: if they accepted the verdict of the commission, which was technically 'not guilty', they were obliged to restore Malhar Rao to his throne. If, on the other hand, they ignored the findings, they would be forced to find some other justification for his deposition. Eventually, after much pressure from the Cabinet, it was decided to remove Malhar Rao on the grounds of 'gross misrule'.[52] Northbrook deeply regretted the Cabinet's decision. He realised that the removal of the gaekwar on the grounds of maladministration would be a breach of his Government's earlier pledge, giving the prince until December 1875 to introduce reforms, and would in addition deny the credibility of the enquiry.[53] The viceroy was well aware that there was already 'some sympathy with the Gaekwar among the Native Princes, not personally, but because of the class of evidence against him – i.e. his own Private Secretary and the Residency servants'.[54]

In refusing to give the gaekwar the benefit of the doubt when the three Indian commissioners concluded that the charge was not proven, Northbrook acted inconsistently with his policy of placing them on the commission in the first place. The damage to relations between Britain and the princes stemmed less from the eventual deposition of Malhar Rao, who was blatantly unfit to rule, than from the obvious British contempt for native ability and integrity. As Salisbury stated,

the Baroda experiment ... has sufficiently indicated to us that an open enquiry and Native members of the tribunal are instruments in advance of present Indian requirements. The moral which the whole of this affair has left written upon Indian history is that the Government is still supreme to punish Princes who do wrong, unfettered by any obligations or customary pledges as to procedure, and with that broad result we have no reason to be dissatisfied.[55]

Minuting in May 1876, Northbrook's successor, Lord Lytton, found nothing in the performance of governments in either Bombay or Calcutta to indicate 'any well considered and well-defined policy' towards the states. In his opinion, Northbrook had 'neglected feudatory policy to his cost'.[56] However during his own viceroyalty in dealing with the ruler of Kashmir, Ranbir Singh, Lytton proved no more proficient in finding a satisfactory means of disciplining the maharaja without moving inexorably towards annexation.

Lytton reported to the secretary of state, Lord Cranbrook, in July 1879 that, despite being under severe pressure from the Punjab Government and public opinion in India to undertake the management of the major famine in Kashmir, he was loath to intervene to stop the 'wholesale corruption and terrible depopulation'. As the viceroy explained,

This I have declined to do, partly because the famine is too far gone to be successfully treated by any system, or at any cost, but mainly because such an attempt would involve the suppression of the whole local machinery, as well as of the Maharaja's authority and ultimately the annexation of Kashmir, after a great and useless expenditure of money by us ... all Native States are badly governed, according to our standard, and if we once begin to interfere in the internal affairs of independent Native Governments, we shall infallibly end by being forced to annex them.[57]

In the view of the viceroy too strong an approach against Ranbir Singh on the grounds of gross, or even criminal, mismanagement of the famine should not be taken, as such an approach 'would have shocked and shaken to the base, the confidence of every one of the Queen's great feudatories throughout India'. Writing to Sir Robert Egerton, Lieutenant-Governor of the Punjab, he expressed his opinion that if the Kashmir administration were put under unprecedented supervision, British action would be regarded by other states as

> that of political Pecksniffs, endeavouring, under a pretence of philanthropy, to secure an extension of political powers, for which no other pretext could be devised. In that case, all our other Native States would, I think, consider themselves to be in the cave of Polyphemus, and each would be wondering whose turn would come next.[58]

However it was recognised that in the case of Kashmir some discipli-nary action must be taken. 'Philanthropic sentiment' had been 'out-raged' by the painful accounts of the famine. In the light of the fact that the maharaja had used the independent political action allowed to him 'to augment his own importance, rather than to promote British interests', the viceroy felt that the prince should be deprived of all pow-ers in relation to the territories of Chitral and Yassin, and told firmly that 'henceforth, he will neither be required, nor permitted, to meddle with the affairs of any state, great or small, beyond the Cashmere fron-tier'.[59] In 1883 Lytton's successor, Lord Ripon, was advised that on the death of the current maharaja strong measures should be adopted. A resident and assistant should remain throughout the year in Kashmir and 'things symbolic of the paramount power be put as ostentatiously forward as they are now studiously suppressed.[60]

Drastic grounds for intervention were also identified in the small north-eastern state of Manipur in 1891, with the eruption of an anti-British revolt second only to the Mutiny of 1857. Following a palace coup, an inadequately armed expedition led by the Chief Commissioner of Assam was despatched to the state to arrest one of the royal princes, Tikendrajit, accused by the Government of India of usurping his brother, the maharaja. The British force was ignomini-ously routed and the political agent, the chief commissioner and four British officers were murdered in cold blood in the palace. A purge of all British influence in the state followed: telegraph offices and lines were destroyed, telegraph operators murdered, a sanatorium burned down and British graves desecrated.[61]

Within a fortnight three columns of British troops converged upon Manipur. The royal palace was looted and razed to the ground to make way for a permanent military camp, and Tikendrajit, the subversive brother of the ruler, was publicly hanged. At home, condemnation of the Government of India resounded both in the press and in parliament. The execution of a prince, albeit a villain, upset Queen Victoria, who protested to the viceroy, Lord Lansdowne, that the behaviour of residents and political agents tended to exacerbate events in a princely state. The viceroy agreed that 'the bearing of our Residents to the Native Princes is not what it should be, and they are often rude and overbearing, their notion being that of governing India by fear, and by crushing, instead of by firmness, joined with conciliation'.[62] However he was determined to maintain the principle that all subjects of native states found guilty of rebellion against the paramount power were, *prima facie*, worthy of death.[63]

There was an assumption by the press in England that Manipur would be annexed with 'a good deal of acceptance in official circles'. Lansdowne was not prepared to admit that annexation must follow as a matter of course. There were points to be resolved: whether by annexation responsibilities would be incurred which would be better avoided, what would be the financial cost of the step, what political effect it would have on other states and 'whether it was beyond the power of the Government to devise an arrangement which would secure all the advantages of annexation, without its disadvantages'.[64] Lansdowne was of the opinion that if the state were not annexed the government should declare that Manipur had forfeited its independence, but that, 'as an act of clemency, we are prepared to restore it, subject to any conditions upon which we may find it desirable to insist'.[65] Following this course of action, the British appointed as heir to the *gadi* Chura Chand, aged five, descended from the same ancestor as the ex-maharaja. Lansdowne was adamant that it was 'most important to show that we are making an entirely new departure and that the new ruler will owe his position altogether to our favour... a long minority under the guidance of a careful British officer will be much the best for this purpose'.[66]

The case of the Manipur revolt demonstrated the degree to which intervention was dictated more by external circumstances and the views of individuals within the secretariat than rational thought and observance of local advice. In the aftermath it was apparent that the alleged palace coup could have been dealt with at the local level without the use of force. However the viceroy, Lord Lansdowne, was much in favour of safeguarding the territory of British India by maintaining a firm hold on frontier states such as Sikkim, Kashmir and Manipur to be used as buffer zones against foreign aggressors. Any unrest within Manipur was perceived as a threat to such a strategy.

By the end of the nineteenth century direct opposition to the orders of the Government of India was in some cases seen as a worse princely crime than actual misrule. The 'final battle' to depose Shivaji Rao Holkar, Maharaja of Indore, rested on relatively minor issues such as decisions by the maharaja to order the permanent expulsion of four innocent people released from prison by the Government of India, and to recant previous statements made in the press of his good intention to rule well. In Curzon's view 'the serious element in the points at issue lies in the fact of direct insubordination to the orders of the Government of India ... Such acts of disobedience, though perhaps small in themselves are, if committed with impunity, more fatal to the Government of India than any evidence of local misgovernment, however gross'.[67]

Highly conscious of the opinions of not only other princes but also the Indian press and British Indian politicians, it was agreed that Holkar's deposition should be made on the grounds of insanity rather than misgovernment. A plea of insanity rendered it 'far easier to pursue action against a prince without taking the political risks usually associated with intervention'. An offer of abdication on Holkar's part was eagerly grasped by the Government of India and publicly announced to be both voluntary and the result of poor health. The abdication was postponed when it was realised that the intended date would prevent Holkar from attending the Coronation Durbar of 1903. The ruler's request to attend the durbar was happily accepted by the British as it

enabled them 'not only to maintain the façade of a voluntary abdication but also to represent its postponement as the magnanimous concession of a benign government'.[68]

Repeated defiance of the Government of India also brought about
the deposition of Zalim Singh, Maharaja of Jhalawar, who 'in obstinate defiance' consistently breached the agreement under which ruling
powers had been restored to him. The Council of India set out its
justification that it was to Britain alone that the subjects of the state
could look for protection against misgovernment, stating that 'Misrule
on the part of a Government which is upheld by British power is misrule in the responsibility for which the British Government becomes
in a measure involved'. It was therefore not only the right but also the
positive duty of the British Government to see that the administration of a state in a critical condition was reformed, and gross abuses
removed.[69]

In the light of the Baroda trial it was nevertheless seen as essential
to adopt the correct judicial procedure for any proposed deposition to
avoid the possibility of antagonising other rulers. In the case of the
maharaja of the central Indian state of Panna, Madhava Singh, who
was directly implicated in a case of poisoning in which his uncle died,
the secretary of state advised Curzon that 'If you have not appointed
your Judicial Commissioner for the trial of the Maharaja of Panna,
I would suggest sending two, and not one, Commissioners. The trial
and deposition of ruling Princes for offences of this kind are somewhat ticklish'.[70] The maharaja was duly deposed and imprisoned, the
eldest son of his uncle nominated in his place and despatched without delay to a princely college.[71]

* * *

The need to abstain from intervention urged upon British political
officers by their superiors in the latter part of the nineteenth century
undoubtedly deterred such officers from maintaining a sufficiently
high profile in state affairs to attain their goal of substituting the
stereotype of the 'Oriental despot' with a model ruler intent upon
the moral and social welfare of his people. Following Mayo's rather
vague pronouncements regarding 'improvement', no positive policy
emerged from the secretariat concerning the nature or implementation

of changes to princely governance. As a result the limited British efforts at reform proved to be negative, in that they were aimed at the avoidance of abuse rather than the development of the individual. Control was applied to prevent rulers from using their autonomy in undesirable ways rather than guiding them in constructive directions. When the Government of India was forced to intervene in cases of undeniable misrule, the fear of the effects upon other princes of severely chastising or even deposing one of their kind resulted in a failure to produce a consistent line of action, which might have provided a yardstick for princely behaviour that could be used by both rulers and political officers.

THE MACHINERY OF GOVERNMENT

Whereas the first section of this chapter on the adult ruler deals with British monitoring of the moral fibre of princely rule in the Indian states, the second section deals with the workings of government. In examining four case studies of states during the period, it can be seen that the single most important factor is the manner in which the imposition of British methods of 'good government' tipped the existing balance of power within a state administration. As the nineteenth century progressed there was less a defined policy operating within states than a series of shifting relationships between the ruler, his minister and bureaucracy, the British resident and, particularly in the case of Rajputana, the nobility.

By operating through the medium of Indian ministers and bureaucracies the doctrine of liberal reform was applied in the states both during and after minorities, justifying British imposition of land reform, law, and efficient and accountable government.[72] The imperial government did not superimpose its political system on states, but rather counted on being able to serve its interests by 'manipulating, through minimal interference, political systems that were not subject to its direct bureaucratic control'. More than minimal interference was almost always considered by British authorities to be undesirable in that it was 'costly, offensive to loyal princes and often productive of British involvement in local intrigues from which they found difficulty in extricating themselves'.[73] The agents of administrative reform were frequently, although not exclusively, the products of education, training and experience in British India. Local aristocracies lacked the kind of education that would equip them for bureaucratic employment. Moreover they disliked the ready access of the diwan to the ruler, and the influence of the diwan in securing the appointment of other outsiders to provide the second level of administration and increasing bureaucratisation. In the view of Robert Stern, of all the British resources that in one way or another permeated state boundaries 'bureaucratic centralisation seems to have had the greatest effect on altering the parameters of politics in the states'.[74]

Once begun, administrative reforms in the states tended to develop an impetus of their own, quite apart from British policy statements. Far from moving towards an ideal of a westernised India ruler firmly overseeing his administration, the momentum of such reforms and the increase in power of the administrators who instigated new systems of government frequently resulted in a considerable loss of a ruler's control within his own state and subsequent loss of status in his relationship with his subjects. As Ashis Nandy suggests, modern colonialism won its great victories not so much through military and technological prowess as through its ability to create secular hierarchies incompatible with the traditional order. These hierarchies opened up new vistas, particularly for those exploited or cornered within a traditional system. To them 'the new order looked like – and here lay its psychological pull – the first step towards a just and equal world'.[75]

The interface between British political officers and Indian ministers and bureaucracies, transformed by their English education and administrative training into an elite, undoubtedly involved a certain loss of control for the British coloniser. If it was, on the one hand, reassuring for the British that Indians became in certain respects 'westernised', on the other hand the adoption of British practices by Indian bureaucrats produced the 'inevitable processes of counter-domination produced by the miming of the very operation of domination',[76] with the result that the identities of coloniser and colonised became less distinct. Such a blurring of identities undoubtedly occurred in British India, however in the princely states where government was in an earlier stage of development, and British personnel thinner on the ground, the relative positioning of the British and states' administrators was even less defined. The inflexibility of rigid control on the part of the paramount power was simply not an option in the states during the period, due to the post-Mutiny requirement to retain the loyalty of Indian rulers and to the paucity of British resources, both in terms of manpower and finances, allotted to princely India. States' administrations would have ground to a halt without a significant amount of negotiation, during the course of which resistance to colonial rule inevitably occurred.

To examine the way in which British indirect rule was capable of dramatically altering the style of administration in princely states during the period, the book considers four case studies with very different scenarios. The states selected are Mewar (Udaipur), the most prominent Rajput state, providing an example of typical British attitudes towards the states of Rajputana at the end of the nineteenth century; Mysore, taken under British rule in 1831 and restored to an Indian ruler 50 years later, the administration of which was under the particular scrutiny of both British and Indians; Baroda, which, following the deposition of its ruler in 1875, was an arena for important and far-reaching administrative reforms; and Hyderabad, the major Muslim state in India, which maintained a delicate balance between the modernisation of the Mughal system of administration and the preservation of traditional institutions and personnel. The financial intricacies of individual administrations are not discussed in any detail, as these varied hugely from state to state over the period. It would require a significant study to cast light on not simply state budgets, but what were at times decidedly murky dealings involved in state and imperial transactions.

The weighting of power varied in the states under examination. Within Mewar (and certain other Rajput states during the period, such as Jaipur) the British were unable to control an unhealthy gain of princely control as they failed to support the nobility or to introduce an effective bureaucracy. In the other three case studies discussed below it can be argued that, conversely, princely authority was diminished due to a British inability or lack of will to curb an unhealthy gain of power held by bureaucracies and the ministers at their head. Neither approach succeeded in producing a model princely administrator.

Mewar

The British treated the states of Rajputana as a special case. The inter-actions of princes and barons in early nineteenth-century Rajput polity were so similar to social practice in medieval Europe that the British tended to identify the Rajput system as feudal. The major influences in shaping British officers' conceptions of Rajput feudalism and sug-gesting, in the broadest terms, imperial policies appropriate to these conceptions were the works of Lieutenant Colonel James Tod and Sir Alfred Lyall. Tod was one of the earliest explorers of Rajputana, when it was still *terra incognita* to the Company, and, as a surveyor and nego-tiator, he played an important role in helping the Company to estab-lish its protectorate over the Rajput states. Lyall was a man of greater official and literary distinction, who in the mid-1870s served as Agent to the Governor-General in Rajputana. Both men believed that the less their government and its officers interfered in the internal affairs of the Rajput states the better. In Tod's view a policy of intervention would only 'destroy the links which connect the prince and his vassals' and would leave the Rajputs with no system at all, 'or at least not a system of feuds, the only one they can comprehend'.[77] A policy of non-interference, on the other hand, would allow feudalism's 'renovation' and a return to its pristine state.

Reflecting on more than half a century of British indirect rule, Lyall judged it to have been 'considerably less than successful' in reaching Tod's goal of renovating Rajput feudalism. He regretted the persistent 'inclination of an English government...toward the support of the central administration' in the Rajput states, declaring that 'To make haste to help the chief to break the power of his turbulent and reaction-ary nobles, in order that he may establish policy and uniform admin-istration over his whole territory, is to an Englishman at first sight an obvious duty, at the second look a dubious and short sighted policy'.[78] Despite believing that British administration had 'rescued' the Rajput states from the anarchy that had followed the decline of Mughal rule, Lyall recognised that the 'listless security produced by our protection' had brought about a 'rapid deterioration' in the effective function-ing of such states.[79] Moreover, despite their belief in the efficacy of

some sort of feudal system in Rajputana, the reluctance on the part
of British officials to interfere on a consistent basis to maintain the
political strength of the *jagirdars* resulted in a failure to provide the
checks and balances within government which might have prevented
a general trend towards Rajput monarchical absolutism.[80] The case of
the state of Mewar clearly illustrates this failure.

The Sesodia maharanas of Mewar had a universally recognised
claim to the highest rank and dignity among the Rajput princes of
India. More than any other Rajput dominion, Sesodia rule exhibited
the ancient and uncorrupted Hindu polity, practically unchanged
by Mughal interference.[81] However the political system of Mewar
'cracked' during the disintegration of the Mughal Empire, when the
country was overrun from without by marauding bands of Marathas
and Pathans and torn from within by feuds between rival *jagirdars* who
rose frequently in rebellion against the prince. In 1818 Mewar entered
into a subsidiary alliance with the British, and an agreement between
the maharana and his chiefs was ultimately reached through tense
negotiations under Tod's supervision.[82] Constitutional and administrative reforms carried out in the two decades following the Mutiny
were due to the initiative of British officials. Consequently reforms
came to be associated with the pro-British party at the *durbar*, headed
by the highly influential minister, Mehta Panna Lal.[83]

The accession of Maharana Fateh Singh in 1884 brought this era of
limited reform to an end. A report on Mewar written in 1901 by the
resident, Major A. F. Pinhey, noted that the maharana worked harder
than any other ruler he had known and was 'always influenced by
laudable motives', however at the same time he was 'uneducated, very
undecided, suspicious of every one and uncompromising in his attitude
towards the *Jagirdars* ... too conservative to appreciate the necessity of
keeping abreast of the times'. The ruler was reduced to a 'position of
isolation' which prevented him from benefiting from the assistance
of his natural advisers in conducting the administration, and every
question, however trivial, was submitted to him before final orders
were passed. Upon the dismissal of Mehta Panna Lal, Fateh Singh
had assumed personal charge of state affairs and, in spite of repeated
British requests, the ruler refused to appoint a new diwan, since he

regarded such an influential officer as a potential ally of the British. It was impossible for the maharana to control his officials adequately, he was scarcely able to leave the capital and his knowledge of what was occurring in the districts was based on whatever unreliable information his officials cared to give him.[84]

Relations between the *jagirdars* and the *durbar* were becoming increasingly more unsatisfactory. Many of the older, more influential *jagirdars* had died recently and their successors were minors, while, as Pinhey noted, 'the *Durbar* has become, with our assistance, far more powerful than it used to be'. *Durbar* officials quite unfitted for the responsibilities of their position managed the estates of *jagirdars* under minorities, missing opportunities to improve the administration and to free the estates from debt. The *jagirdars* had been 'from ancient times hereditary counsellors and pillars of the state', however they were seldom associated with the maharana in the administration. When they came to Udaipur with their grievances they were treated with 'scant respect' by state officials and found it impossible to obtain an impartial hearing. The *jagirdars* were no doubt largely to blame for this state of affairs as they failed to attend at the capital when requested and annoyed Fateh Singh by setting themselves up as virtually independent rulers. Nevertheless the resident was convinced that they were thoroughly loyal to the maharana as the head of the clan, and that if he met them with more sympathy yet firmness their grievances could be amicably settled.[85]

Highly conscious of the heroic past of the Sesodias, the great ambition of Fateh Singh was to restore to the position of maharana the dignity enjoyed by his predecessors and to resist all innovations. In spite of British objections he stopped work on a projected railway line from Udaipur to Chittor on the grounds that funds were not available. Moreover Mewar remained the only important princely state free from the obligation to supply troops to the British.[86] The State Education Committee, appointed by the previous maharana, was abolished and control for that department given to the *durbar*, which showed no inclination to spend the accumulating sums allocated to education.[87] In addition the virtual breakdown of earlier agreements between Fateh Singh and his *jagirdars* seriously affected the administrative capacity of the state to cope with the devastating famine of 1899. Distrustful of his officials, he attempted to centralise government into his own hands, with the result that he was overwhelmed by 'a mass of confusing details'. The powers of *jagirdars* in civil and criminal cases were not defined and the state police exercised little or no authority over the greater nobles. The latter, although outwardly submissive to the maharana, constantly disobeyed his orders.[88]

In 1906 a confidential note from Pinhey discussed the possible death of the maharana and the action of the resident if he were to take over the administration of the state. In many ways Pinhey was still adhering to the principles laid down by Tod and Lyall, advising that

Local conditions and customs should be scrupulously respected and no change should be introduced merely because it coincides with some preconceived idea of how a thing should be done or because a different system prevails in British India ... As few outsiders should be introduced as possible, at any rate until it has been definitely demonstrated that local men are really incompetent or untrustworthy if properly supervised ... It would be a great mistake to entirely lose sight of old traditions or to attempt to transform an essentially Rajput state into a model British province. The Rajput element should be fostered and encouraged and the more important and better-educated Rajput nobles should be taken unreservedly into our confidence.[89]

In Pinhey's view it would be impossible to improve the administration as a whole unless the *jagirdars* were involved and felt that they had a real stake in the country.[90] This was particularly the case as far as judicial and police matters were concerned, but also applied in areas relating to education, medical and sanitary arrangements, and the extension of irrigation and famine programmes. The first move should be to reappoint the committee of officials and nobles nominated by the maharana's predecessor. Secondly, a Court of Wards should be established under a European officer for the proper management of the *jagirs* under minority administration in order to restore their prosperity. Where the recognition of traditional rights did not interfere with the administration of the state under modern requirements, these rights should be conceded.[91]

However, despite the obvious imbalance of power in the state, the Government of India was reluctant to interfere in Mewar affairs. While generally concurring in the line of action proposed to reform the administration, senior government officials felt that it was most important to show the maharana plainly that it had 'no intention of pressing reforms upon him against his will' and it would be 'wise to leave largely to his initiation the actual undertaking of improvements'.[92] As a result Fateh Singh was able to maintain, as far as possible within the limitations of treaty relations with the British, a deeply conservative and safely autocratic position until forced to step down in favour of his son after the First World War.[93]

Mysore

The Mysore of Haider Ali and his son, Tipu Sultan, was a Muslim state created in 1761 by a coup against the Hindu ruling house. The new Mysore was maintained by rigorous revenue management and a growing emphasis on the power of the sultan, posing a threat to British dominance through an increased military capacity which challenged the Company's army. Following Tipu's death fighting Wellesley's armies in 1799 Mysore was made over by the British to Krishnaraja Wadiyar III, a member of a Hindu family which had once ruled a small portion of the state.[94]

The establishment of colonial government in Mysore was greatly facilitated by the use of the old diwan as a *de facto* ruler, however when the young maharaja failed to maintain law and order the state was taken under direct British rule in 1831. After 1857 the emerging imperial strategy to treat the Indian princes as allies resulted in a decision by the British Government to restore Mysore to native rule in 1881, by which time the British would have prepared the adopted son of the maharaja for rule. The task of the princely regime to win British favour after reinstatement was helped by the policies of the British Commission prior to 1881. When Maharaja Chamarajendra Wadiyar was reinvested with his powers, he was presented with a fully developed administrative structure based upon Madras and Bombay models. The British also inserted an Indian official of the highest calibre as diwan, and a tradition was soon established of a strong centralisation of power in his hands. This tradition was carried on by a number of accomplished successors who were able to maintain the high quality of administration given to them by the British. Consequently before the end of the century knowledgeable and otherwise highly critical British observers cited Mysore as 'the best administered native state in India'.[95]

There was a strong continuity in direct British day-to-day contact, as many British officers were retained in control of several important areas such as the Public Works, Judicial and Police Departments. At least 40 Europeans remained in the Mysore Government.[96] However the viceroy, Lord Mayo, had earlier seen the need to introduce natives into the minority administration to retain British credibility in Mysore. He regretted the fact that 'This Country is almost wholly wanting in the class of "Good Native Families" from whom we ought to be able to select well educated young men' and felt that it might be advisable to establish a special class in the high school for a number of Indian youths to be educated towards service in the higher ranks of the state government.[97] As a later despatch from the India Office made clear, the task would not be an easy one, due to the complexity of the administration introduced by the British during the young prince's minority. The Mysore structure was 'too much encumbered by forms' with 'too intricate departmental systems' to be worked satisfactorily by a native government, and it was feared that the transfer of such an administration to native hands would 'ensure the failure of the restored government'. This result would have the worst possible effect upon the people and princes of India, who had been watching the experiment with interest and 'who would not hesitate to impute to us the worst motives in failing to accomplish its success'.[98]

In 1878 the viceroy, Lord Lytton, stressed that it was extremely desirable to introduce 'constitutional principles', not to give the new native government 'any recognised representative character' but to organise it 'upon the basis of a certain balance in the administrative powers of the State'. Safeguards were to be built into the financial administration: a specific sum was to be fixed for the civil list of the maharaja, to be kept firmly apart from the revenues of state, and the administrators of the Mysore revenue department would be responsible not to the maharaja personally but to the state, 'of whose financial interests the Suzerain Power would still remain guardian'. There was to be a legislative body, 'by no means necessarily elective', whose decisions would be made 'subject to the ratifications sanctioned by the Viceroy in Council, as Representative of the Suzerain Power of all India'. These stringent measures, which in effect would drastically curtail the young maharaja's ability to exercise power over his own state, were deemed necessary

> to provide against the possibility of all the powers of the new Native State falling eventually into the hands of any one man – be he the Prince himself, or a popular and powerful Minister – over whose use of them the Government of India could exercise no adequate control without hostile, and possibly violent intervention.[99]

However by 1894 there was little evidence that such a balance of power was being maintained. A memorandum from Colonel P. D. Henderson, Resident at Mysore, to the Foreign Secretary of the Government of India stated that, although in many ways the current administration had been 'a brilliant success', there had been 'more or less autocratic rule' by the diwan, K. Seshadri Iyer, under cover of the maharaja's name. Native Mysoreans were driven to seek a living outside the province. There was a tendency to fill almost all positions from the 'lowest Amin upwards' with Brahmins who formed 'a powerful and impenetrable clique', and the non-Brahminical classes had little chance of obtaining even the most humble government posts. The Muslim population was particularly discontented with Brahminical rule and complained that it did not receive justice in revenue matters from Brahmin officials. In the courts much the same situation existed, and officials treated Muslims with an absence of consideration for their social position. The Mysorean Brahmins were discontented at the preponderance of imported Madras Brahmins, ignorant of the language of the country and out of sympathy with the people. The diwan's 'pet hobby, that of filling the higher grades of the Civil Service by successful candidates at a competitive examination open to all India is unfavourably regarded as filling the service with foreigners'. A wider representation of all classes in government was needed, along with the regulation of admissions to the Civil Service in all grades to prevent a monopoly by any one class.[100]

Nevertheless to the British the accountability and efficiency that Seshadri Iyer's regime had brought to state affairs made any internal differences within the administration pale into insignificance. A report by Sir Donald Robertson, the resident in 1902, referred glowingly to the way in which Mysore was 'governed on enlightened principles' and the fact that the administration was 'practically the same as that in force in the fifty years of British occupancy which terminated in 1881'. In Robertson's view, the 'liberal policy and enlightened statesmanship of the late dewan, Sheshadri Iyer, have produced results probably finer than anything in British India'.[101] That the maharaja had had little to do with this major achievement appears to have been immaterial to British officials. In fact the British insistence upon bureaucratic procedures which resulted in the removal of power from the palace had been stated clearly by the secretary of state and quoted in a memorandum from the resident in 1895:

> it is obviously necessary that a large part of the details of current business should be disposed of by His Highness's Ministers ... we consider it essential under this system of personal government that all important acts and orders shall necessarily have passed through certain departmental formalities, and shall have undergone certain processes of examination and joint consultation before they issue in the Maharaja's name and by his will.[102]

In 1903 it was reported that the new diwan, Krishna Murti, was displaying many of the same 'autocratic' characteristics as his predecessor. The resident complained that he was hardly involved in administrative measures since his role was confined to securing 'adequate recognition' for the maharaja and 'fair play' for the 'sanctioned scheme of administration in all its branches'.[103] He was entirely dependent for information upon stray conversations with visitors, newspaper reports and belated monthly proceedings. It was suggested that Krishna Murti was not giving the young ruler the 'real support and assistance' he had a right to demand of his diwan. The diwan was firmly of the opinion that he was head of the administration, and orders promulgated by the maharaja which were not exactly in accord with his wishes were 'unjustifiable curtailments of his power and dignity'. He had resorted to 'sundry stratagems' such as holding back papers indefinitely and keeping councillors in the dark over the issuing of orders and had started a 'Camp Office', a 'most mischievous and undesirable' institution, which was an 'entirely unnecessary adjunct to the administrative machinery' and unfair to the secretariat as papers went missing.[104] In attempting to assert his position the maharaja had been diverted from profitable work and the completion of his education.[105] The resident admitted that 'the science of good government' was 'almost as well known to the clever officials of Mysore as to us'. Nevertheless there was 'a feeling that most Brahmins entertain, namely that should the Palace party assert itself the authority of the hitherto all-powerful Brahmin element must decline'.[106]

Yet the 'Palace party', like the much-lauded Representative Assembly which was inaugurated in 1881, was to prove no threat to the diwan and his bureaucracy. Notes written at the beginning of the twentieth century by the resident, Sir Donald Robertson, dismissed the assembly as a 'harmless institution' consisting of 'raiyats, pleaders and merchants' elected to represent certain qualified areas, which met annually at the capital for a few days.[107] It had, he claimed, been of 'little practical use either to the people or the State' and its aims had been 'mistakenly described as securing popular representation'. In future it should be encouraged merely as a means of affording the people an opportunity of paying homage to their ruler at the festival of Dassara, or of making direct representations to him. On any other basis it would probably in time prove both 'anomalous and mischievous' in an Indian state.[108] At first the assembly was not even allowed to be called 'representative' as it was feared that such an expression might give rise to misunderstandings. According to Hindu political theory councils and assemblies were 'organs in the body politic', with the maraja as the supreme head and the diwan as executive arm, therefore no power existed that was not derived from the ruler's person. However in the long run it was not possible to maintain the assembly as a body of 'royal sycophants', and by the beginning of the twentieth century debates were dominated by the struggle between Madrassi and Mysorean bureaucrats,[109] with little recognition of the maharaja's traditional role as leader of government.

Baroda

In 1817, after the final defeat of the Peshwa, the Gujarati lands of western India claimed by the Marathas were divided between the British and the local warlords. The area under the Gaekwar dynasty became known as Baroda state.[110] The power of the dynasty was based originally on an informal alliance between the ruling gaekwar, various local Gujarati notables and some rich Vania financiers, however this structure provided little stability. The final downfall of the system was brought about by the personal misrule of two gaekwars, Khande Rao and his successor, Malhar Rao, who, as discussed in the first section of this chapter, was deposed by the British in 1875 on the grounds that the Baroda government was riddled with corruption and that Malhar Rao was not capable of carrying out necessary reforms.[111]

The British created an artificial minority by replacing Malhar Rao with a 12-year-old boy from an obscure branch of the Gaekwar family, Sayaji Rao III, and the state was placed in the capable hands of the diwan, T. Madhava Rao, following his departure from Travancore. Before 1875, when the young maharaja began his reign, Baroda was under a 'patrimonial' system of government whereby office holders owned their positions personally and ran their offices with the help of their followers, relatives and friends. Under T. Madhava Rao's imposition of a modern bureaucratic system of government local notables and hereditary office holders lost their power to officials appointed by merit, who were paid regular salaries by the state. In his study of Baroda as a 'progressive' state, David Hardiman suggests that what had once been considered as 'an office holder's worthy solidarity with kith and kin came to be seen as nepotism and corruption'. State-employed officials became the local political controllers and also the representatives of the people. This change in administrative practice inevitably brought considerable dislocation. However, despite the discontent which resulted, Baroda succeeded in instigating a modern bureaucratic system similar to that found in British India.[112]

Under the new system, power was concentrated into the hands of the diwan and his subordinates. An executive council existed, consisting of the diwan, deputy diwan and two leading officials, and there was no provision for the nomination of non-officials before 1940. The same applied to the legislative council, which was founded in 1907. Although Baroda was far in advance of most princely states in having such a body at all,[113] it was also under the control of the bureaucracy. The diwan was president, the council could only give 'advice' and there was a majority of officials and government nominees among the 18 members. At the local level the new bureaucratic system followed the British pattern closely, with each of the four districts of the state placed under a revenue officer.[114]

The Baroda bureaucracy maintained its political power through the control of state expenditure. In the past most of the state revenue had gone towards the upkeep of the gaekwar and the maintenance of his army, the police and princely administration. Between 1876 and 1934 state expenditure in these areas declined from 70 per cent to 33 per cent, and by 1934 most of the revenue was spent by the bureaucracy on public works, education and various improvement projects to aid the development of Baroda. For instance, between 1876–7 and 1933–4 education expenditure rose from 1 per cent to 17 per cent of total state spending. During the same period expenditure on public works rose from 5 per cent to 13 per cent.[115]

Following a rivalry which grew up between T. Madhava Rao and Sayaji Rao's tutor, Frederick Elliott, the minister retired prematurely in 1882. The period of Elliott's influence lasted from 1881 to 1895[116] and was a time of continuing reform in the state. However, according to the Agent to the Governor-General in Baroda, the administration 'under the cloak of codes, laws, regulations and highly paid officials' was anything but sound. Elliot, despite at times preventing friction between residency and *durbar*, was not qualified to act as an adviser in matters relating to civil and political administration and, unable to distinguish between his clear duty to his own government and his 'fancied duty' to the young man he had educated, upset one minister after another.[117] During this period British officials in the service of the state, instead of 'forwarding' the policy of the Government of India did their utmost to foster the gaekwar's ill will towards Britain and vied with each other in supplying him with arguments with which to combat the agent to the governor-general. The administration of which they were supposedly in charge was a 'pale copy' of that existing in British India 'with all its defects magnified and its vivifying spirit wholly wanting'. It was considered that any benefit that the empire at large might derive from proposed reforms in Baroda was counterbalanced by the antagonism to British rule.[118] Due to his championing of Baroda interests Elliott was by no means popular in British circles, and in 1895 he was forced to revert to British service.[119]

A report of 1895 on Baroda affairs written by Colonel J. Biddulph, Agent to the Governor-General in Baroda, emphasised the unsatisfactory attitude of the gaekwar towards the Government of India during Elliott's term. It referred to the ruler's efforts at 'pulling the whole administration to pieces and building up an unworkable system that [he] has been taught to believe is superior to anything in British India'. Having adopted Machiavelli's *The Prince* as his political guide, the gaekwar subscribed to the belief that the Baroda state was politically equal with the British Government, 'which has no more right to interfere with Baroda affairs than it has to interfere in the affairs of Denmark or Portugal'. Colonel Biddulph's report suggested that, despite attempts at reform during this period, major problems still existed in the state. The official class was very corrupt in spite of high salaries. A large proportion of officials consisted of men imported into the state for the purpose of building up a Maratha administration and 'only concerned to make money and convey it into British territory', with the result that there was constant intrigue between Marathas and Gujaratis and 'a substitution of regulations for personal responsibility'. Bankers had been ruined by previous regimes and their grievances never remedied. Petty landlords were subjected to great oppression, as the policy of the state was to get as much land as possible into its hands. Although Baroda College was satisfactory the Education Department was mismanaged, and compulsory education, which had 'started with a great flourish of trumpets in 1893', was 'a sham'. The judicial service was highly paid but, although there were attempts at 'honourable independence', some of the younger judicial officers were very corrupt and the *durbar* did not hesitate to interfere with and disregard judicial verdicts when it pleased.[120]

However Biddulph's view was not necessarily the definitive picture of the Baroda administration. Captain W. Evans-Gordon, supervising the gaekwar's army, in 1894 expressed the opinion that the prince was 'an extremely able man with apparently a perfect knowledge of every detail concerning the condition of his people and the administration of his state'. The gaekwar had pointed out to British officials that a ruler could never guarantee how accurately his opinions on administrative matters were represented to the Government of India. The residency was the channel for all communications 'and they are coloured in the passage by the personal feelings, character, and opinions of the individual in charge ... Supposing a Resident to be adverse, the Government of India hear the worst side only'. In the gaekwar's opinion the system was faulty in principle, and this had been accentuated by the frequent changes of resident which had occurred in recent years. The only remedy would be 'a closer and more intimate knowledge by the Viceroy and the Foreign Secretary of the Chiefs themselves; and a fuller representation of their views by Political Officers, as apart from the personal opinion of the latter'. In meetings with the viceroy the gaekwar 'sometimes could not fail to detect the tutoring hand of the Resident or the Foreign Secretary' which made him uneasy. Colonel Biddulph in particular, he asserted, was determined 'to interfere in everything', undermining the ruler's influence. The viceroy had once told the gaekwar that he wished the 'Rulers of Native States should govern them in fact as well as theory', but this would prove an impossible task if the political officer took pains to show the people that their ruler's authority was 'little more than nominal'. Such an attitude might be necessary in a badly governed, backward state, but in states such as Baroda where there had recently been a genuine attempt at improvement 'it paralyses the usefulness of the best Native Chief'.[121]

No doubt partly due to the frustration of having to spar constantly with British political officers, during the latter period of his reign Sayaji Rao spent increasingly more time away from Baroda and he was not involved in the day-to-day administration of the state, relying increasingly on ministers who lacked adequate arrangements for the continuation of work in his absence.[122] The outgoing resident at Baroda, Major C. Pritchard, reported in 1906 that the gaekwar 'leaves very much to his Dewan and Council' and that the latter was responsible for the 'sometimes unsuitable style of correspondency' with the Residency with the object of contesting the orders of the Government of India, belittling the Resident and his assistants and reducing the Residency to 'a mere pillar box'.[123]

During Curzon's viceroyalty there was yet again an official difference of opinion as to the calibre of the Baroda ruler. The viceroy was of the opinion that, although Sayaji Rao professed to have enlightened standards of government, his famine administration in 1900 had been 'slack and abominable'.[124] Moreover his frequent and lengthy absenteeism on European visits, which he was accused of financing through the imposition of an income tax in Baroda, had convinced a succession of viceroys of his readiness to abandon his subjects and their needs.[125] However the secretary of state, Lord Hamilton, having met the ruler in England, refuted Curzon's dismissal:

> He has thought and read a good deal, and being selfish and self-seeking, he analyses with great acumen the motives and guiding influences of his fellow-countrymen... contrasting him with other Native Princes, he undoubtedly shows far more aptitude than the majority for governing and managing his own affairs.[126]

In Hardiman's view Sayaji Rao was an extremely effective and popular ruler, imbued with the faith that western institutions could greatly enhance the power and prestige of his state. He was not an original thinker, but he was extremely receptive to the original thought of others and depended a great deal on good advisers.[127] Had he been encouraged more by British officers and had his genuine efforts at reform received a more receptive audience from them it is possible that he, rather than the bureaucracy which supposedly served beneath him, might have gained more credit by the end of the nineteenth century as the power behind one of the most progressive of Indian states.[128]

Hyderabad

Since 1766 the Company had occupied the rich coastal districts of Hyderabad, the domain of the former governors of the Mughal Empire, the nizams. During the following decades the nizam's control over the Telegu warriors of his outlying districts became so weak that the annual tribute which the Company continued to pay for these districts was crucial to the survival of the state. A new subsidiary alliance in 1798 enforced the nizam's dependence upon the British and expelled the French battalion which had given him some room for manoeuvre. The British already had a powerful group of supporters at Hyderabad, consisting of Shia Muslims and north Indian Hindus, who looked to the British for protection against the Marathas. After Hyderabad lost more of its outlying districts in 1800–1, it was drawn firmly into the British orbit, as a succession of powerful residents built up an alliance with the diwans of the day.[129]

The policies and practices of the diwan, Salar Jung I, effective ruler of Hyderabad from 1853 to 1883, initiated a modernising administration. In 1853 Hyderabad was in severe financial straits, and the Government of India threatened to take over the state through loans, cession of land or direct administration. To preserve Hyderabad's independence the young diwan had to reorganise the revenue system and the bureaucracy, both to achieve financial stability and to meet British criticism of its corruption and inefficiency.[130] The diwan understood that the importation of British Indian administrative practices and personnel could have a significant cultural and political impact upon Hyderabad society. Personally opposed to the cultural changes accompanying western education and the use of English elsewhere in India, his main goal was to preserve Hyderabad's Mughal political traditions and culture.[131] Therefore he developed policies to prevent and control change, whereby the Hyderabadi nobles, the new administrators and British officials were kept isolated from each other, from the nizam and from political power as centralised in the diwan. In addition to the regulation of social contacts, there was a prohibition on British entry into the old walled city to insulate the nobility and court from British political and cultural influence. The insularity of the old city and its inhabitants proved politically useful for Salar Jung, and on several controversial matters during his 30-year diwanship he forestalled reforms urged by successive residents by 'citing cultural backwardness' on the part of the nizam or nobles.[132] Recurring issues were the implementation of judicial reforms, the reduction of Arab troops, use of the Hyderabad Contingent[133] and the construction of the railway through Hyderabad.[134]

Since both the British and the new diwani officials were denied access to leading Hyderabadi representatives, they became allies. In their efforts to construct a modern bureaucracy the officials were constrained by a strong diwan, a powerful traditional aristocracy and a nizam secluded with his palace retainers. Many of the new administrators had come from the Indian Civil Service, and the Hyderabad diwani administration was modelled upon British Indian administration.[135] In 1888 the journalist William Digby[136] bemoaned the fact that Hyderabad and other states removed from the British provinces

the best of their Mahomedan and Hindoo sons ... statesmen for whom there is no room in our scheme of rule. Without begrudging him to the Nizam we want Mehdi Hasan in the Chief Justiceship of the North-West Provinces, not in that of Hyderabad. We want British India to receive some of the many benefits which follow from the judicial and administrative efforts of such men.[137]

In some respects the departmental secretaries in Hyderabad had more power than their counterparts in British India. These administrators were familiar with the modernising policies of British India and their implementation, and they were aware of developments occurring in other Indian states. There was impatience with the obstacles to modernisation set up by elder members of the Hyderabad nobility and a distaste for the use of 'antiquated Urdu'. Moreover in Hyderabad they were confronted with a civic culture which they judged to be a regional and inferior version of the Mughal heritage then disintegrating in British India.[138]

By 1890 it was clear that non-Hyderabadis dominated the diwani administration. The Civil List of 1894 included 680 gazetted officers; the number of non-Hyderabadis had nearly doubled, from 230 to 447 men, in the eight-year period since 1886, and the number of Hyderabadis had actually decreased.[139] Salar Jung II, who took over the diwanship after his father's sudden death in 1883,[140] had started as an old friend of the young nizam, Mahbub Ali Khan,[141] and was in fact appointed by the nizam against the wishes of the Government of India who viewed the new minister as 'without ability, strength of character, or official training'.[142] However the diwan's apparent manipulation by diwani and residency officials soon provoked conservative opposition to him. The nizam declared that Salar Jung wished to 'exclude him altogether from interference in public affairs', and that the minister's misrepresentation of matters to the resident was creating 'constant mischief'.[143] Palace officials, such as the ruler's secretary, Sarwar Jung, and others of the old order who had the ear of the nizam turned Mahbub Ali Khan against his diwan, obstructed proposals which did not suit their interests and encouraged the nizam in extravagant spending, with the result that the finances of the state degenerated to a drastic degree.[144]

It was apparent that over the years political officers had been unable to convince Hyderabadi rulers of the benefits of subscribing to British advice, thus failing to strengthen the nizam's position vis-à-vis his minister. However the officiating resident, Colonel K. J. Mackenzie, observed in 1894 that British officials were to some extent responsible for this princely mistrust:

> While I am here my constant endeavour will be to induce the Nizam to see and feel that I am his friend, that I wish to see him strong and a real power for good, that if I differ from him, it is ... because the difference of opinion is an honest one, dictated purely in the interests of himself and his State and with no ulterior motives whatever ... it has been a great misfortune that

we have so often backed Ministers personally distrusted by or distasteful to the Nizam of the day, and frequently have kept them in power for years against his wishes. The natural result was that the Nizam either sulkily effaced himself, or secretly intrigued against us.[145]

A later resident, Sir David Barr, also regretted the lack of British support for the nizam:

I am more than ever convinced that there is no state in India more dependent upon the Government of India and indirectly upon the Resident than is Hyderabad. If the Resident is on good terms with the Nizam his power is almost unlimited. Every one in the State recognises this – and the consequence is that intrigues are discouraged, and the authority of the Nizam is upheld.[146]

To achieve changes in the Hyderabad administration efforts were made by British officials to diminish what was perceived as 'despotic' power on the part of the minister in favour of increased control by the bureaucracy beneath him. Sub-ministers were to be invested with 'definite' powers to be exercised 'without reference to others'. The Cabinet Council, to which all business of importance was to be referred, was to meet three times a month and was designed to check the exercise of individual authority by making the whole body of ministers answerable for the treatment of major issues. Finally, attempts were made to prevent the nizam from 'divesting himself of the responsibility of a ruler of a great state'. The proceedings of the Cabinet Council were to be reported regularly to him, and he could modify decisions at will.[147] However the nizam continued to be 'peculiarly inaccessible'. The minister and other Hyderabad officials could only obtain rare interviews with the ruler, and consequently great delay resulted in dealing with state affairs. The confidence which the nizam placed in his secretary, Sarwar Jung, 'made it easier to play upon the traditional jealousy with which the Chief of a Native State is apt to regard his Minister, and so bring the administration almost to a stand-still'.[148]

Official files suggest that by the end of the century the British were over-preoccupied with the relationship between nizam and minister, leaving the diwani administrators much to their own devices. Overambitious secretaries, who acquired the real power in the state, disregarded the views of sub-ministers. Grave financial mismanagement occurred and public scandals were frequent.[149] The resident admitted that he saw more value in acting behind the scenes as a 'lightning-conductor ... carrying off, harmlessly, storms which might otherwise wreck the administration', rather than entering officially into the formal fray of government.[150] In 1898 the Foreign Secretary to the Government of India, W. J. Cuningham, warned the viceroy that 'the personal question naturally looms largely' in Hyderabad.[151] The only solution to save both nizam and state appeared to rest in the prevention of the downfall of the minister, Vikar-ul-Umra, upon which the nizam was intent, as demonstrated by his establishment of a Nobles' Council as a rival body to the minister's Cabinet Council.[152] Cuningham declared that

> authoritative interference in superseding the Nizam's power is as big an act of State as the Government of India have ever touched in connection with the Native States of India. It would be of course denounced most vehemently in Hyderabad itself where the ideas of the State's political independence are very exalted ... Everything which lends support to the contention that the Minister and the Resident in collusion have brought the affairs of the Nizam to a crisis, will weaken the position of the Government.[153]

However it was required that the nizam govern his state in a reasonable manner in order to avert 'danger and confusion'. In the last resort it was the duty of the British Government to save the state from such consequences.[154] Initial attempts by the British Comptroller-General to examine the Hyderabad financial situation succeeded only in generating much official secrecy over existing accounting procedures.[155] In 1901 the weakness of the position of diwan was recognised by the secretary of state, Lord Hamilton, who saw the need to find a 'competent European' to overhaul the current state of finances in Hyderabad: 'It is very improbable that you would be able to find any Native outside Hyderabad, capable of coping both with the Nizam and Hyderabad nobles, as Dewan. If you can once get through a reliable European control over the finances, the Dewan's weakness or mal-administration is of secondary importance'.[156]

In the meantime the diwani administration became a largely autonomous bureaucracy, constituting itself as an elite. No longer checked by the nizam, the diwan or powerful nobles, it was left to make decisions that affected the structure of Hyderabadi society. The accelerated modernisation and expansion of the administration enhanced its political power, and the Mughal bureaucracy was 'effectively dismantled and its personnel disinherited at all levels'.[157]

* * *

Having been strongly advised to refrain from interfering in state politics, the reforming zeal of political officers appears to have been concentrated upon achieving high standards of administrative procedure. This was attempted through bureaucracies operating according to British Indian models rather than grooming a prince as an exemplary figure at the head of an invigorated administration, a task that would have required blatant intervention in state affairs.

In Rajputana the British appear to have been mesmerised by the mystique of traditional 'feudal' government. However despite appreciating that an essential part of such government was provided by utilising the balance of baronial power, British officials failed to maintain *jagirdars* as a power base, choosing rather to introduce where possible a somewhat limited bureaucracy to further their own interests. As a result several rulers in Rajputana, such as Fateh Singh, Maharana of Mewar, moved gradually towards autocracy, curbed neither by their nobles nor by the Government of India, which was reluctant to meddle in what it perceived as the tried and tested art of Rajput politics.

The importance of Mysore as an example of a 'model state' after its return to native rule in 1881 and the inheritance of a sophisticated British administration necessitated the employment of a powerful, highly competent diwan and an educated bureaucracy imported largely from British India and versed in British methods. There was little role for the maharaja beyond that of a signatory on a checklist and, in the interests of sound, accountable government, the British appeared reluctant to remove power from diwan and bureaucracy in order to change the ruler's role from symbolic head of state to instigator of administrative reforms in the state.

On the contrary, the power base of Sayaji Rao Gaekwar of Baroda was not threatened by an intellectually superior diwan. The ruler was seen by some British officials to be a wise and innovative administrator, determined to replace traditional elements within Baroda society with a powerful class of bureaucrats owing more to merit than patronage. However a loss of British support resulted from the fact that opposing officials were rankled by his leaning towards independence and his supposed antagonism towards the paramount power. Princely disillusionment led to a lack of interest in state administration, and Britain failed to maximise the skills of a potentially able ruler.

In Hyderabad a bureaucracy imported from British India and isolated from both resident and nizam by a powerful diwan succeeded in establishing an unassailable position over the state administration. Nizam Mahbub Ali Khan, conservative by nature and an easy prey to subversive influences, failed to control state expenditure or to participate in any positive way in government. The British in their turn, and by their own admission, failed to pay heed to the nizam's dislike of the autocratic methods employed by successive diwans or to push him to any great extent to mend his ways. As in Mysore and Baroda, while the individual figures of rulers and ministers waxed and waned an elite class of administrators accumulated greater power, steadily achieving its independence from the indirect control of the Political Department and the greater authority of the Government of India.

5

SERVANT OF THE EMPIRE

Following the Queen's Proclamation a highly detailed hierarchical structure of Indian society was designed by British officials, within which princely subordination to British rule and the person of the British monarch was repeatedly reinforced. By 1876 an effort had been made to group the princes by region, with a fixed assignment of rank vis-à-vis other rulers in their area.[1] The size of a prince's estate, the amount of his revenue, the date at which he had become an ally of the East India Company, the history of his family, his standing in relation to the Mughal Empire and his acts of loyalty towards the British could all be weighed and an index established to determine the rank of every ruler. In the view of Francis Hutchins the hierarchical ordering of Indian society was attractive to the British in perpetuating a structure that was under threat in an increasingly democratised Britain, observing that 'India seemed to offer the prospect of aristocratic security at a time when England itself was falling prey to democratic vulgarity'.[2]

David Cannadine suggests that the hierarchical principle underlying the British perception of empire was not exclusively based on the collective colour-coded ranking of social groups but depended as much on the 'more venerable colour-blind ranking of individual social prestige'.[3] When the British thought of the inhabitants of their empire in individual terms rather than collective categories they tended to be more concerned with rank than with race, and in negotiations it was natural for them 'to search for overseas collaborators from the top of the indigenous social spectrum, rather than from lower down, whom they supported, whose cooperation they needed and through whom they ruled'.[4] However, whereas there is little doubt that as collaborators the Indian princes were placed in an elevated position in the social hierarchy fabricated by the British, such elevation was something of a two-edged sword. The system was used by the British as much to reinforce Indian subordination at the highest level as it was to bolster the native rulers as the natural leaders of Indian society.

Efforts to reposition the princes in the imperial hierarchy occurred in a highly centralised and formal manner.[5] Protocol for ceremonial events, increasingly remote from the ceremony of pre-colonial India, was rigidly standardised in memoranda issued from the Foreign Department of the Government of India, and individuals were ranked strictly by precedence. Any deviation from the unyielding instructions was a source of immediate concern at the highest level of British administration. However, although such rigid adherence to detail would suggest the full weight of imperialism bearing down upon the princes, the reality was that in the case of the imperial system of honours and rewards the British were forced to adopt a considerably more flexible approach. Such an approach was dependent upon a continuing exchange of interests between rulers and the paramount power, as the section on the award of the Star of India makes clear.

Over the second half of the nineteenth century there was evidence of a growing awareness of the need to sustain princely support in the face of the rulers' increasing subordination to the British Crown, and to maintain the high regard in which princes were held by their subjects. Believing that Northbrook had neglected feudatory policy to his cost, Lytton planned to make it a focal point of his viceroyalty in order to secure the princes' effective cooperation by associating their personal concerns with the imperial administration. The proposals for Imperial Service Troops and an Imperial Privy Council, although in the latter case unworkable, illustrate the awareness of a need for a decidedly more ambitious approach to the utilisation of the princes as servants of the empress than had previously been the case. Since it was recognised that the profile of the princes within these institutions would be highly visible both in India and Britain, many of the sources researched on these subjects deal with policy making at the highest level.

The Durbar

Traditionally the Indian royal ritual process was highly fluid and capable of being adapted to meet the requirements of the current political situation. Ritual performances were visual statements of variable honour and status, and under Mughal rule a prince, as the supreme authority within his state, was able to a great extent to orchestrate ritual display to meet his own ends. However under British control in the latter part of the nineteenth century bureaucratic rules and regulations increasingly forced ceremonies into a straitjacket of rigid format in which a ruler was deprived of the opportunity to dazzle or influence his subjects on a political level.[6] By the end of the nineteenth century the ceremonial *durbar* became separate from the administrative *durbar*, with the former becoming only a ritual (and increasingly Europeanised) celebration of Diwali, Dassara and other major festivals. The administrative *durbar*, which had previously represented an open discussion of the affairs of state between the ruler and his kinsmen as well as the prominent non-kindred interest groups of the state, was transformed into the more restricted meetings of the new 'state council' which began to rule individual states under increasing British influence.[7]

As part of the re-establishment of political order in 1858 Canning undertook a series of extensive tours through north India to clarify the new relationship proclaimed by the queen. As one of their main features the viceroy's tours included *durbars* with large numbers of Indian princes, notables, and Indian and British officials, at which honours and rewards were presented to Indians who had demonstrated loyalty to the British in the 1857 Mutiny. At such *durbars* Indians were granted titles such as raja, nawab and rai sahib and presented with special clothes and emblems, granted special privileges and some exemptions from normal administrative procedures, and rewarded in the form of pensions or grants. The *durbar* model derived from court rituals of the Mughal emperors, and was utilised by Hindu and Muslim

eighteenth-century rulers, then adapted in the early nineteenth century with British officials acting as Indian rulers. As Manu Bhavagan
points out, while the use of Mughal imagery theoretically validated
British authority throughout India, 'it also wrote native rulers into
the colonial narrative and joined modernist imperialist visions with
perceived ancient, traditional forms of rule'.[8] The result was a bizarre
mixture of European and Indian rites.

The central ritual in the Mughal *durbar* was the act of incorporation.
The person to be honoured offered *nazar* (gold coins) and/or *peshkash*
(valuables such as elephants, horses, gold or other precious objects).
The emperor, or his deputy, would present *khilats*, which consisted of
specific and ordered sets of clothes but could also include horses and
elephants with various accoutrements as signs of authority. The number
of such items and their value was always carefully graded. Under
the Mughals and other Indian rulers ritual presentations were not
understood as simply an exchange of goods and valuables. The *khilat*
was a symbol of continuity or succession, implying that the recipient
was 'incorporated through the medium of clothing into the body
of the donor'.[9] This 'incorporation', according to F. W. Buckler, was
based on the idea that the king stood for a 'system of rule of which
he is the incarnation ... incorporating into his body ... the persons of those who share his rule'.[10] The offering of *nazar* in the coins
of the ruler was the officer's acknowledgment that the ruler was the
source of wealth and well-being, and its presentation was reciprocal
to the receipt of the *khilats*. Both were 'acts of obedience, pledges
of loyalty, and the acceptance of the superiority of the giver of the
khilats'.[11]

The British in the seventeenth and eighteenth centuries tended to
misconstrue the acts of the *durbar* by seeing them as economic in nature
and function. Offerings of *nazar* and *peshkash* were seen as 'paying for
favours, which the British then translated into "rights" relating to their
trading activities'.[12] Objects which formed the basis of a relationship
through incorporation, such as cloth, clothes, gold or silver coins,
animals, weapons or jewellery, were seen by the British as utilitarian
goods which were part of their system of trade. At the end of the eighteenth century, parliament and the directors of the Company began

to limit the acquisition of private fortunes by Company employees by eliminating private trading activities and defining as 'corruption' the incorporation of officials of the Company into the ruling native groups through the acceptance of *nazar*, *khilats* and *peshkash*, which were declared to be forms of bribery. In addition Company officers were prohibited by their employers and parliament from participating in rituals and entering into improper relationships with Indians who were their subordinates. However in relationships with territorial rulers who were allied with the British, it was recognised that loyalty to the Company had to be symbolised in some form. Reversing roles, the British therefore began the practice of presenting *khilats* and accepting *peshkash* in formal meetings that could be recognised by Indians as *durbars*.[13]

Although the British, as 'Indian rulers' in the first half of the nineteenth century, continued the practice of accepting *nazar* and *peshkash* and giving *khilats*, they tried to restrict the occasion for such rituals to highly significant ceremonies such as the installation of a ruler.[14] The giving of *nazar* as a ceremonial payment by a ruler to the British when an adoption *sanad* was bestowed by the paramount power was encouraged as an act of obedience and pledge of loyalty, although seen to be in need of regularisation 'with due regard to the circumstances of each case'. A despatch of April 1873 declared that Her Majesty's Government had been under the impression that payment of *nazarana* was 'not only in accordance with Native custom under Mughal and Mahratta Rule, but was also entirely consonant to the feelings of the Chiefs, as indicating, by its receipt, a direct recognition, by the Paramount Power, of the succession on account of which it was accepted'. Although the levy of *nazarana* had been discontinued during the earlier period of British rule, it was suggested that its reintroduction would be 'readily if not gladly witnessed'.[15]

When a prince or notable visited Government House in Calcutta or when the governor-general, governors, commissioners and lower British officials went on tour, a *durbar* would be held. *Khilats* were always granted in the name and by the permission of governors of presidencies or the governor-general. Items offered by Indians as *nazar* and *peshkash* were never kept by the official to whom they were given.

Valuations and minute listings were made of the objects presented, which were ultimately deposited in the *Toshkana*, the special government treasury for the receipt and disbursement of presents. Unlike Indians, the British 'recycled' the presents which they received – either directly, by giving one Indian what had been received from another, or indirectly, by selling at auction in Calcutta what they received and using the proceeds to buy objects to be given as presents. The British always 'tried to equalise in economic terms what they gave and received by instructing Indians of the exact worth of objects or cash they would be allowed to give'.[16]

An official description of the installation of Sultan Jahan, Begam of Bhopal, in 1901 illustrates the manner in which palace ritual was defined by the British in monetary rather than symbolic terms. It was reported that articles composing the *khilat* for the begam from the viceroy 'to the value of Rs. 10,000' were brought into the Sadr Manzil palace where the agent to the governor-general tied an emerald-and-pearl necklace from the *khilat* around the ruler's neck and seated her on the chair of state. Her Highness presented the 'usual *nazar* of gold *mohurs*', expressing her determination to abide by the traditions of her house. The nawab-consort was invested with the 'usual *khilat*, valued at Rs. 10,000', by placing a pearl and ruby necklace on his neck; affixing a *sarpech*, or head jewel, on his turban; wrapping a shawl around his shoulders; and 'girding him with the sword of honour'. The nawab then presented *nazar* of 101 gold *mohurs* and 'expressed in suitable terms his gratitude to the Paramount Power'. The report emphasises unequivocally that 'articles for the *khilats* for both Her Highness the Begam and the Nawab Consort were provided by the state, and the *nazars* presented in return were credited to the state treasury'.[17]

The Mughal ritual might appear to have been retained, but the meaning had changed. What had been under Indian rulers a ritual of incorporation had now become 'a ritual marking subordination, with no mystical bonding between a royal figure and chosen friend or servant'.[18] A contractual relationship was formed by converting what was a form of present giving into an economic exchange between a British official and Indian subject or ruler.

A precise code of conduct was established for princes and chiefs for their attendance at a viceregal *durbar*. The clothes they wore, the weapons they could carry, the number of retainers and soldiers that could accompany them to the viceroy's camp, where they were met by British officials in relation to the camp, the number of gun salutes fired in their honour, the time of the entry into the *durbar* hall or tent, whether the viceroy would rise and come forward to greet them, where on the viceregal rug they would be saluted by the viceroy, where they would be seated, how much *nazar* they could give and whether they would be entitled to a visit from the viceroy were all 'markers of rank' and could be changed by the viceroy to raise or lower their standing.[19]

The status of a prince's representation at a *durbar* was not always to that ruler's satisfaction. With the exception of Maharana Sajjan Singh, who was a minor at the Imperial Assemblage of 1877, no ruler of Udaipur had made obeisance after other Indian princes, and the sug- gestion that at the 1911 Coronation Durbar Maharana Fateh Singh would be not able to occupy a position of superiority was seen as a 'bitter pill', resulting in great loss of '*izzat*'.[20] The problem was solved by his appointment as 'Ruling Chief in Waiting' to King George V and his participation in the ceremonies as such.[21] Some British officials, such as Charles Tupper and William Lee-Warner, spent years sorting out the correct relationship between the queen-empress's regal status and that of the Indian princes. Tupper confidently declared the princes to be 'chiefs' but not kings, citing Pudukkottai as a prime example of a state whose diwan had to be reprimanded after daring to call his raja a 'royal person'. Quoting Sir Henry Maine from a memorandum dated 1864, Tupper reminded his readers, 'There may be found in India every shade and variety of sovereignty but there is only one independ- ent Sovereign, the British Government'.[22]

The *durbar*, reinvented on a national level as the Imperial Assemblages of 1877, 1903 and 1911, became a place where the Indian princes, redefined as feudal allies, expressed their allegiance to the British Crown. The new format 'transformed the physical performance of the princes from one which symbolised incorporation, equality and respect, into one of homage'.[23]

Imperial Assemblages

The Royal Titles Act, officially recognising Queen Victoria as Empress of India, was passed and received the royal assent on 27 April 1876. The need to overcome the acrimonious debate following vociferous Liberal opposition to the bill and adverse newspaper coverage, especially as it found its way into Indian newspapers and was discussed by western-educated Indians, became part of the rationale for planning an Imperial Assemblage in India to celebrate the new title. At the heart of the Conservative defence of the bill it was argued that, given the constitutional relations between India and Great Britain, the Indian princes were indeed 'feudatories'. With the imperial title the hierarchical order would become clear-cut and unequivocal, and the ambiguity existing in the relationship of the princes to British paramountcy would be reduced. The claim was reiterated that the British were successors to the Mughals, who had held an imperial position which Indians of all status understood, and in 1876 to fulfil this role the British monarchy was 'refurbished and reinvented as an imperial crown of unprecedented reach, importance and grandeur'.[24]

Much has been made of the symbolism and pageantry employed in the planning of the assemblage,[25] however great emphasis was also placed upon the political implications of the event, both at home and in India. As Lytton explained to the queen, the celebrations would help Britain from a strategic point of view. In a letter of November 1876 he declared that if there were a threat of European war, which might bring Europe 'into collision' with Russia in central Asia, it would be 'essential to the success of our military operation that we should, as soon as possible, rouse the enthusiasm, secure the confidence, and confirm the loyalty of the Native States of India, in order that we may be able to withdraw troops from the interior without any risk to the stability of our rule'.[26] The Secretary of State for India, Lord Salisbury, agreed that Britain should 'try and lay the foundations of some feeling on the part of the coloured races towards the Crown other than the recollection of defeat and the sensation of subjection'.[27]

Lytton recognised that the new title of empress was only potentially popular in India. If the major princes were put to trouble and expense simply to be informed that the queen had assumed a title which Her Majesty and her government regarded as a mere technicality and 'unconnected with any practical advantage, or benefit to themselves' they would leave the assemblage disappointed and angry. The viceroy appreciated that 'Here is a great feudal aristocracy which we cannot get rid of, which we are avowedly anxious to conciliate and command, but which we have as yet done next to nothing to rally round the British Crown as its "feudal head"'.[28]

Salisbury warned Lytton that the plans for the assemblage, although admirable for the purpose of 'conciliating the native population', were likely to be 'antagonistic to the English', advising the viceroy that when making his pronouncements he must bear in mind 'the killjoys upon this side ... modulate the tone of your language to something which shall be a compromise between Oriental requirements and occidental fastidiousness'.[29] The secretary of state was of the opinion that 'English ridicule and abuse is able to destroy the value of any expression of goodwill' and that the viceroy could be subject to 'a storm of satire and abuse' when parliamentarians were faced with the reality of the financial drain which seemed certain to result from the assemblage.[30] However Lytton considered that although the opposition speeches in both houses of parliament had resulted in the suspicion in India that the queen's new title of empress had been 'adopted out of caprice, or else in connection with some covert design against the rights and privileges of the Indian Princes', he was nevertheless reassured by the fact that 'the enthusiasm of Asiatics is never spontaneous'. The princes could not imagine that the Prince of Wales would visit India or the queen assume a new title publicly without some special political purpose and they hoped that this purpose, when more clearly revealed, could prove beneficial to their own interests.[31]

In order that the 1877 assemblage could succeed in its task of articulating the new social order and legitimating the position of the British monarch at the head of it, while firmly relegating the Indian rulers to the role of native aristocracy, a great deal of effort was devoted to enhancing the trappings of princely status. A strong element of psychological manipulation lay behind the mountain of bureaucratic detail involved in the organisation of this mass gathering, and viceregal and other official correspondence dealing with the arrangements reveal a certain amount of racism in British attitudes towards the Indian rulers. The susceptibility of Indians to symbols and show was assumed. The British, Lord Lytton famously declared, could gain the allegiance of the rulers, 'without giving up any of our power ... the further East you go, the greater becomes the importance of a bit of bunting'.[32] Although the viceroy suspected that he might appear 'fussy, or frivolous' in his attention to detail, he stressed to Disraeli the importance of display: 'The decorative details of an Indian pageant are like those parts of the animal which are not used at all for butcher's meat, and are even unfit for scientific dissection, but from which augurs draw the omens that move armies and influence princes'.[33]

As was to be their role throughout the assemblage, the princes attended as recipients of largesse and honour bestowed upon them by their empress.[34] Somewhat surprisingly princely reactions indicated that the majority of the most powerful rulers were by no means unwilling to accept their new role of loyal servants of Queen Victoria. Much attention was given to the question of suitable recognition for Jayaji Rao Scindia, Maharaja of Gwalior, one of the most influential princes, whose position was already so elevated by previous 'marks of favour from the Suzerain Power, that it was hard not to lower it by the honours and privileges to be given to princes of lower rank and smaller salutes'. Upon being informed that he would receive the Grand Cross of the Order of the Bath, Scindia spoke of the queen using a word which in its original meant 'the power of issuing absolute orders which must be obeyed'. Delighted, Lytton assured his sovereign that this reference 'permanently and publicly fixes your Majesty's suzerain, and more than suzerain, power in India, beyond all possibility of future question'.[35] However, to make sure that the maharaja was left in no doubt as to his position in the new hierarchy, Lytton stressed the point that for a viceroy to travel to Gwalior for the investiture would be 'improper'. Scindia was therefore instructed to visit Calcutta to receive the order.[36]

In a similar vein a sycophantic letter from Tukoji Rao Holkar to the Prince of Wales rejoiced in the fact that the queen was 'pleased to confer upon the Native Princes new dignities commensurate with their ranks, and admit them also to participate in her new greatness, so that the whole political fabric of India may appear together as one harmonious group, tending, by its united effort, to exalt the British name'. However Holkar's true suspicions are reflected in the last paragraph, in which he expressed the hope that the 'independence' of native princes would continue to be respected 'according to treaties which have been ratified by Her Majesty's Proclamation of 1858'.[37] Unfortunately Lytton could not give the princes any such guarantee of their independence. He admitted to Salisbury that the rulers presented a dilemma which was not to be solved by a devolution of power, 'For whilst on the one hand, we require their cordial and willing allegiance, on the other hand we certainly cannot afford to give them any increased political power independent of our own'.[38]

The sheer mass of detail of the assemblage succeeded in impressing upon the princes the fact that, for all their personal wealth and influence, they were unable to place themselves on an equal footing with their imperial overlords. Scindia's minister, Dinkur Rao, was heard to say that

> If any man would understand why it is that the English are, and must necessarily remain, the masters of India, he need only go up to the Flagstaff Tower, and look down upon this marvellous camp. Let him notice the method, the order, the cleanliness, the discipline, the perfection of its whole organisation, and he will recognise in it at once the epitome of every title to command and govern which one race can possess over others.[39]

Holkar confided to Lytton that 'India had been till now a vast heap of stones, some of them big, some of them small. Now the house is built and from roof to basement each stone of it is in the right place'.[40] The ruler of Indore, 'the most avaricious and stingy Prince in India', was so pleased with the promise to rectify one of his boundaries, that he subscribed £800 to famine expenses. Moreover the attitude of Ranbir Singh, Maharaja of Kashmir, at the assemblage showed a respect for the paramount power which had not hitherto been apparent, dismissing his councillors and declaring to Lytton, 'I am now convinced that you mean nothing that is not for the good of me and mine. Our interests are identical with those of the Empire. Give me your orders and they shall be obeyed'.[41]

The only state whose officials failed to admit that the Imperial Assemblage provided incontrovertible proof of British supremacy was Hyderabad. Salar Jung's delusions of grandeur were at their most blatant during the celebrations, when he referred to relations between the nizam's administration and the British Government as 'equal in sovereignty', although 'unequal in strength'. Lytton reported to the queen that, at the presentation of the banner and medals to the nizam, when

> I alluded to your Majesty's reliance on the loyal allegiance of His Highness, Salar Jung translated the words 'loyalty' and 'allegiance' by the words 'friendship' and 'alliance'. My interpreter having noticed this, I corrected the intentional mistranslation and caused the young Nizam to be informed that I meant not only friendship and alliance, but obedience and fidelity.[42]

The viceroy was swift to demand a 'written acknowledgment of the supremacy of your Majesty's Government over that of His Highness' and, after several unacceptable drafts, such an acknowledgment was received, leaving relations with Hyderabad 'on a more safe and dignified footing' and firmly placing the nizam publicly in 'the true position of ... one of your Majesty's feudatories'.[43]

It is somewhat ironic that Queen Victoria was bathed in an omnipotent light while her deferential Indian counterparts were increasingly perceived as lesser mortals, since the British royal establishment and Indian *durbars* had much in common in their loss of real sovereignty. Just as the Indian rulers were disempowered as a result of the process of indirect rule, by the latter part of the nineteenth century the political power of the Crown at home had been much diminished. Queen Victoria's reign marked the gradual establishment of a modern constitutional monarchy. A series of legal reforms, notably the Reform Act of 1832 which targeted the unhealthy pressure of royal patronage upon elections, saw the power of the House of Commons increase at the expense of the House of Lords and the monarchy, with the queen's role becoming gradually more symbolic. Both in India and Britain

with the reduction of political influence the ritual performance of royalty assumed greater significance, as evidenced by the 1903 Coronation
Durbar to proclaim Edward VII Emperor of India.

Curzon was determined to give princely morale a further boost by securing the active participation of the leading princes in the 1903 ceremony.
Each prince in turn mounted the dais and offered a message of congratula-
tion to the king-emperor, and in place of the presentation of *nazar* Curzon
simply shook hands with each ruler as he passed. Some such interchange of
'homage and courtesy', Curzon insisted, had been 'an immemorial feature
of Indian Accession *Durbars*'.[44] However, although like its predecessor of
1877 the Coronation Durbar provided an elaborate display of traditional
Indian rule, it was intended above all to demonstrate the power and majesty of the British Empire. Never before, Curzon exalted, had there been
a gathering of the 'Asiatic feudatories of the British Crown' from such a
'sweep of territory', extending over 'fifty-five degrees of longitude' from
Aden to Burma. By bringing together this great number, Curzon hoped
to give India's ruling elite a sense of 'common participation in a great
political system and of fellow citizenship of the British Empire'.[45]

The secretary of state, Lord Hamilton, suggested to the viceroy
that the rulers might be given ideas above their station: 'you and the
Ruling Princes necessarily were "en evidence", and the performers in
the series of functions, and the rest of the officials, nowhere: will this
not give the Native Princes a more exaggerated sense hereafter of their
own importance and make them more difficult of management by
their agents?'[46] However Curzon was convinced of the rulers' awareness of their supporting role as figureheads rather than prime movers
in the durbar, as in the Indian Empire: 'I believe that they went away,
not only conscious that they had played a prominent and glorious part
in a magnificent pageant, but proud of their honourable position as
partners and pillars of the Empire'.[47]

Investitures of the Star of India

In India, as throughout the empire, the creation of orders of knighthood grew throughout the latter part of the nineteenth century.
In addition to the award of Indian titles, a special English order of

knighthood was created in 1861 at the behest of Victoria and Albert and entitled the Star of India or 'Eastern Star', to give it the title bestowed by Albert, who designed its ribands and mottoes in consultation with the secretary of state, Sir Charles Wood. Restricted to the most influential princes and senior officials, it at once became the most coveted of all the distinctions at the disposal of the viceroy and a means of strengthening the personal bonds of loyalty between the British monarch and the princes who had not rebelled in 1857.[48] At first the order of the Star of India, which included both Indian and British knights, was restricted to 25 members consisting of the most important Indian princes and distinguished senior British civil and military officers. In 1866 it was expanded by the addition of two lower ranks, and by 1877 there were several hundred holders of knighthoods in the order, which were granted by the queen.[49] However the fact that the most senior princes, such as the maharajas of Mysore, could reasonably expect to receive the Star of India in every generation suggests that it was not necessarily as exclusive an honour as it seemed to be. Moreover within the order the rulers were on the same footing as senior British officials. As David Cannadine points out,

> many a ruling prince posed for his portrait in the mantle, star, collar and sash of the Order of the Star of India, as did the governors of Bombay, Madras and Bengal, and also the viceroy himself: another sign of ordered hierarchy and honorific equality, as the British proconsuls and Indian princes were merged together.[50]

In the view of Bernard Cohn the investiture and holding of chapters of the order added an important European component to the ritual that the British were establishing in India. The accoutrements of the order were 'English and "feudal"': a robe or mantle, a collar, a medallion with the effigy of the Queen (the wearing of such a human effigy was an anathema to Muslims) and a jewelled pendant'.[51] A report of the investiture ceremony stated that 'on the ground, in front of the dais, is a crimson carpet, with a large oval frame of scrolls worked in relief, in gold, and the Lion and Unicorn with *"Dieu et mon droit"* in the centre'.[52] The ceremony was conducted in a European style with the reading of the warrant and a presentation of the insignia, the newly entitled knight kneeling before the monarch's representative. The 'contractual aspect of the entitlement was painfully clear to the Indian recipients, as the accoutrements given had to be returned on the death of the holder', unlike symbolic accessories received from Indian rulers in the past which were kept in treasure rooms as objects to be viewed and used only on sacred occasions. Statutes of the order required the recipients to sign a bond that the valuables would be returned by their heirs.[53]

However the 'contractual aspect' of orders such as the Star of India did not exclusively favour the British donor. The caricature of Indian princes vying with each other to curry favour with the paramount power for 'empty' titles and the ceremonial trappings of imperialism is in many cases far from a true portrayal of the relationship between the conferrer and the recipient. The honours that were bestowed upon rulers carried considerable weight as the recognition of the cooperation and exploitation of mutual interests without which indirect rule would not have been feasible. The example of Ram Singh, Maharaja of Jaipur, demonstrates the ability with which a client prince was able to ask his imperial patron to requite the *durbar's* loyalty by being sensitive to the maharaja's interests even when they were different or on occasions opposed to that of the empire.[54] At the same time the position of the British in the Indian states was legitimised to some extent by their collaboration with a ruler in the pursuit of the 'improvement' of his subjects.

For a prince of a modern inclination in Rajputana there were many opportunities to earn imperial honours and serve one's own immediate interests by catering to imperial concerns with reform and progress. In 1861 the maharaja opened Jaipur's Nobles College, which brought much favourable notice to its founder for some years until it became clear that the institution was failing. In 1864 the establishment of a royal council, over the objections of barons and 'old officials', attracted considerable British attention as having the potential to strengthen, modify and improve internal government. This potential was never attained due to the fact that the maharaja used the bureaucratic administration primarily as an instrument to control the nobility either directly or indirectly, however the council

served the interests of both the maharaja and the imperial government in maintaining order in Jaipur against the threat of baronial
turbulence.[55] In the light of this cooperation in 1864 the maharaja
received his initial imperial accolade, becoming the first Rajput
prince to be knighted in the order of the Star of India.[56]

Following drought and famine in the state in 1868 Ram Singh
abolished duties on grain, giving the British access to supplies for
garrisons in Rajputana and a free grain trade along the high road
from Ajmer to Agra for the merchants of British India. The abolition
of duties also resulted in a breakthrough in lifting 'vexatious' tar-
iffs as commerce passed though *jagirdars'* customs posts throughout
Rajputana. By his decision to renounce the revenue from grain duty
on the part of both his *durbar* and his *thakurs*, thus benefiting the
imperial economy, the maharaja was able once again to enlist British
support for his general policy of subordinating the Jaipur nobility to
his *durbar*, despite the declared British intent to balance princely and
noble power.[57] The ruler was perceived to be playing a major role in
promoting progress in his state and was honoured by the imperial
government with an addition of two guns to his salute. This was not
a matter to be taken lightly; additional gun salutes were awarded
with carefully calculated economy to maintain scarcity value and
after exhaustive consideration at every government level. Moreover in
1869 Ram Singh was invited to serve on the Viceroy's Council as an
additional member.

From 1870 the Jaipur *durbar* also gained from the Government of
India's dependence upon it to protect the empire's considerable invest-
ments in railway and salt developments in the state. The politically
and economically advantageous running of the railways as military
and commercial high roads through Rajputana was dependent on
a strong and capable central administration in Jaipur. At the same
time the railways allowed Ram Singh to monopolise the collection of
customs duties in the state, and *jagirdars* who wished to share in the
benefits were forced to act through the prince. With the production of
salt Ram Singh also successfully exploited the complementary aspects
of British interests and his own. The government's great investment
at Sambhar Lake increased the reliance of the British on the Jaipur

durbar, and the rents, royalties and duties on the salt extracted from Sambhar became the *durbar's* major source of non-agricultural revenue. The mutually beneficial dealings in salt between the British and the maharaja went over the heads of the nobility and were to become for them political and financial losses.[58]

The maharaja's symbolic gestures of loyalty kept pace with the advancing prosperity of the state, and in 1875 the viceroy presided over the opening ceremony in Jaipur city for the largest and most modern medical facility in Rajputana, Mayo Hospital. In 1876 Ram Singh commissioned Sir Swinton Jacob to design and construct a large museum and general facility for public enlightenment, the Albert Hall.[59] At the same time armed-robbery and boundary conflicts between *jagirdars* were rare, revenues were increasing, commerce was thriving, railways were secure and profitable and the salt monopoly was not undermined by smuggling. State expenditure in the building of roads was the highest in Rajputana. Lastly the British derived satisfaction from Ram Singh's gestures towards social reform; prisons were maintained satisfactorily, *sati* was officially discouraged and there were attempts to reduce female infanticide and general indebtedness.[60] The empire bestowed virtually all the distinctions and honours possible for an individual ruler on the Jaipur maharaja. In 1875 he was one of two Indian rulers (along with Scindia of Gwalior) selected by the British to serve on the commission set up to investigate charges of attempted murder and misrule on the part of Malhar Rao of Baroda,[61] and in recognition of Ram Singh's efforts towards education the viceroy in 1876 established a medal in his name to be awarded each year to the best student at Maharaja College in Jaipur. At the Imperial Assemblage in Delhi in 1877 the ruler's personal salute was raised to the highest grade of 21 guns and he became a Councillor of the Empress, and in 1880 he was made a Knight Grand Commander of the Order of the Indian Empire.[62]

Other princes and diwans were also honoured for furthering imperial interests. Nawab Faiz Ali Khan, Ram Singh's prime minister, was recommended for the Companion of the Star of India in 1870 for the 'progress, public works, good order and general good native government' of Jaipur,[63] as were the rulers of Jind and Nabha in 1879, distinguished by their assistance to the Government of India and 'the excellence of the contingents which they have furnished for service in the field'.[64] In 1898 Mulam Tirunal, the Maharaja of Travancore, was formally promoted to a salute of 21 guns, as during his 12 years of rule he had in every way proved himself a 'wise and sympathetic ruler' and expressed an 'unselfish subordination of personal to public interests'.[65]

However the removal of such honours could also act as one of the final sanctions that might be served against the rulers in cases of grave misconduct. The absence of Takht Singh, Maharaja of Jodhpur, from Mayo's viceregal *durbar* at Ajmer in 1870, on the grounds that he was unable to 'sit on an equality' with the Maharana of Udaipur, was one such instance; a reduction in his gun salute was deemed to be insufficient punishment and the 'only other possible penalty' suggested by the viceroy was to deprive him of the Star of India on the grounds that he had committed a 'misdemeanour derogatory to his honour'. Mayo took an unequivocal stand:

> I can look upon the conduct of the Joudhpore Raja in no other light than a deliberate and premeditated insult to her Majesty's Representative. I hold that if the Viceroy desires the attendance of the feudatory chiefs in *Durbar*, it is for him and not for any particular Chief to settle any question of precedence – the greatest care is taken in this matter that ancient custom and well ascertained right should be strictly adhered to – and it is most desirable that all these questions of Precedence should be determined on and finally settled.[66]

The maharaja was told to leave British territory, his 17-gun salute was reduced and his punishment was published in the Government of India's *Gazette*.

However it was perfectly possible for a royal family to eradicate such a stain of dishonour at a later date through the promotion of imperial causes. An addition to the gun salute of Takht Singh's successor, Jaswant Singh, was recommended in 1878 because of the prince's 'admirable conduct' in recent salt negotiations. Lytton expressed his appreciation of the fact that

> He has not only met all our wishes, unreservedly and cordially, in reference to his own State, but has exerted his powerful influence throughout Rajputana, setting an example which has secured to us the good will of all the other Rajput States in this important business ... By his active support of our salt policy, [he] has, with great public spirit, exposed himself to a certain amount of local unpopularity, by disregarding the economic heresies of his advisers, and it is, therefore, particularly important that he should receive an open generous support from the Government in a form which his own people will appreciate. Otherwise, when we next require his assistance, in some imperial matter, we shall have weakened both his will and his ability to give it.[67]

In order to avoid any possible degradation of the British system of honours, attempts on the part of the Indian princes to create their own order were firmly curtailed. In 1885 the viceroy, Lord Dufferin, wrote to the secretary of state, Lord Kimberley, that a 'sudden fancy had seized the Nizam for instituting an Order and distributing decorations'. Dufferin appreciated that Indian princes were entitled to grant 'titles' of honour at their discretion to their own subjects, so 'we cannot plead that the Empress is the sole fountain of honour'. However it was 'not desirable that every petty Rajah or Maharajah should be sowing stars and ribands broadcast over India'. A distinction should be made between a 'purely Indian ornament and one which should imitate the insignia of our Western Orders'.[68] A further rebuke was delivered later in the century to the raja of the Punjab state of Kapurthala, informing him that personal orders with insignia in any way resembling British decorations would not obtain recognition.[69] Dufferin's successor, Lord Lansdowne, warned the queen that although the expectation of a honour was always 'a useful stimulus' to a ruler, there was a danger that decorations could do more harm than good: 'The Chiefs watch very closely the manner in which such awards are distributed and are quick to notice the selection of an undeserving member of their class'.[70]

Until 1875 British holders of the Star of India far outnumbered their native counterparts. A total of 38 British knights of the order existed, as against 13 native knights, and 69 British companions of the order as against 31 native companions. Northbrook put forward the suggestion in 1875 that there should be a fixed proportion between British and native holders of both the KCSI and CSI, resulting in a ratio of 40 British to 20 native knights and 80 British to 40 native companions. Nevertheless the numbers were still heavily weighted in favour of the British holders of the order.[71]

Imperial Service Troops

Over and above honours, it was deemed highly desirable to give the Indian rulers a role in which they could be seen to be a valued and cooperative ally of the empire while maintaining *izzat*. Having guaranteed the defence of Indian rulers by treaty in the early nineteenth century, thereby removing the principal *raison d'etre* of state armies, the British in the last decades of the century made a concerted effort to find a profitable means of satisfying the traditional princely requirement for military display. To Lytton a military role for the princes fitted admirably into his conception of a 'feudal' empire, expressing also the reality that the armies of the princes were a 'formidable mass which may some day give us more anxiety than assistance'. In order to minimise this threat, the viceroy suggested that princely military power be harnessed to that of British forces for the common good, since many of the rulers were in any case bound to assist the queen in times of war. In the viceroy's view relations with the states could be modified to contribute to the security of the empire, and it was a 'sound policy to utilise some of the native armies which we cannot suppress, and which are at present a great anomaly'.[72] In giving the rulers the chance to aid the imperial cause their resources would be employed in a desirable direction:

> We allow these princes to maintain huge military establishments, which are perfectly useless to us in times of peace, and considerably in excess of what is strictly necessary for police

purposes; and yet we will not allow them to make use of their military power even in our own service? We leave them vast revenues and great powers from which we ourselves derive no benefit, and for which as yet they have no adequate employment... The whole social structure of this Empire is essentially feudal and eminently fitted for the application of the salutary military principle of the feudal system.[73]

The possibility of war with Russia in 1878 made the question of British utilisation of states' armies more immediate. The embarkation of a British Indian army force to the Mediterranean produced 'remarkable enthusiasm' among princely *durbars*. Lytton reported that

> The Begum of Bhopal has written to place the whole resources of her kingdom, military and financial, such as they are, at our unrestricted and unconditional disposal in the event of war. Kashmere offers his best troops for the defence of the frontier. Scindia is fretting for permission to furnish and lead a contingent; and numbers of our young hill Rajas are offering to raise regular cavalry regiments ... the Maharajah of Ulwur has telegraphed to me offering to raise at least two regiments of 500 infantry and 600 cavalry, at his own expense; and I yesterday received a telegram from the Co-Regents at Hyderabad, earnestly requesting that, in the event of war, all the military forces of that state might be employed by the British Government.[74]

However doubts were expressed at home where the viceroy's proposed scheme met with considerable opposition from the Council of India. In a note dated February 1879, council member Sir Frederick Halliday declared that he was quite unable to reconcile the policy of the Government of India with the line of action laid down in 1878 that forces maintained by states should not exceed either in numbers or equipment their requirements for police and ceremonial purposes. He stressed that 'Our wisest and best statesmen have always looked upon armed bodies in the pay of such feudatory states as a source of danger... which of [the rulers] will not now hope that his turn will come round, and that to his loosely organised and badly armed rabble will be granted the boon of arms and organisation, as it has now been granted to some of his compeers? As for the supposed loyalty by which these offers of service are dictated, it may be politic not absolutely and openly to deny it. But he that really believes it, and puts his trust in it, and persuades the English people to believe it, is, in my poor judgment, a very simple person'.[75]

Despite his belief in the advantages of the scheme, Lytton agreed that such largesse on the part of rulers, although supporting imperial interests in the short term, could in time pose a possible threat to British dominance, in that the princes were bound to demand some form of power-sharing in return for their generosity. Lytton had no doubt that 'our larger feudatory chiefs and neighbours count on eventually getting from us a substantial "quid pro quo" for any military or financial assistance we may hereafter accept from them'.[76] However the viceroy remained convinced that the existing military relations with the states were 'by no means creditable to English statesmanship' and had one of the great Continental powers been in control of India it would have certainly found the means of utilising the 'martial proclivities' and resources of the princes.[77] This conviction was shared by the secretary of state, Lord Randolph Churchill, who seven years later wrote to the viceroy, Lord Dufferin, with his vision of a total transformation of the armies of the states in which they would be

> incorporated effectually in the military resources of India, each state maintaining a certain military quota calculated upon its population and revenue, which should be efficient as our own native troops in equipment, skill, and discipline, and frequently inspected by British officers and brigaded with British troops. This would lead to a tremendous reduction in point of numbers of the Native armies, but the Princes would be so gratified by the superior efficiency and responsibility that I do not think they would object. Here you might find your outlet for native military aspirations which our policy since the Mutiny has unduly, I think, repressed.[78]

In 1885 the Government of India first introduced the Imperial Service Troops scheme, founded against the backdrop of a potential Anglo-Russian conflict in Afghanistan. Under the scheme, Indian princes were invited to designate existing or recently organised units of their armies to be trained and equipped by the British to the levels of military efficiency of comparable units in the Indian Army. British officers were assigned to these Imperial Service units for the purposes of 'advising, superintending and instructing' them in the ways of modern armies, but not to command them.[79] Imperial Service units were not contingents of the peacetime Indian army. Rather, they were elite corps of their separate state armies, available for imperial service in times of need but ordinarily commanded by their own Indian officers and under the political control of their princes. Lord Frederick Sleigh Roberts, Commander-in-Chief of the Indian Army and a leading proponent of the scheme,[80] was of the opinion that, because they were isolated in their states and scattered over the map of India, Imperial Service units were themselves unlikely to be the cause of serious disturbance, moreover the scheme would force princes to reduce their numbers of ill-armed and undisciplined retainers. He remained 'convinced that our wisest policy...is to let the chiefs see that we are prepared to trust them', and congratulated the government 'at having obtained a material addition to its available military forces at a comparatively insignificant cost, and on having at the same time secured... important political advantages'.[81]

This new potential for a display of princely largesse immediately met with success. In 1887 the Nizam of Hyderabad offered to make a contribution of 60 *lakhs* towards the defence of the Indian frontier on the occasion of the Golden Jubilee celebrations for Queen Victoria. Similar offers of help were received from rulers of states such as Jaipur and Kashmir. Although in the eyes of the Government of India it was deemed not 'altogether desirable or proper to accept grants of money from states, some of which can ill afford to make them', there was an opportunity to train and equip portions of states' armies for use in time of war, starting with Kashmir and the Punjab, then 'useful material' in Rajputana, to protect and defend the passes leading from Afghanistan to India.[82] Such an opportunity would provide an opening for the sons of many great Indian families 'who have at present no career before them, and whose lives are passed in idleness and often in discontent'.[83] A scheme was put forward in 1889 to add 25,000 men to the effective force of the empire, and by 1892 more than 15,000 had been recruited.

During his viceroyalty Curzon utilised Imperial Service Troops outside India for the first time by sending a brigade to China during the Boxer Rebellion, and in 1899 Imperial Service Troops accompanied British forces in the Second Boer War, providing crucial aid in the form of 1,200 horses for the use of mounted infantry. Making a break from the earlier emphasis on the voluntary nature of participation, Curzon unsuccessfully resurrected the question of a compulsory financial contribution by the princes to imperial defence, stressing that only 23 out of the 100 princes at the Coronation Durbar had made a donation despite the fact that the prosperity of the states had benefited from the peace and facilities of extended trade resulting from the development of British India. The India Office was greatly opposed to the suggestion, as public pronouncements had stressed that princely offers were 'spontaneous and unsolicited' and it was suspected that the move would antagonise the princes.[84] The lukewarm response from the rulers, fuelled by suspicion of fresh monetary levies and greater intrusion into state revenues, confirmed this view. At the same time Curzon failed in implementing measures to improve the military efficiency of the Imperial Service troops, although his initiatives did lead to an increase in the number of troops assigned for imperial service over the following years. By 1906 Curzon's efforts had led to offers of 3,000 additional troops from different states, with the result that the Imperial Service Troops comprised 16,942 fighting men, 4,485 transport animals and 1,594 carts. These proved to be of great value in the crisis of military manpower generated during the First World War.[85]

The utilisation of Imperial Service Troops provides an excellent example of how collaboration between Britain and selected social groups was sustained. Despite their ongoing concerns regarding the potential threat of states' forces, the British pursued a policy of military collaboration with the princes because it enabled them to augment armed forces without meeting the ensuing costs. At the

same time the well-publicised picture of the paramount power placing trust in the rulers in the defence of India served to legitimise
imperial rule. The policy was also politically expedient in providing
the princes with a role as loyal imperial allies and a platform for prestigious martial display on the all-India stage. However the rulers'
muted response to Curzon's financial proposals reflected an aversion
to falling in line with a policy that was contrary to their interests.[86]
The wholehearted support of the collaborators was only ensured when
they believed that they would benefit personally from participating
in an imperial project.

Imperial Privy Council

Whereas there could be a mutual recognition of interests between the
British and individual princes, as the sections on the award of the Star
of India and the scheme for Imperial Service Troops make clear, any
suggestion of a highly visible partnership between Indian rulers and
the paramount power in matters of state was dismissed out of hand
both in London and Calcutta. The proposal for the establishment of an
Imperial Privy Council, Lytton's most ambitious plan for the princes,
demonstrates the difficulty of raising the imperial profile of the rulers while denying them a voice of any substance. It also reveals the
somewhat surprising amount of interest in the situation of the princes
which existed in Britain in the latter part of the nineteenth century,
and a sensitivity towards their treatment under the Government
of India.

Putting forward his original suggestion to Disraeli in April 1876
that members of the proposed Privy Council, the 'great Indian mag-
nates', should be admitted to the Imperial Legislative Council, Lytton
made it clear that it would not give 'the least real power' to the rulers
but would

> flatter their 'amour propre', please the whole native
> population... [and] furnish an inducement for visiting the
> Viceregal Court and paying their respects to the Queen's
> Representative. As such visits are public acts of obeisance to

the supremacy of the British Power, and as they will offer the Viceroy opportunities, now rarely offered to him, to exercise a personal influence over the Native Chiefs, I think they ought to be encouraged.[87]

The secretary of state, Lord Salisbury, was quick to question whether the bestowal of honorary seats in the Legislative Council was 'a necessary portion' of Lytton's plan for creating a Privy Council. The proposed council represented the queen's relationship to those parts of India not subject to the jurisdiction of the Legislative Council, due to the fact that the most conspicuous members would be princes. Therefore there was no reason to invest them with a share of power in the government of British India. Moreover Anglo-Indians might object to having laws made for them by 'a majority consisting of coloured men'. A Privy Council in India would be an imperial body, whose duty it would be to advise the viceroy in the government of the empire, and for that reason it would contain councillors, 'white and coloured', to inform him of the needs in all areas. However the secretary of state stressed that it should not be a legislature: 'It gives him [the viceroy] no authority; it receives such authority as it has from him. Its strong point will be dignity, not power'. In Salisbury's view the council should be considered entirely separate and distinct from any existing institution.[88]

The viceroy agreed that his original proposition that native members of the Privy Council should participate in the Legislative Council ought to be abandoned for the present. The Privy Council was to include, as 'ex-officio' members, all governors, lieutenant-governors and members of the Viceroy's Executive Council, to 'enhance the importance of the native position'. Lytton emphasised that since this new 'purely consultative' body would meet only at the summons of the viceroy, there would be 'no surrender of substantial power'. The proposed constitution of the Privy Council would 'swamp' native members, yet still secure the 'prestige of their presence and assent'. It was expected that in such consultation the greatest princes would always agree with the decision of the viceroy, moreover the viceroy would be careful to summon only those rulers on whom he could count. If the rulers were allowed to meet and deliberate by themselves 'they would instantly put spokes into the government wheel'.[89] It was decided not to include local councils in the Privy Council, as such an inclusion would entirely drown the native element who, if they found themselves not only in an overwhelming minority but also outnumbered by British officials of no rank or status, would regard the council as a mockery. Moreover if the queen were to be sovereign of the council, and members of the royal family honorary members, it would not be appropriate to include 'all the scrubs of the local Councils'.[90]

Salisbury, looking for more precise details of the council's function, expressed his anxiety as far as its development was concerned: 'Especially I should be careful not to attribute to it any kind of authority over the internal government of the British territory'. The secretary of state saw the council primarily as a platform on 'the common weal of the Empire' which, hopefully, would divert the Indian rulers from potentially dangerous 'isolated communications'. He was convinced that the princes should not look upon the council as a machine for checking and guiding the viceroy in his dealings with them, but as a means of guiding the viceroy in the dealings of the empire with those who existed outside it: 'Eton schoolboys may like to place constitutional checks on the Headmaster; yet a meeting for devising the best means of beating Harrow at cricket would be more popular than a meeting for drawing up a code of regulations under which boys should be flogged'.[91]

The secretary of state recognised that some of the more astute princes might object to the formal subjection to the empress which the Privy Council would imply, and felt it would be wise to ascertain the opinions of maharajahs Holkar and Scindia at least before making an official announcement.[92] Salisbury admitted that there was

a wide gulf between the nominal and the real relation of the Indian Government to the feudatory Chiefs. In theory they are sovereigns – independent, except as far as they have bound themselves by particular stipulations, affecting chiefly their external relations and their military habits. In fact, their power within their own dominions is constantly diminishing, the sphere within which their authority is unrestricted is steadily contracting, the range of subjects upon which we assume to give authoritative advice is being slowly but constantly enlarged. By a process which is not traced out by any set policy or design, but simply results from the ascendancy which strength acquires over weakness when the two are long in contact, the Native Chiefs are tending to the position of glorified Lieutenant-Governors.[93]

The risk of antagonising the rulers in India was mirrored in Britain by the risk of raising adverse public opinion. Lytton's friend, the lawyer and writer James Fitzjames Stephen, who served in India for three years from 1869 as Law Member of the Viceroy's Council, expressed his alarm that the viceroy was 'getting into a channel where there are some dangerous rocks, and an ominous possibility of sudden and violent squalls'. Stephen was of the opinion that if the Privy Council were merely titular it would not 'harmonise' well with the general austerity of British rule, and if it were to act in any way as a council, 'i.e. if it is ever to deliberate and advise upon political affairs either with or without definite results', he considered that its establishment would be illegal. The Indian Councils Act of 1861 and other legislation provided a parliamentary constitution for India headed by the Council of India, and if the viceroy by an executive act called into being another council and publicly consulted with its members on imperial matters this action would be in 'direct opposition to the spirit of the Indian Councils Act'. Although this was technically not the same thing as a positive break in the law, 'it is so near an approach to it that the consequences might in practice be not very different'. Stephen stressed that although not in other ways a particularly powerful body, retired Indian civil servants had a considerable influence over the India Office, as well as English opinion in Indian matters, and 'would be apt to exclaim against anything which honoured their successors in a manner in which they had not been honoured, to say nothing of the jealousy with which they would view any measure capable of being represented as a departure from the traditions of Indian government'.[94] Moreover it was feared that the formation of a council on a model of the English equivalent might give rise to expectations on the part of the princes and people of India which could not be realised.

There was strong opposition from the India Council in London, many of whom were Liberals and disliked both the queen's new title and the display involved. It was widely suspected that parliamentary action would follow such opposition and 'Every kind of ridicule would be thrown by one set of opponents upon what they would term the sham honours with which you had tried to bribe the native princes into allegiances. On the other hand, other, perhaps less responsible speakers, would treat the office you have created as intensely real, would urge the Princes to take advantage of it, and act fully up to it, and to claim a substantial part in directing the policy of the Empire'.[95] As a result of these major concerns the viceroy was informed that, since parliament had formally constructed his own council both for purposes of policy and legislation, it was not open to him to set up another council constructed on very different principles.

Salisbury himself regretted that the Privy Council was not more popular at home, since he believed that Indian opinion was now 'enlightened, bewildered and irritated by such rays of English opinion as come to it across the globe concentrated and somewhat distorted through Reuter's lenses'. The necessity of 'guiding or disguising the naked action of absolute power' was paramount after the deposition of the ruler of Baroda, and for this reason an official link between the viceroy and the princes appeared highly desirable. Left alone, there seemed no grounds for believing that the rulers would bother to explore the difference between their titular and their actual condition, but 'the growing proximity of Europe is a menacing element in the future task of governing India ... Average Englishmen, from Dukes to Common Councillors, evidently took the Indian Princes seriously, and talked of them as if they were little less than independent. The same tone prevailed in foreign books of travels, in Russian newspaper articles, and other expressions of superficial Western thought'. It was feared that such language would in the end affect the most important rulers and 'put wind into their heads', resulting in the need for the Government of India to assert its paramount power by 'unmistakeable action' which would then be criticised in England. However it would be impossible to argue seriously that the princes had international rights as independent sovereigns if they accepted the position of Privy Councillors of the queen.[96]

Agreement was finally reached between London and Calcutta that in the long term a formal association of princes and other Indian nobles had the potential to be 'politically dangerous'. Authorisation was given to confer upon chosen chiefs the title of 'Councillor of the Empress', but it was admitted that holders of this title would be unable to form part of any organised body and could not be summoned for 'collective deliberation', although consultation between the viceroy and one or more members of the councillors might strengthen the hand of the executive government in an emergency.[97] When Lytton left for home in 1880 his scheme for a council of princes was put into cold storage, where it remained until resurrected by Lord Chelmsford in 1916.

* * *

During the latter half of the nineteenth century Indian rulers were subject to major changes in ceremonial practice. In the pre-colonial period a person was ranked 'not according to an absolute scale, but in relation to the changing assets and achievements of others in a specific ritual context'.[98] Under British rule an Indian prince safe on his *gadi* unless found guilty of gross misrule, no longer had a requirement to influence his kinsmen or rivals, and was unable to consort with his fellow rulers except under extraordinary circumstances such as Imperial Assemblages. Ceremonies which had been sufficiently fluid to display pomp and wealth to influence individual audiences, and sufficiently adaptable to change the parameters of local politics, evolved into rigidly formatted meetings between British officials and individual princes in which the Indian rulers deferred to the paramount power.

As the century progressed, the Indian ruler was increasingly bound by the strictures of a rigid hierarchical system within which he owed allegiance to the British monarch and was frequently consigned to a position of equality with British officials. Recognising the loss of princely status resulting from the new social structure, there was an awareness of the need for tools to encourage loyalty to the empire while providing the rulers with a role of significance in an all-India context. In examining imperial policy on the award of honours it is evident that a collaboration between the paramount power and an individual prince could carry significant weight, and institutions such as the

Imperial Privy Council and Imperial Service troops were designed to incorporate the princes into the imperial fabric in an effort both to raise the princely profile and to legitimise British rule. Although the princes proved up to a point to be willing collaborators in a military capacity, the failure of the Imperial Privy Council to come to fruition was evidence of the reluctance of the British to relinquish power to the Indian rulers at the highest level of government, despite the political advantages of securing their loyalty.

EPILOGUE

In October 1906 the Governor of Bombay, Lord Lamington, urged the new viceroy, Lord Minto, to initiate a policy of freeing the Indian princes from 'so much Government supervision and interference'.[1] Minto needed little encouragement, deploring what he saw as the aggressive and dictatorial behaviour of his predecessor, Lord Curzon, towards the states. A year later he informed John Morley, the secretary of state, that Madho Rao Scindia of Gwalior had declared, 'the tyranny of Curzon's rule towards the Native Chiefs had been so unbearable that nothing would have induced them to put up with it and they would have united together without regard to religion or caste to throw it off'.[2] With the appointment of Harcourt Butler at the head of the Foreign Department in 1907,[3] Curzon's ideas were officially discarded and replaced by a policy of non-interference in states' affairs.

Various factors had led to the adoption of such a policy. It had been deemed necessary to reduce the demands made of the overworked and understaffed Foreign Department, and after much open resentment to relieve the rulers of the constant overseeing of their private affairs. In addition the new viceroy believed strongly that, given the Home Government's determination to introduce constitutional reforms in the Indian provinces, in order to appease critics of the Raj he was morally bound to grant a corresponding concession to its most faithful allies. Minto and Butler were persuaded by an argument put forward by the gaekwar in 1909[4] that 'a looser leash on the princes would improve, rather than retard, the standard of their administrations'.[5] Above all, however, the policy was designed to ensure that the princes would act to support the British position in India.

Confronted with the rise of extreme nationalism following Curzon's partition of Bengal in 1905, Minto and Butler reached the conclusion that the Indian rulers could be both 'capable and willing alliance partners'. At the beginning of the discussions which led to the Indian Councils Act of 1909, Minto suggested that a Council of Princes might serve as a possible counterpoise to the Indian National Congress, the vehicle for the nationalist movement. Morley doubted the wisdom of the suggestion on the grounds that 'if the princes were allowed to combine and confer they might conceivably use the opportunity to unite against the Government'.[6] However although Minto failed to secure constitutional recognition for the princes, he was determined that his viceroyalty would not leave them empty-handed. In a speech at Udaipur in November 1909 he unveiled the principles of the new policy of non-interference, declaring:

> I have always been opposed to anything like pressure on *Darbars* with a view to introducing British methods of administration. – I have preferred that reforms should emanate from the *Darbars* themselves, and grow up in harmony with the traditions of the State. It is easy to overestimate the value of administrative efficiency – it is not the only object to aim at, though the encouragement of it must be attractive to keen and able members of the Political Service, and it is not unnatural that the temptation to further it should for example appeal strongly to those who are temporarily in charge of the administration of State during a minority, whether they are in sole charge or associated with a State Council. Their position is a difficult one – it is one of peculiar trust – and though abuses and corruption must of course as far as possible be corrected, I cannot but think that Political Officers will do wisely to accept the general system of administration to which the Chief and his people have been accustomed. The methods sanctioned by tradition in States are usually well adapted to the needs and relations of the ruler and his people. The loyalty of the latter to the former is generally a personal

loyalty, which administrative efficiency, if carried out on lines unsuited to local conditions, would lessen or impair.[7]

The Udaipur speech makes it clear that Minto was well aware of the fact that 'the value of administrative efficiency', by which the more determined political officers set such store, had frequently undermined the traditional structure of rule in the Indian states, thereby diminishing the status of a ruler vis-à-vis his subjects. The precise details of the new policy were formulated by Butler in the *Manual of Instructions to Officers of the Political Department*. In sharp contrast to the methods of Curzon, the political officer was now given strict instructions that he was not to interfere in the domestic affairs of the princes unless misrule was rampant.[8] Paragraph six of the introduction to the *Manual* insisted that

> He should leave well alone; the best work of a Political Officer is often what he has left undone ... Having guaranteed internal independence to the states, and having undertaken their protection against external aggression, the Imperial Government have assumed some responsibility for the maintenance of order and fairly efficient government of them and cannot consent to being an indirect instrument of oppression. The degree of misrule which will call for interference is a question for decision on the merits in each case. It may be stated generally that, unless misrule reaches a pitch which violates the elementary laws of civilisation, the Imperial Government will usually prefer to take no overt measures for enforcing reform; and in any case, the attempt to reform should, so long as is possible, be confined to personal suasion.[9]

The declaration of government policy towards the states during Minto's viceroyalty was accompanied by an equally significant development among the princely ranks. A new type of prince, 'anglicised in outlook and social habits', began to emerge. Curzon's administration had done much to stimulate this development. In attempting to foster a new sense of responsibility among the princes, Curzon, despite his strong opposition to European travel by the rulers, was largely responsible for 'dismantling the traditional barriers of isolation' which had prevented a prince from looking beyond the narrow confines of his own state. As has been discussed, British influence, particularly in the area of education, had produced westernised princes such as Jai Singh, Maharaja of Alwar, and Ganga Singh, Maharaja of Bikaner, both products of Mayo College. However these men were not representative of the princely order as a whole and the transition was not always wholly successful.[10] A prince could become both physically and culturally estranged from his subjects, endangering the traditional respect for authority which was still seen to validate the existence of princely regimes.

Such estrangement was not inevitable. In a few isolated cases, as Manu Bhagavan has suggested, 'by bridging the gap between the colonial and the colonized' princes and their bureaucracies could use 'modern' ideas successfully to provide model examples of states. Wearing one hat, they could claim to be loyal representatives of the empire and, wearing the other, the last line of defence protecting the Indian people from the 'full onslaught of English evil'.[11] The packages of reforms pursued by the administrations of Krishnaraja Wadiyar of Mysore and Sayaji Rao, Gaekwar of Baroda, during the first three decades of the twentieth century were warmly received by their people, who expressed their general contentment by rejecting frequent calls for agitation against their governments.[12] However for many princes less ambitious in their outlook the 'methods sanctioned by tradition' to which Minto referred at Udaipur were no longer an option either in internal state government or palace life. In December 1915 Madho Rao Scindia, Maharaja of Gwalior, described the irreversible situation created by the loss of his traditional role, informing the viceroy, Lord Hardinge, that although political officers had used minority periods to remove long-standing abuses and improve the finances of the states, their methods had 'shaken the adherence of the people to their traditional customs and ways', weakening the ties of personal loyalty and obedience between subjects and prince.[13]

As the possibility for a political partnership increased, relations between the British and the princes came to be characterised more by consultation than control of subordinate by superior, particularly after the establishment of the Chamber of Princes in 1921 which allowed rulers direct access to the Delhi authorities. Pre-eminent among those rulers who played a prominent role in institutions such as the Chamber of Princes and the Committee of Ministers were Ganga Singh of Bikaner, Udaibhan Singh of Dholpur, Dijvijaysinhji of Nawanagar, Bhupinder Singh of Patiala, and Sultan Jahan Begam and Nawab Hamidullah of Bhopal. However the impressive status achieved by these rulers on the all-India stage was unable to hide the fact that in most cases the traditional source of power of the princely rank had been severely undermined by British efforts to reform the Indian states and their rulers during the last decades of the previous century. From examining the intricate workings of indirect rule during the period, this book draws the following conclusions.

The British determination to 'modernise' Indian princes failed to a large extent due to the inadequacy of members of the political service, understaffed and unsupported by their superiors, to deal with the complexities of *durbar* practice, and the fact that the regulation and transparency required to produce well-ordered and open government were on the whole alien concepts to the first generation of westernised Indian rulers. During the period, with the exception of matters of succession and minority rule in which the heavy hand of imperialism was evident, the Government of India appears to have lacked the interest or commitment to provide a consistent policy towards the conduct of political officers or to provide a useful role for the princes, both within their states and in an all-India context. When forced to act, as in cases of gross misrule, officials at the highest level were capable of dramatically misreading the situation.

Lacking a consistent line of command as government views shifted over time in response to the changing interests and outlook of the British in India, the overzealous intentions of local British officers to arrive at 'good government' were frequently met by a significant amount of opposition from various parties within states. In the case of education, for example, there was much resistance to the efforts of tutors and political officers from the members of the *zenana* and from *durbar* officials. However in matters of marriage and other mutually beneficial dealings between the British and the princes, such as the granting of honours to reward loyalty, there is evidence of a surprisingly active accommodation, enhancing the status of both parties and demonstrating that indirect rule was by no means a one-way process in which the colonial state invariably reigned supreme. Moreover as the princes were increasingly drawn into the newly established imperial hierarchy during the period British measures countenanced to confront the effects of both actual and perceived subordination – in particular, the formation of Imperial Service Troops and proposals for the Imperial Privy Council – although not successful in involving the rulers at a high level of the Indian administration (and undoubtedly politically motivated) demonstrate at least the consideration of a British policy to work in some form of partnership with the princes.

As far as government was concerned, in the urgency to introduce visible and sound methods of administration into states there appeared to be too little emphasis on ensuring that an adult ruler was given sufficient time and encouragement to abandon traditional ideas of largesse and autocracy in order to become a cost-conscious head of state. Research shows that political officers often neglected rulers in the intricacies of state politics and the pursuit of well-regulated government. For many members of the Political Service the ends were seen to justify the means and even at the most significant stage of a prince's life, during which he was theoretically at the head of a state administration, a ruler could be sidelined with relative ease if he failed to subscribe wholeheartedly to the pursuit of efficiency and accountability. However it is hardly surprising that in many cases political officers were content to leave their princely charges as figureheads rather than prime movers in the government of a state, if such a government was in any case progressing in line with liberal ideals. Indeed it could be argued that British officers were more successful in moving towards their goal of 'good government' by so doing.

This book makes it clear that for the purposes of modelling aware and progressive rulers of the Indian states, British methods of indirect rule during the crucial phase of princely development proved to be inadequate. The evidence suggests that the weakening of the bonds between princes and their traditional power bases was not a result of deliberate British policy but the inadvertent outcome of colonial ideals and political expediency. Considerable effort was expended by the British to regulate palace life and to lay the groundwork for a modern monarchy by exposing young heirs to a *gadi* to western thought. However attempts to integrate a relatively untrained, and often unwilling, ruler into the administrative procedure proved frequently to demand more time and trouble than they were worth, particularly with the endless rounds of negotiation required between the various parties involved in state politics. Deprived of the opportunity to act as an essential cog in the wheel of a sound, modernised government, the Indian princes were by no means experiencing a golden age during the last decades of the nineteenth century. Traditionally the protectors and sustainers of the social fabric, they were dramatically diminished in status by the process of enforcing in their administrations the virtues of 'Clearness, certainty, promptitude, cheapness' advocated so enthusiastically by James Mill and the early Victorian liberal reformers.[14]

APPENDIX: INDIAN PRINCES AND DIWANS

Dates refer to reigns or terms in office

Alwar

Sheodan Singh, Maharao Raja	1857–1874
Mangal Singh, Maharaja	1874–1892
Jai Singh, Maharaja	1892–1937

Baroda

Malhar Rao Gaekwar, Maharaja	1870–1875
Sayaji Rao Gaekwar, Maharaja	1881–1939
T. Madhava Rao, Diwan	1875–1882

Bhopal

Shah Jahan, Begam	1868–1901
Sultan Jahan, Begam	1901–abdicated 1926

Bikaner

Ganga Singh Rathor, Maharaja	1898–1943

Gwalior

Jayaji Rao Scindia, Maharaja	1843–1886
Madho Rao Scindia, Maharaja	1894–1925

Hyderabad

Mahbub Ali Khan, Nizam	1884–1911
Salar Jung I, Diwan	1853–1883
Salar Jung II, Diwan	1884–1887

Indore

Tukoji Rao Holkar, Maharaja	1844–1886
Shivaji Rao Holkar, Maharaja	1886–1903

Jaipur

Ram Singh, Maharaja	1835–1879
Madho Singh II, Maharaja	1880–1922

Jhalawar

Zalim Singh, Maharaja	1884–deposed 1896

Jind

Ranbir Singh, Raja	1899–1948

Jodhpur (Marwar)

Takht Singh, Maharaja	1843–1873
Jaswant Singh II, Maharaja	1873–1895
Sardar Singh, Maharaja	1895–1911

Kashmir

Ranbir Singh, Maharaja	1857–1885
Pratap Singh, Maharaja	1885–1925

Mewar (Udaipur)

Sajjan Singh, Maharana	1874–1884
Fateh Singh, Maharana	1884–1930

Mysore

Chamarajendra Wadiyar IX, Maharaja	1881–1894
Krishnaraja Wadiyar IV, Maharaja	1902–1940
K. Seshadri Iyer, Diwan	1883–1896

Pudukkottai

Ramachandra Tondaiman, Raja   1839–1886
Martanda Bhairava Tondaiman, Raja   1894–abdicated 1928
A. Sashiah Sastri, Diwan   1878–1894

Travancore

Mulam Tirunal, Maharaja   1885–1924
T. Madhava Rao, Diwan   1860–1872
A. Sashiah Sastri, Diwan   1873–1877

GLOSSARY

amildar	lowest level of revenue officer
ashraf	respectable class
atar	fragrant essential oil of jasmine, roses and other flowers
begam	Muslim female ruler, married Muslim woman
Brahmin	Hindu priestly caste
devadasi	woman 'married' to a god in a temple, ritual dancer
diwan	senior minister, head of administration
durbar	royal court, formal assembly
durbari	courtier
faringhi	foreigner
gadi	throne
Gaekwar	surname of Maratha family who formed state of Baroda
haveli	private mansion
Holkar	surname of Maratha family who formed state of Indore
izzat	honour, respect, prestige
jagir	hereditary estate
jagirdar	grantee of hereditary estate
karkhana	office or place where business is conducted
khalsa	state owned or controlled
kharita	formal letter to or from a ruler

khilat	robe of honour worn on ceremonial occasion
Kshatriya	Hindu military caste
kumar	heir of raja, every son of rulers of Gujarat and Kathiawar
lakh	a hundred thousand (unless otherwise specified, rupees)
madrasa	Muslim school of learning originally attached to a mosque
mahal	division of a district yielding revenue
maharaja	princely ruler; variants include *maharana* and *maharao*
maharani	wife of princely ruler
mohur	gold coin worth 15 rupees
munshi	clerk
nautch	intricate traditional dance performed by professional dancing girls
nawab	Muslim princely ruler
nazar, nazarana	offerings of presents or coins to signify loyalty to a ruler
nizam	Muslim princely ruler, originally Mughal governor
pan	betel vine prepared as a savoury
panchayat	literally, 'council of five'; generally, caste or village council dealing with disputes relating to personal law
pandit	Hindu theology teacher
patel	village headman
patwari	village accountant
peshkash	tribute
purdah	veil or curtain, practice of keeping women in seclusion
purdahnashin	veiled or secluded woman
raj	ruling regime
raja	ruler
ryot	peasant cultivator
sahibzada	son of Muslim ruler
samaj	religious community
sanad	grant or deed conferring rights or title
sardar, sirdar	honorific title of a leader

sati	self-immolation of a Hindu widow
Scindia	surname of Maratha family who formed state of Gwalior
sepoy	soldier
shariat	Islamic law
shastras	sacred Sanskrit texts
sheristidar	secretary, registrar
Shia and Sunni	the two principal Muslim sects
tahsildar	collector of revenue in a *tahsil* (subdivision of a district)
taluqdar	revenue official presiding over district, landed aristocrat in Awadh
thakur	minor Rajput ruler
til	sesame
ulama	scholar of Islamic jurisprudence, learned man
vakil	agent, attorncy
vizier	Muslim high official
zamindar	landholder, landed aristocrat in Bengal and elsewhere
zamindari	large agricultural estate
zenana	women's quarters

NOTES

Preface

1. See Thomas R. Metcalf, *The Aftermath of Revolt: India 1857–1870* (Princeton, 1964), p. 323 and Francis Hutchins, *The Illusion of Permanence: British Imperialism in India* (Princeton, 1967), p. 171.

Introduction: The Indian States and the British

1. Descriptive note on the Indian States, 1931, quoted Stephen R. Ashton, *British Policy towards the Indian States, 1905–1939* (London, 1982), p. 1.
2. C. A. Bayly, *Indian Society and the Making of the British Empire* (Cambridge, 1988), p. 8.
3. Ashton: *British Policy*, pp. 2–3. For an account of British relations with the Indian states at the beginning of the nineteenth century, see Edward Thompson, *The Making of the Indian Princes* (London, 1943). Ian Copland discusses the diversity of the states in the twentieth century in *The Princes of India in the Endgame of Empire, 1917–1947* (Cambridge, 1997), pp. 8–11.
4. Ashton: *British Policy*, pp. 2–3.
5. Jagirdars could and did present considerable challenges to Indian princes. They could trigger internal revolts, influence succession and drain off resources.
6. See Sir Michael O'Dwyer, *India As I Knew It: 1885–1925* (London, 1925), pp. 151–5.
7. Barbara Ramusack, *The Indian Princes and Their States* (Cambridge, 2004), pp. 171–3.

8. Ibid, p. 173.

9. Terence Creagh-Coen, *The Indian Political Service: A Study in Indirect Rule* (London, 1971), p. 7. The Muslim state of Janjira was an oddity, founded by Abyssinian pirates.

10. Bayly: *Indian Society*, p. 58.

11. *Vakils* were normally recruited from the Islamicised service elite of scholars and administrators who traditionally served in such positions across India. The key difference between the Mughal and British systems of dealing with subordinate states was that the rulers who were *mansabdars*, or military commanders acting in the name of the emperor as in Amber and Jodhpur, could send their *vakils* to the Mughal court whereas, under the East India Company, the British could send their representatives to the princes but the princes could not send their agents to the British capitals.

12. Michael H. Fisher, *Indirect Rule in India: Residents and the Residency System, 1764–1858* (New Delhi, 1991), p. 49. By the end of the eighteenth century there was a gradual shift in British usage from the words 'king' to 'prince' and 'royal' to 'princely', which represented a conscious or unconscious effort to subordinate Britain's Indian allies as they were drawn into an evolving subsidiary alliance system. However in the past decade or so some scholars and the tourist industry have begun to refer to the Indian princes and their palaces as 'royal'.

13. Robin Jeffrey, Introduction, *People, Princes and Paramount Power: Society and Politics in the Indian Princely States* (New Delhi, 1978), pp. 263–8.

14. Fisher: *Indirect Rule*, pp. 222–4.

15. Fisher: *Indirect Rule*, p. 414.

16. Princes still communicated with other princes to arrange marriages and spent several weeks or even months at wedding sites. Princely pilgrimages to sacred sites also allowed rulers to maintain relations with each other.

17. William Lee-Warner, *The Native States of India* (London, 1910), p. 220.

18. Fisher: *Indirect Rule*, p. 230.

19. Fisher: *Indirect Rule*, pp. 196, 282.

20. Ian Copland states that the word 'paramountcy' crops up with impressive regularity in documents about Britain's feudatory policy: 'Essentially it meant supremacy and it is usually in this sense that the Raj was described as the "Paramount Power" in the subcontinent. But it also implied a condition of suzerainty as between lord and vassal and just as the act of commendation was supposed to confer rights on the feudal superior, so the Government of India was held to possess certain rights of intervention in the internal affairs of the princely states. The problem was to establish what those rights were. Was the superiority of the Paramount Power unlimited, or were there

conventions which had to be observed?' Ian Copland, *The British Raj and the Indian Princes: Paramountcy in Western India, 1857–1930* (New Delhi, 1982), p. 211.

21. Ashton: *British Policy*, p. 6.

22. Lee-Warner: *Native States*, p. 201.

23. Ibid.

24. Ashton: *British Policy*, p. 11.

25. Extract from Munro to Lord Hastings, 12 August 1817, quoted Ashton: *British Policy*, p. 11.

26. See Martin I. Moir, Douglas M. Peers and Lynn Zastoupil (eds), *J. S. Mill's Encounter with India* (Toronto and New York, 1999).

27. James Mill, *The History of British India* (Chicago, 1975), p. 226. See also John Stuart Mill, *On Liberty* and *Considerations of Representative Government* (New York, 1947).

28. James Mill: *British India*, Vol. II, p. 47, Vol. V, pp. 474, 521, quoted E. Stokes, *The English Utilitarians and India* (Oxford, 1959), pp. 56, 146.

29. Evidence to House of Commons Committee, 16 February 1832, quoted Metcalf: *Aftermath of Revolt*, p. 31.

30. Elphinstone to T. H. Villiers, 5 August 1832, quoted Ashton: *British Policy*, p. 13. Elphinstone, having read Mill's *History of British India,* found the book offensive and deplored Mill's ignorance and 'cynical, sarcastic tone'. Quoted David Gilmour, *The Ruling Caste: Imperial Lives in the Victorian Raj* (London, 2005), p. 13.

31. Malcolm to T. H. Villiers, 26 March 1832, quoted Ashton: *British Policy*, p. 13.

32. John William Kaye, *The Life and Correspondence of Major General Sir John Malcolm* (London, 1854), Vol. 2, p. 324.

33. Minute by Lord William Bentinck on Oude, 30 July 1831, quoted Ashton: *British Policy*, p. 14.

34. Dalhousie's minute, 30 August 1848, PP 1849, Vol. XXXIX, p. 83.

35. Sleeman to Dalhousie, 1848, quoted Creagh-Coen: *Indian Political Service*, pp. 17–18.

36. GoI FD to SoS, No. 43A, 30 April 1860, PCI, Vol. 85.

37. Bernard Cohn, 'Representing Authority in Victorian India' in Hobsbawm and Ranger (eds), *The Invention of Tradition* (Cambridge, 1983), p. 165.

38. Queen Victoria's Proclamation, 1 November 1858, in C. H. Philips (ed), *The Evolution of India and Pakistan, 1858–1947: Select Documents* (London, 1962), pp. 10–11.

39. Miles Taylor, 'Queen Victoria and India', *Victorian Studies* (Winter 2004), p. 266.

40. Taylor: 'Queen Victoria', p. 271.
41. Canning to Wood, 13 June 1860, quoted S. Gopal, *British Policy in India, 1858–1905* (Cambridge, 1965), p. 8.
42. *The Annual Register*, 100 (1858), p. 250, quoted Copland: *British Raj*, p. 95. Before 1875 there were ten rupees to the British pound, therefore a rupee was worth two shillings. However, in that year the value of silver-based currencies began to fall. The rupee was worth only one shilling and seven pence in 1885 and had fallen to below one shilling and three pence by 1892. From 1899 it stabilised at one shilling and four pence, or 15 rupees to the pound. Gilmour: *Ruling Caste*, p. xxi.
43. GoI to SoS, No. 43A, 30 April 1860, PCI, 1792–1864, Vol. 85, quoted R. J. Moore, *Sir Charles Wood's Indian Policy, 1858–1866* (Manchester, 1966), p. 164.
44. Ibid.
45. Minute from Frere to Canning, 19 June 1860, enclosure Canning to Wood, 26 June 1860, Wood Collection F78, Vol. 4.
46. Wood to Canning, 26 July 1860, Wood Collection F78, Vol. 4.
47. SoS to GoI, No. 59, 26 July 1860, PCI, 1792–1864, Vol. 440.
48. Metcalf: *Aftermath of Revolt*, p. 225.
49. *Hindu Patriot*, 26 August 1858, quoted Metcalf: *Aftermath of Revolt*, p. 226.
50. *Soma Prakesh*, 21 September 1863, quoted Metcalf: *Aftermath of Revolt*, p. 226.
51. B. Qanungo, 'A Study of British Relations with the Native States of India, 1858–62', *Journal of Asian Studies* 26 (February 1967), p. 265.
52. From 1858, to reflect the governor-general's role as the representative of the monarch to the feudal rulers of the princely states, the term Viceroy and Governor-General of India was used.
53. GoI to SoS, No. 43A, 30 April 1860, PCI, 1792–1864, Vol. 85.
54. Elgin to Wood, 9 September 1862, quoted T. Walrond (ed), *Letters and Journals of James, 8th Earl of Elgin* (London, 1872), pp. 419–20.
55. Lepel Griffin, 'Native India', *Asian Review* (April 1886), pp. 452–5.
56. Created by royal warrant in 1861 as a means of remedying the faults of the previous system, whereby military officers were withdrawn for unlimited periods from the regiments to meet the expanding needs of the public services.
57. Copland: *British Raj*, p. 73.
58. The term 'Political Service', or 'Indian Political Service', is used throughout, following the examples of Creagh-Coen and Copland; however, it was not coined until 1937, after the 1935 Government of India Act had removed all matters relating to the Indian states from the Foreign and Political

Department of the GoI to the Crown Representative, reporting directly to the British Government. In fact, the viceroy also held the office of Crown Representative and no major changes occurred.

59. Resolution of the Govt. of Bombay No. 5605 of 10 September 1873, quoted Ian Copland, 'The Other Guardians: Ideology and Performance in the Indian Political Service' in Jeffrey (ed): *People, Princes*, p. 288.

60. Memorandum by Lee-Warner, 8 July 1892, quoted Copland: *British Raj,* p. 78.

61. In the larger states there was a more substantial British support system. Residents' offices tended to be supported by a small group of technical experts with their clerks: principally an executive engineer, a doctor known as the residency or agency surgeon, and a military advisor from the Indian Army to inspect the local forces.

62. Copland: *British Raj*, p. 85.

63. Copland: 'Other Guardians', p. 280.

64. Copland: 'Other Guardians', p. 281.

65. Copland: 'Other Guardians', p. 295. Since relatively few political officers could achieve the plum jobs of lieutenant-governors or secretariat postings, by the early decades of the twentieth century the Political Service became the refuge of less-ambitious or less-competent Indian Civil Service (ICS) officers. The service also became a haven for both ICS and military officers who did not like the growing democratisation at home and in India.

66. At the highest level a number of viceroys, notably Northbrook and Lansdowne, displayed a significant lack of interest in the states. Ironically both men were forced to deal with major cases of misrule: Northbrook in Baroda and Lansdowne in Manipur.

67. Copland: *Princes of India*, p. 14. It is noticeable that correspondence at the highest level, for example between viceroy and secretary of state, tended to be significantly more Orientalist in tone in its preconceptions of the East than the correspondence of the men on the ground in the states as they 'muddled through'.

1. Succession

1. '*Gadi*' in a princely context indicates a *rajgadi*, 'an ensemble of cushion with cotton or silk coverings that was the Hindu equivalent of a European throne'. Usually a *rajgadi* was on the floor but sometimes it was placed on a chair of wood, silver or stone. When a prince was enthroned on the *rajgadi* and his body was in direct contact with it, 'sanctified royal qualities were transmitted to him'. Ramusack: *Indian Princes*, p. 138.

2. Under the Mughal Empire, virtually every political authority from raja down to village headman 'held' from some larger authority. What most held was a written, dated document, known as a *sanad* in Mughal-influenced areas, which stated the holder's name, rights and recompense, duties and length of tenure. Such a document was signed and sealed by the appropriate Mughal official. Stewart Gordon, 'Legitimacy and Loyalty in Some Successor States' in J. F. Richards (ed), *Kingship and Authority in South Asia* (New Delhi, 1998), p. 330.
3. Gordon: 'Legitimacy and Loyalty', p. 335.
4. Robbins Burling, *The Passage of Power: Studies in Political Successions* (New York, 1974), p. 58, quoted Gordon: 'Legitimacy and Loyalty', p. 334.
5. Fisher: *Indirect Rule,* p. 265.
6. Dalhousie's minute, 30 August 1848, PP 1849, Vol. XXXIX, p. 83.
7. See Bisheshwar Prasad, *Paramountcy under Dalhousie* (New Delhi, 1964).
8. Fisher: *Indirect Rule*, p. 258.
9. Fisher: *Indirect Rule*, p. 259.
10. Qanungo: 'Study of British Relations', p. 264.
11. Ibid.
12. Quoted Fisher: *Indirect Rule*, p. 260. The terms of the adoption *sanad* granted to the Gaekwar of Baroda can be found in Philips (ed): *Evolution of India and Pakistan,* p. 416.
13. Creagh-Coen: *Indian Political Service*, p. 68.
14. Salisbury to Lord Lytton, 21 September 1877, Lytton Collection E218, Vol. 4B. Under the viceroyalty of Sir John Lawrence the ruler of Gwalior had been allowed to adopt an heir, but later wished to annul the adoption on the grounds that the youth had plotted against his life. Permission for the annulment was used by the British on one hand to apply pressure for the retention of the British fort in Scindia's territory, and on the other to close the deal on a loan of three-quarters of a million rupees at 4 per cent from the ruler for the Agra to Gwalior railway. Northbrook to Duke of Argyll, 9 and 26 September 1872, Northbrook Collection C144, Vol. 9.
15. SoS to GoI, No. 24, 9 September 1875, PSCI, 1875–1911, Vol. 1.
16. Lee-Warner, Lee-Warner Collection F92, quoted Philips (ed): *Evolution of India and Pakistan,* pp. 421–2.
17. Ibid.
18. Following the defeat of the Muslim ruler of Mysore, Tipu Sultan, in 1799 the governor-general, Lord Wellesley, rejected the restoration of a relative of the ruler on the grounds of Muslim 'racial characteristics', family traditions of hostility to the British and Francophilia. Selected instead was a member of the ancient Wadiyar family of Hindu rulers of Mysore, whom the

Company had recently liberated from prison. Under his personal direction the state went into debt.

19. Ashton: *British Policy*, pp. 19–20.

20. Mysore Instrument of Transfer, Philips (ed), *Evolution of India and Pakistan*, pp. 418–21.

21. See Donald R. Gustafson, 'Mysore 1881–1902: The Making of a Model State', PhD Thesis, University of Wisconsin at Madison, 1968.

22. Note by W. Lee-Warner, 11 February 1885 to Sec. GoI, FD R/1/1/703.

23. Ibid.

24. H. M. Durand to Chief Sec. Govt. of Bombay, 19 June 1885, R/1/1/703.

25. The three principal factory locations of the East India Company developed to become the centres of military and political control in British India as the Company's influence grew during the eighteenth and nineteenth centuries. These centres became known as the presidencies of Madras, Bombay and Bengal since a president headed the council of each area.

26. Political memorandum to the Marquis of Hartington, SoS for India, from the Viceroy's Council, 28 September 1880, L/PS/7/388. Ironically, in the light of the Council's somewhat cavalier attitude towards the use of judicial procedure to settle disputed successions, the viceroy at the time was the Liberal, Lord Ripon.

27. Ibid. In her study of the South Indian district of Ramnad, Pamela Price makes it clear that the referral of disputed *zamindari* successions to British Indian law courts was far from satisfactory. In the absence of *durbar* assemblies for the negotiation of the parties concerned, the Anglo-Indian legal system quickly became important in providing officially recognised, formal arenas for representation, ranking and competition. The use of the colonial courts appealed to men and women of considerable wealth and local authority, due to traditions of 'looking to superior lords for confirmation of ruling status and access to domain privileges'. However, the winner of a suit was not selected because the imperial government wanted a weaker or stronger ruler on the throne, or because he represented a powerful faction which needed to be appeased. Winners of litigation were picked, against local practice, on the basis of 'criteria which served the wider needs of government from a British imperial vision: the need for a standardised law to ensure, theoretically, that justice would be given fairly to all on an equal basis'. Pamela Price, *Kingship and Political Practice in Colonial India* (Cambridge, 1996), pp. 40, 52.

28. Col. Sir Edward Bradford to Col. C. K. M. Walter, Res. Mewar, 5 May 1885, R 2/179/343.

29. Col. C. K. M. Walter, Res. Mewar, to Col. E. R. C. Bradford, AGG Rajputana, 26 December 1884, R/1/1/690.

30. Offg. Sec. GoI to AGG Rajputana, 27 January 1885, R/1/1/690.
31. Edward S. Haynes, 'Alwar: Bureaucracy versus Traditional Rulership' in Jeffrey (ed): *People, Princes*, p. 38.
32. Councils of regency reorganised administrative structures and judiciaries, state-managed forests and, most importantly, land-revenue settlements. According to Barbara Ramusack, 'These settlements measured land, defined who was responsible for land taxes, the major source of state income, and set rates. They were crucial in shaping economic and social hierarchies in the princely states where agriculture was even more dominant than in British India, as well as enhancing state revenues at the expense of both nobles and peasants'. Ramusack: *Indian Princes*, p. 108. See also Shakti Kak, 'The Agrarian System of the Princely State of Jammu and Kashmir: A Study of Colonial Settlement Policies, 1860–1905' in Waltraud Ernst and Biswamoy Pati (eds), *India's Princely States: People, Princes and Colonialism* (London, 2007), pp. 68–84.
33. Malhar Rao's deposition is discussed more fully in the chapter on administration.
34. Northbrook to Salisbury, 20 May 1875, Northbrook Collection C144, Vol. 12.
35. Memorandum by T. Madhava Rao, Minister Baroda, 13 May 1875, R/2/539/321.
36. GoI to SoS, No. 110, 31 August 1883, PSCI, 1875–1911, Box III.
37. Princely rulers were entitled to be saluted by the firing of an odd number of guns between 3 and 21, with a greater number indicating greater prestige. Both Baroda and Hyderabad were eligible for a 21-gun salute.
38. SoS to GoI, No. 21, 8 March 1877, PSCI, 1875–1911, Vol. 3.
39. Ibid. Minorities were not always seen as the most desirable route to increased British power in a state. When the nizam appeared to be dying in 1876 the viceroy, Lord Lytton, suggested that a puppet ruler in Hyderabad could solve British problems: 'might it not be good policy for the British Government to step in boldly and insist on deciding the succession itself, as the Paramount Power? Select not a minor, nor an octogenarian, but a man of sufficient mental and physical vigour to assert his independence'. Lytton to Salisbury, 3 September 1876, Lytton Collection E218, Vol. 18.
40. The state of Pudukkottai features fairly frequently in the book; however, it should be stressed that, although it has attracted two influential studies, by Nicholas Dirks and Joanne Punzo Waghorne, it was only 1,179 square miles in area and, but for a twist of fate, would have been a *zamindari*, not a princely state. It certainly lacked the population, territory and economic resources of major states such as Hyderabad, Mysore and Baroda.

41. SoS to GoI, No. 117, 22 November 1877, PSCI, 1875–1911, Vol. 3. The chapter on education makes it clear that in the case of the adopted grandson, Martanda Tondaiman, an English 'training' did not produce a model ruler.
42. SoS to GoI, No. 104, 25 September 1879, PSCI, 1875–1911, Vol. 5. Rajkumar College is discussed in detail in the chapter on education.
43. The size of the state of Idar was only 1,669 square miles, but it attracted much attention due to the colourful personality of its ruler, Pratap Singh.
44. Literally an offering of presents or coins. Under the British, a ceremonial payment made by an Indian ruler to the paramount power on a significant occasion such as an installation or marriage.
45. Political agent, Mahi Kantha to Sec. to Govt. Bombay, Political Dept., 24 February 1901, PSCI, 1875–1911, Box XXXV. See also R/2/157/178.
46. Charles Allen, *Lives of the Indian Princes* (London, 1984), p. 95.
47. H. S. Barnes, Sec. GoI, FD to J. L. Jenkins, Offg. Sec. Govt. Bombay, Political Dept., 18 July 1901, R/1/1/270. Pratap Singh abdicated nine years later to take over as regent of Jodhpur in order to support his nephew, the young maharaja, as discussed in the chapter on education. The personification of a Rajput warrior, at the age of 70 he accompanied his troops into the trenches of France and later into Palestine. Allen: *Lives of Indian Princes*, p. 94. Pratap Singh was described by the viceroy, Lord Hardinge, as 'The best pig-sticker in India ... of Spartan simplicity ... truly a white man among Indians'. Lord Hardinge, *My Indian Years, 1910–1916* (London, 1948), p. 48.
48. G. T. Mackenzie, Res. Travancore and Cochin, to Chief Sec. Govt. Madras, 18 December 1899, R/2/892/278.
49. Opinion by V. Bhashyam Iyengar, 12 February 1900, GoI FD to Res. Travancore and Cochin, 30 April 1900, R/2/892/279. As one of the royal adoptees, later the Senior Maharani of Travancore, revealed, 'The idea was that whoever between the two of us got the first child, he would be the next Maharaja'. Allen: *Lives of Indian Princes*, p. 14.
50. See Siobhan Lambert-Hurley, *Muslim Women, Reform and Princely Patronage: Nawab Sultan Jahan Begam of Bhopal* (London, 2007).
51. M. J. Meade, Pol. Agent, Bhopal, to R. J. Crosthwaite, AGG CI, 23 June 1893, R/1/1/158. See also R/1/1/1179. Other than in Bhopal, women were subject to rigid rules of succession. A woman could rule as a wife (or widow) or as a mother (and regent), but never as a daughter or sister of a former ruler. In practice this meant that a woman ruler had to operate in the milieu of her in-laws. Once she married into a royal house, she was cut off from her own kinsmen.

52. Nawab Sadik Mohammed Khan of Bhawalpur to L. W. Dane, Chief Sec. Govt. Punjab, 4 June 1897.
53. W. J. Cuningham, Sec. GoI, FD to Chief Sec. Govt. Punjab, 25 October 1897, R/1/1/199. See also R/1/1/207.
54. H. S. Barnes, Offg. Sec. GoI, FD, to Sec. Govt. Bombay, Political Dept., 13 May 1899, R/1/1/222.
55. A. Younghusband, Commissioner Sind, to Sir George Sydenham Clarke, Gov. Bombay, 6 March 1909, R/1/1/372. Shruti Kapila discusses the British treatment in the 1930s of the 'insanity' of a later Mir of Khairpur, Faiz Mohammed, in 'Masculinity and Madness: Princely Personhood and Colonial Sciences of the Mind in Western India, 1871–1940', *Past and Present*, 187 (May 2005), pp. 121–56.
56. Maharaja of Kashmir to Lord Minto, 4 July 1906, R/1/1/341.
57. Note by Sir Louis Dane, Sec. GoI, FD, 15 June 1906, R/2/1074/200.
58. Francis Younghusband, Res. Kashmir, to Sec. GoI, FD, 31 October 1906, R/1/1/341.
59. Dane to Younghusband, 15 June 1907, R/2/1074/200. The Maharaja of Kashmir may have been wise in opposing the succession of either Amar Singh or his son. Younghusband managed to prevent Hari Singh from being poisoned, but in the 1920s the gullible prince became the victim of a blackmail plot 'which contained all the ingredients of a good scandal'. Patrick French, *Younghusband: The Last Great Imperial Adventurer* (London, 1994), p. 270.

2. Education

1. Thomas R. Metcalf, *Ideologies of the Raj* (Cambridge, 1995), p. 29.
2. Thomas Babington Macaulay, *Minute on Indian Education*, 2 February 1835, in Harlow and Carter, *Imperialism and Orientalism* (Malden, MA, 1999), p. 61.
3. Gilmour: *Ruling Caste*, p. 60.
4. Bernard S. Cohn, 'Recruitment and Training of British Civil Servants in India 1600–1860' in Ralph Braibanti (ed), *Asian Bureaucratic Systems Emergent from the British Imperial Tradition* (Durham, NC, 1966), p. 136. The district officer John Beames recalled that his father had informed him of his nomination to Haileybury with regret, as he had anticipated a successful career at the Bar for his son. John Beames, *Memoirs of a Bengal Civilian* (London, 1961), p. 60.
5. Quoted Gilmour: *The Ruling Caste*, p. 44.
6. B. Spangenberg, *British Bureaucracy in India: Status, Policy and the ICS in the Late Nineteenth Century* (Columbia, 1976), p. 21.

7. After the Salisbury system was abolished in 1892 and the age limit raised to 23, Jowett had his way. In the last years of his life, over half the ICS recruits were Oxford graduates and another quarter had been at Cambridge. Gilmour: *Ruling Caste*, p. 63.

8. Lepel Griffin, 'The Indian Civil Service Examinations', *Fortnightly Review* 17 (1875), p. 523, quoted Gilmour: *Ruling Caste*, p. 63. According to the *Dictionary of National Biography*, Sir Lepel was 'a dandyish, Byronic fig- ure, articulate, argumentative, and witty', a man of 'languid foppishness and irreverent tongue' as well as possessing an 'overt disdain for modesty'. C. W. Walton, 'Sir Henry Lepel Griffin' in Sir Sidney Lee (ed), *Dictionary of National Biography: Second Supplement* (New York, 1912).

9. Martin Moir, *A General Guide to the India Office Records* (London, 1988), p. 38.

10. Letter from Col. G. Malleson to Lord Mayo, 29 August 1869, enclosed Mayo to Argyll, 9 September 1869, Argyll Collection B380, Vol. II.

11. Mayo to Argyll, 25 January 1871, Argyll Collection B380, IOR Neg. 4236.

12. SoS to GoI, No. 133, 3 October 1873, PCI, 1792–1874, Vol. 16.

13. SoS to GoI, No. 104, 22 May 1871, PCI, 1792–1874, Vol. 14.

14. W. S. Seton-Karr, Sec. GoI, to L. B. Bowring, Commissioner Mysore, 12 December 1868, R/2/44/408.

15. Col. G. Malleson to Sec. GoI, FD, 1 January 1875.

16. Salisbury to Northbrook, 17 June 1875, R/2/44/403.

17. Retrospective Note on the Education of the Maharaja of Mysore, 8 September 1892, R/1/1/164. A similar school modelled on English lines was opened in 1875 for the young Gaekwar of Baroda and the sons of *sirdars* of the state. Baroda's minister, T. Madhava Rao, was convinced of the virtues of such an education, believing that 'England repudiates ignorance as a basis of strength or stability ... and bids Princes and people alike to be enlight- ened and happy'. Thomas Henry Thornton, *General Sir Richard Meade and the Feudatory States of Central and Southern India* (London, 1898), p. 240. He was the first Indian to be appointed Acting Principal of the Madras High School, a fellow of Madras University and diwan regent of Baroda during the gaekwar's minority from 1875 to 1881. Vikram Menon, 'Popular Princes: Kingship and Social Change in Travancore and Cochin 1870–1930', PhD Thesis, University of Oxford, 1998, p. 263.

18. Seton-Karr to Bowring, 12 December 1868, R/2/44/408.

19. Diwans T. Madhava Rao and A. Sashiah Sastri were both educated at Kumbakonam.

20. A. Vadivelu, *Some Mysore Worthies* (Madras, 1900), p. 15. This scheme never came to fruition. As will be seen in the chapter on marriage, the maharaja

eventually agreed to a marriage with the elder daughter of the Rana of Vana, a Rajput 'connected with other ruling Chiefs' in Kathiawar.

21. Quoted Vadivelu: *Mysore Worthies*, p. 17.

22. Vadivelu: *Mysore Worthies*, p. 63.

23. Report on Education of Wadiyar Bahadur for January 1896 by J. J. Whiteley, R/2/33/314. See also R/2/32/300.

24. S. M. Fraser was appointed in 1896 at a salary of Rs. 1,600 rising to Rs. 2,500 a month, plus travelling expenses and a free house, under the strict conditions that he would stay until the maharaja came of age, not apply-ing for long leave unless sick during that period. W. Mackworth Young, Res. Mysore, to K. Seshadri Iyer, Diwan, 9 April 1896, R/2/29/267. Later Sir Stuart Fraser, KCSI, CIE, he became an officer of great distinction who died a few weeks short of 100 years old after serving as resident in Kashmir, Mysore and Hyderabad.

25. Quoted Vadivelu: *Mysore Worthies*, p. 63.

26. As his military leader, Haider Ali had usurped the power of the Wadiyar ruler of Mysore. Haider Ali's son, Tipu Sultan, consolidated his power over the state and was defeated by the British in 1799.

27. Fraser to J. A. Crawford, Res. Mysore, 16 November 1901, R/2/8/64.

28. J. J. Whiteley to W. Lee-Warner, 26 May 1895, R/2/33/314. The maha-rani, Vanivilas Sannidhana, features strongly in the chapter on marriage and royal women.

29. Whiteley, Reports on Education of Maharaja of Mysore, August 1895 and January 1896, R/2/32/300.

30. Sir Richard Meade was a highly distinguished member of the Political Service, working in Gwalior, Indore, Mysore, Baroda and Hyderabad.

31. Thornton: *General Sir Richard Meade*, p. 286. See also V. K. Bawa, *Hyderabad under Salar Jang I* (New Delhi, 1996), pp. 108–9.

32. Memorandum by Sir Richard Meade, Res. Hyderabad, 24 March 1881, attached to No. 461, GoI to Res., 25 May 1881, PSCI, 1875–1911, Box I.

33. Lytton to Salisbury, 24 September 1877, Lytton Collection E218, Vol. 19. Salar Jung's somewhat autocratic stance appears with regularity throughout this book. However British efforts were not entirely in vain; the Reverend H. Fitzpatrick wrote in 1881 to Major F. A. Wilson, superintendent of the nizam's education, that he was 'particularly struck with the clear way in which the first Parliament assembled in the reign of Edward I was described by the young ruler, with "ingeniously phonetic" spelling'. Letter dated 4 November 1881, attached to No. 16, 6 February 1882, GoI to SoS, PSCI, 1875–1911, Box II.

34. Trevor Chichele Plowden, Res. Hyderabad, to nizam, 6 September 1894, R/1/1/164.

35. Chichele Plowden to W. J. Cuningham, Sec. GoI, FD, 5 May 1894, R/2/67/19.

36. Chichele Plowden to nizam, 6 September 1894, R/1/1/164. As Foreign Secretary Sir Henry Durand recognised the problems inherent in attempting to control the education of the son of such a prominent ruler, suggesting 'I would interfere as little as possible. Better a spoilt and uneducated heir-apparent than a discontented Nizam'. Extract from memorandum by Sir H. M. Durand, 20 April 1894, R/1/1/164.

37. Chichele Plowden to Cuningham, 19 March 1895, R/1/1/164. See also R/2/67/21.

38. Extract from private letter from Lord Elgin, 3 February 1898, attached to No. 275, PSCI, 1875–1911, Box XXV.

39. Nizam to Res. Hyderabad, 15 January 1898, R/1/1/201. Other candidates for the job of tutor to the sahibzada were Capt. J. R. C. Colvin of the political dept., tutor to the Nawab of Rampur; J. W. D. Johnstone of the education dept., tutor to Scindia, Maharaja of Gwalior; and Theodore Morison of Aligarh College. R/2/67/27. It is perhaps surprising that the nizam failed to choose a man with Muslim connections over and above Egerton, who had served exclusively in Rajputana.

40. Cuningham to Chichele Plowden, 10 August 1897, and viceroy to SoS, 16 February 1897, R/1/1/201.

41. Sir David Barr, Res. Hyderabad, to Walter Lawrence, 8 July 1900, R/2/68/38.

42. Nizam to Barr, 6 November 1903, R/1/1/299.

43. Res. Western Rajputana to 1st Asst. to AGG Rajputana, 14 December 1895, R/2/182/360. Pratap Singh's association with undesirable companions places him in a rather less rosy light than that suggested in the chapter on succession.

44. Ibid.

45. A. Martindale, Res. Western States Rajputana, to 1st Asst. to AGG Rajputana, 24 December 1897, attached to No. 77, PSCI, 1875–1911, Box XXVI.

46. GoI to SoS, No. 165, 16 December 1897, PSCI, 1875–1911, Box XXIV.

47. Sir Louis Dane to Foreign Secretary GoI, attached to No. 165, 16 December 1897, PSCI, 1875–1911, Box XXIV.

48. The Phulkian *sirdars* were rajas and aristocrats of the Punjab, tracing their ancestry to the twelfth-century Raja of Jaisalmer, Rewal Jaisal. The founder of this Sikh dynasty was Chaudary Phul, governor of an area south east of Delhi, whose descendants established the four states of Patiala, Nabha, Jind and Faridkot. In 1809 the Phulkian states sought protection from the British against the rising power of Ranjit Singh, first Maharaja of the Sikh Empire.

49. Dane to Maharaja of Patiala and Raja of Nabha, and President of Jind Council, No. 870, 23 September 1897, PSCI, 1875–1911, Box XXIV.
50. Raja of Nabha to Lt. Gov. of Punjab, 13 August 1897, attached to No. 165, PSCI, 1875–1911, Box XXIV.
51. Dane to Capt. F. E. Bradshaw, 23 September 1897, attached to No. 165, PSCI, 1875–1911, Box XXIV.
52. For differing views on Sayaji Rao's anti-British stance see Ian Copland, 'The Dilemmas of a Ruling Prince: Maharaja Sayaji Rao Gaekwar and "Sedition"' in P. Robb and D. Taylor (eds), *Rule, Protest, Identity: Aspects of Modern South Asia* (London, 1978), pp. 24–8; Charles W. Nuckolls, 'The Durbar Incident', *Modern Asian Studies*, 24, 3 (1990), pp. 529–59; and Manu Bhagavan, *Sovereign Spheres: Princes, Education and Empire in Colonial India* (New Delhi, 2003), pp. 47–69.
53. Sayaji Rao Rao to Lord Reay, 20 January 1897, quoted J. P. Sergeant, *The Ruler of Baroda* (London, 1928), pp. 280–1.
54. In the gaekwar's reply to the Governor of Bombay's address at the ruler's investiture, he declared that Elliott's contribution to his education had produced 'an indelible impression'. Enclosure No. 21, P. S. Melvill, AGG Baroda, 'Investiture of Gaekwar', 2 January 1882, attached to GoI to SoS, No. 10, PSCI, 1875–1911 Box II. Elliott was given a wide brief in his subsequent duties in Baroda, and in 1885 was despatched to England for three months to arrange for the care and education of young men whom the gaekwar wished to be trained as 'Engineers, Surveyors, Artists and Doctors'. GoI to SoS, No. 108, 11 July 1885, PSCI, 1875–1911, Box V.
55. Lawrence James, *Raj: The Making and Unmaking of British India* (London, 1997), p. 337. Sayaji Rao was also a great believer in the education of women. At the time of their arranged marriage, his wife, Chimnabai, had been 14 and illiterate. Her husband immediately arranged for her to receive tuition and many years later wrote, 'An educated lady in the house is more able to shed the light of happiness than one who is ignorant'. Sayaji Rao 'My Ways and Days', *Nineteenth Century and After*, XLIX, p. 223, quoted James: *Raj*, p. 337. Her education bore fruit in a book launched in 1911 entitled *The Position of Women in Indian Life*, giving an international view of the 'women's movement' and containing a number of 'radical ideas and assertions'. It examined the successes and failures of women in Europe, America and Japan, and contrasted the status of women elsewhere with that of women in India. Bhagavan: *Sovereign Spheres*, p. 58. However Sayaji Rao was to display a less-enlightened attitude to female independence when his daughter, Indira, having severed her betrothal to Madho Rao Scindia of Gwalior, married the future Maharaja of Cooch Behar in a registry office in London. Her parents did not attend the wedding.

56. Report of interview between the Baroda Res., Col. M. J. Meade, and gaekwar, 14 February 1908, R/1/1/288.

57. Ibid. File R/1/1/293 sets out the bitter objections of the gaekwar to Curzon's circular on foreign travel.

58. Extract from memorandum by Sir H. M. Durand, 20 April 1894, R/1/1/164.

59. Nicholas B. Dirks, *The Hollow Crown: Ethnohistory of an Indian Kingdom* (Cambridge, 1987), p. 392.

60. Sashiah Sastri was born into a poor family, educated at Scottish mission schools in Madras and received the 1st Prize of the Madras Council of Education. He was later Head *Sheristidar*, or Secretary, of the Madras Revenue Board, the highest position to which an Indian could rise, and a fellow of Madras University. Menon: 'Popular Princes', p. 263.

61. Joanne Punzo Waghorne, *The Raja's Magic Clothes* (Pennsylvania State University, 1994), p. 74.

62. Quoted Punzo Waghorne: *Raja's Magic Clothes*, p. 77.

63. Pudukkottai *Durbar* Files, Administration Report for 1888–9, quoted Punzo Waghorne: *Raja's Magic Clothes*, p. 75.

64. Dirks: *Hollow Crown*, pp. 390–1.

65. Ibid.

66. Note by 'JFP', 11 February 1897, R/2/892/268.

67. Chief Sec. Govt. Madras to Sec. GoI, FD, 6 August 1897, R/2/892/271.

68. Dirks: *Hollow Crown*, p. 391. See R/2/892/268 for government criticism of Crossley.

69. Paolo Durisotto, 'Traditional Rule and Modern Conventions: The Maharajas of Bikaner and Their Relationship with the Raj, 1887–1947', PhD Thesis, Royal Holloway College, University of London, 2001, p. 45.

70. During the hot season Ganga Singh had previously spent holidays in Mount Abu in the companionship of Maharaj Kunwar, the heir to the Jodhpur *gadi*, in order that friendly relations would be established between the two Rathor families. Col. C. K. M. Walter to Sec. GoI, FD 16 January 1888, R/2/182/356. Mount Abu was, and remains, a popular Rajput pilgrimage destination, due to its significant number of Jain and Hindu religious sites.

71. Durisotto: 'Traditional Rule', p. 52.

72. K. M. Panikkar, *His Highness the Maharaja of Bikaner: A Biography* (London, 1937), p. 42.

73. Durisotto: 'Traditional Rule', p. 53.

74. Pannikar: *Maharaja of Bikaner*, p. 42. Ffrench-Mullen was a member of the Indian Medical Service posted in Rajputana, so it is possible that his opinion was a medical one.

75. Pannikar: *Maharaja of Bikaner*, p. 47.
76. Durisotto: 'Traditional Rule', p. 56.
77. Bayly: *Indian Society*, p. 111.
78. Durisotto: 'Traditional Rule', p. 56. The Maharaja of Bikaner, no doubt partly due to the influence of an English tutor, also turned out to be inordinately fond of foreign travel. In 1902 Curzon feared that, although 'very opinionated, and decidedly vain', he was 'much the most attractive in manner and style' of the Indian rulers and would be made 'the darling of London Society'. Curzon to Lord Hamilton, 21 May 1902, Curzon Collection F111, Vol. 161. As shown in the chapter on royal marriage, western ideas also had a dramatic effect on the maharaja's choice of bride.
79. Sultan Jahan Begam, *An Account of My Life* (London, 1912), Vol. I, pp. 17–18.
80. Sultan Jahan: *Account*, Vol. I, pp. 23–9.
81. Sultan Jahan: *Account*, Vol. I, p. 217.
82. Sultan Jahan: *Account*, Vol. I, pp. 330–2. Sir Swinton Jacob was the 'high priest' of Indo-Saracenic architecture, discussed later in the chapter.
83. SoS to GoI, No. 59, 15 June 18/6, PSCI, 1875–1911, Vol. 2.
84. SoS to GoI, No. 13, 1872, PCI, 1792–1874, Vol. 15.
85. The Nawabs of Palanpur, Tonk and Rampur, as well as one or two lesser Muslim rulers, shared a common ancestry as descendants of Pathan tribesmen from Afghanistan who entered India in search of the traditional 'Zan, Zar, Zamin' – women, gold and land. Allen: *Lives of Indian Princes*, p. 44.
86. Chief Sec. Govt. Punjab to Sec. GoI, FD, 22 April 1899, PSCI, 1875–1911, Box XXIX.
87. Chief Sec. Govt., NWP and Oudh, to Lt. Gov.'s Agent in Rampur, 15 September 1899, R/2/801/6. Another, more famous Indian studying at Cambridge in the 1890s was Ranjitsinhji of Nawanagar, who would eventually use his contacts in England (and his fame as a cricketer) to put pressure on the Government of India to reverse its position on whether he should succeed to the *gadi* of Nawanagar.
88. The education of royal offspring in Britain provided an excellent opportunity for lavish travel. Curzon was particularly anxious to make his princely charges accountable when major expenditure occurred which might affect states' subjects. Referring to a request from the Maharaja of Cooch Behar for £40,000 to cover a foreign trip, the viceroy aired his suspicion that the money for 'this unnecessary and ill-advised visit to London' had either been 'taken from the pockets of the peasants in Kuch Behar or filched from the allowance which the Maharaja undertook to set apart for the future maintenance of his children'. The Government of India should stop rulers

'gallivanting' over Europe with the disastrous financial consequences that 'commonly ensue'. With a son at Eton the ruler in question had a 'plausible excuse' for travel, however such 'intermingling ... was not dissociated from financial transactions'. Curzon to Hamilton, 28 May 1903, Curzon Collection F111, Vol. 162.

89. Fowler to Elgin, 15 June 1894, Elgin Collection F83, Vol. 1.

90. Curzon to St. John Brodrick, 2 February 1905, Curzon Collection F111, Vol. 164.

91. See Lucy Moore, *Maharanis* (London, 2004), p. 113. The marriage of Suniti Devi to the Maharaja of Cooch Behar in 1878 caused a split in the Brahmo Samaj. She wrote and published the first autobiography by a maharani.

92. Strictly speaking, the term 'public schools' only applied initially to the English schools covered by the Public Schools Act of 1868, and not to independent schools elsewhere in Britain.

93. J. A. Mangan, *The Games Ethic and Imperialism* (London, 1986), p. 125.

94. Quoted H. Sherring, *The Mayo College 1875–1895* (Calcutta, 1897), Vol. I, p. 2.

95. Ibid.

96. Article from *The Pioneer* of 17 October 1870, attached to letter from Mayo to Argyll, 2 November 1870, Argyll Collection B380, Vol. II.

97. *Progress of Education in India*, Fourth Quinquennial Review, 1897–8 to 1901–2, p. 182.

98. J. Chailly, *Administrative Problems of British India* (London, 1910), p. 222.

99. Report on Mayo College at Ajmer, attached SoS to GoI, No. 109, 28 September 1876, PSCI, 1875–1911, Vol. 2.

100. Mangan: *Games Ethic*, p. 128.

101. Thomas R. Metcalf, *An Imperial Vision: Indian Architecture and Britain's Raj* (London, 1989), p. 69.

102. Metcalf: *Imperial Vision,* p. 76.

103. G. H. R. Tillotson, *The Tradition of Indian Architecture: Continuity, Controversy and Change since 1850* (New Haven and London, 1989), p. 46. See also Tillotson, 'Orientalizing the Raj: Indo-Saracenic Fantasies' in Christopher W. London (ed), *Architecture in Victorian and Edwardian India* (Bombay, 1994), pp. 15–34. Tillotson considers that the term Indo-Saracenic was poorly chosen, as the Islamic element in Indian buildings was not strictly Saracenic. India's Muslim conquerors were not Arabs, but Afghans and Central Asians who drew many of their cultural ideas from Persia. However, given the nineteenth-century association of Islamic with Saracenic, the term was clear, if inexact, in its application to the architecture of the Mughals and their predecessors.

104. Quoted Metcalf: *Imperial Vision*, p. 77.

105. Note by Hardinge, 13 January 1913, quoted Metcalf: *Imperial Vision*, p. 81.

106. Speeches by Lord Curzon, Curzon Collection F111, Vol. 559, pp. 60–7.

107. 'Report on Mayo College at Ajmer', attached to SoS to GoI, No. 109, 28 September 1876, PSCI, 1875–1911, Vol. 2. Sidney and Beatrice Webb were informed that parental pressure was still lacking when they visited Mayo College in March 1912. Sidney and Beatrice Webb, *Indian Diary* (Oxford, 1987), p. 160.

108. SoS to GoI, No. 5, 17 January 1878, PSCI, 1875–1911, Vol. 4.

109. Article, *The Pioneer*, 24 December 1870, quoted Copland: *British Raj*, p. 134.

110. Chester Macnaghten, *Common Thoughts on Serious Subjects: Addresses Delivered between the Years 1887–9 to the Elder Boys of Rajkumar College in Kathiawar* (London, 1912), pp. 20–1. Macnaghten eventually broke down under the relentless strain of being the only European in the school.

111. Copland: *British Raj*, p. 135.

112. Mangan: *Games Ethic*, p. 131.

113. V. A. Stow, *A Short History of the Mayo College 1869–1942* (Ajmer, 1942), p. 3.

114. Mangan: *Games Ethic*, p. 131.

115. Extract from 'Annual Report on Mayo College 1875–76', quoted Stow: *Short History*, p. 5.

116. Stow: *Short History*, p. 18.

117. Sherring: *Mayo College*, Vol. I, p. 201.

118. Mangan: *Games Ethic*, p. 132.

119. Sherring: *Mayo College*, Vol. I, p. 77.

120. Sherring: *Mayo College*, Vol. I, p. 86. Emulating no doubt those English public-school products who were 'worthy rulers' of the empire. As the secretary of state, Lord Hamilton, wrote to Curzon, 'I often ponder over the secret of young Englishmen being so extraordinarily successful as administrators and governors of races and countries other than their own; and I believe their success is more the result of the sense and spirit of fair play which the average Englishman possesses, but which is so much fostered early in life by public school training'. Hamilton to Curzon, 28 April 1899, Curzon Collection F111, Vol. 158.

121. *The Times*, 11 May 1895, p. 5, quoted Mangan: *Games Ethic*, p. 133. Macnaghten taught cricket to the famous Indian batsman Ranjitsinhji, Jam Sahib of Bhavnagar.

122. Sir Bhavasinhji Takhtsinhji, Maharaja of Bhavnagar, *Forty Years of the Rajkumar College 1870–1910* (London, 1911), Vol. II, p. 3.

123. Address by Chester Macnaghten, 'Prize Giving at Rajkumar College by the Duke of Connaught', *The Indian Magazine 1889*.

124. 'Local Education Report for Delhi College, 1845' in *General Report on Public Instruction in the N. W. Provinces of the Bengal Presidency for 1853–4*, V/24/905, p. 75.

125. Avril A. Powell, *Muslims and Missionaries* (Richmond, Surrey, 1993), pp. 200–1.

126. *General Review of Benares College 1844–5*, V/24/905, p. 75.

127. 'Local Education Report', V/24/905. p. 3.

128. Sherring: *Mayo College*, Vol. I, p. 171.

129. Narullah Khan, *The Ruling Chiefs of Western India and the Rajkumar College* (Bombay, 1898), pp. 8–9.

130. Article contributed to the *Calcutta Review*, 1879, Vol. XLVIII, quoted Bhavasinhji: *Forty Years*, Vol. VI, p. 11.

131. Letter from Holkar to W. J. Cuningham, 25 January 1895, R/1/1/154. See also R/1/1/129. Holkar later revealed surprisingly firm views on the education he wished for his own son: 'a Prince should learn to read and write, to understand accounts and to go deep in the administration instead of becoming proficient in playing polo, football etc. In saying so it is not meant that I do not approve of these manly sports, but that they should have a secondary consideration'. Holkar to viceroy, 30 July 1900, R/1/1/253.

132. *Kharitas* from viceroy to Holkar, 28 March 1894 and 19 March 1895, R/1/1/154. The Indore ranis were not to be trifled with, as the chapter on royal women makes clear.

133. Quoted Sherring: *Mayo College*, Vol. I, p. 80.

134. Quoted Durisotto: 'Traditional Rule', pp. 49–50.

135. Satadru Sen, *Colonial Childhoods: The Juvenile Periphery of India, 1858–1945* (London, 2005), p. 184.

136. Khan: *Ruling Chiefs*, p. 3.

137. Mangan: *Games Ethic*, p. 137.

138. Sherring: *Mayo College*, Vol. I, p. 161.

139. Sir Walter Lawrence, 'Confidential Report on Chiefs' Colleges', 31 August 1901, Curzon Collection F111/257, p. 100. For some Rajput princes, colleges such as Mayo had a political use. As Edward Haynes points out in his study of Alwar, the power of Maharaja Mangal Singh was more secure than that of any of his predecessors on the Alwar *gadi*. Following a period of rebellion of Alwar *thakurs* against their prince, the recalcitrant *thakurs* were forced out of the state, and their *jagirs* were resumed and regranted to younger and, in the eyes of the British, 'presumably more pliant'

heirs. These young *jagirdars* were then sent to the newly established Mayo College to join Mangal Singh, who had entered the school in 1875 as the first student. With the careful isolation of possibly dissenting Rajput lineages the Alwar ruler achieved a position that a British officer described as 'something more than *primus inter pares*, as there are no very great nobles whose power might, if combined, overshadow the throne, as is so often the case in the Rajput States'. Thomas Holbein Hendley, *Ulwar and Its Art Treasures* (London, 1888), p. 5, quoted Haynes, 'Alwar: Bureaucracy versus Traditional Rulership' in Jeffrey (ed): *People, Princes*, pp. 37–8.
140. Robert W. Stern, *The Cat and the Lion* (New York, 1988), p. 159.
141. Stern: *Cat and Lion*, p. 124.
142. Barbara N. Ramusack, 'Punjab States, Maharajas and Gurdwaras: Patiala and the Sikh Community' in Jeffrey (ed): *Princes, People*, pp. 177, 179.
143. *Chiefs and Leading Families in Rajputana* (Calcutta: Office of Superintendent of Government Printing, 1894), Introduction.
144. *Chiefs and Leading Families*, p. 9.
145. *Chiefs and Leading Families*, p. 87.
146. Haynes, 'Alwar: Bureaucracy versus Traditional Rulership' in Jeffrey (ed): *People, Princes*, pp. 52–3.
147. *Chiefs and Leading Families*, p. 86.
148. Sir Thomas Raleigh, *Lord Curzon in India: Being a Selection from His Speeches As Viceroy and Governor General 1898–1905* (London, 1906), p. 244.
149. Persuading the Punjab Government to ensure that the Raja of Jind (an orphan of 11) was sent to Aitchison, the *Civil and Military Gazette* warned in 1890 that 'If he is not sent here, the conclusion will inevitably be drawn that the College is not fulfilling its function … "If", another Raja may be excused for thinking "the Aitchison College is not good enough for Jind, it is not good enough for my son and heir". And once distinctions of this kind begin to be drawn, they show a marvellous aptitude for sliding downwards'. *Civil and Military Gazette*, Punjab, 1890, Curzon Collection, quoted Sen: *Colonial Childhoods*, p. 199.
150. Stow: *Short History*, p. 20.
151. Durisotto: 'Traditional Rule', p. 50.
152. 'Report of the Proceedings of the Conference at Ajmer in connection with Chiefs' Colleges, 10–16 March 1904', enclosed A. H. T. Martindale to Sec. GoI, 5 April 1904, Curzon Collection F112/442.
153. Mangan: *Games Ethic*, p. 140. Curzon considered that *thakurs* and *jagirdars* should be trained in agricultural science, civil engineering, land records and knowledge of stock and plants, while for young princes emphasis should be placed on history, geography, mathematics, political economy

and science. Speech by the viceroy opening Conference on the Chiefs' Colleges, Calcutta, 27 January 1902, F111/257.

154. L/PS/10/5 is a huge file, devoted entirely to the future policy for the chiefs' colleges following the impetus of the conference.

155. Quoted Bhavasinhji: *Forty Years*, Vol. II, p. 75. In 1889 when there was a vacancy for the Principal of Rajkumar College the viceroy, Lord Lansdowne, wrote that it was of the 'utmost importance that we should get a first-rate man to take charge' and wondered if there was a 'really strong candidate in England'. Unfortunately the salary was hardly compelling at a mere Rs. 750 per month. Lansdowne to Lord Cross, August 1889, Lansdowne Collection D558, Vol. 2.

156. Conference on the Chiefs' Colleges, Calcutta, 27 January 1902, Part II, Curzon Collection F112/442.

157. Portman excelled at running, tennis, cricket and racquets. Sadly his enthusiasm reached such heights that he literally ran himself to death, racing with his pupils before breakfast during their training for the school sports day. *The Radleian*, 3 March 1906, p. 314, quoted Mangan: *Games Ethic*, p. 136.

158. Stow: *Short History*, pp. 9, 11. At the beginning of the twentieth century there was undoubtedly an increase in masters who had been educated at public schools. J. C. Mayne, educated at Tonbridge and Oxford, taught at Brighton College and several Indian schools before becoming Principal of Rajkumar College in 1903. C. W. Waddington, educated at Charterhouse and Oxford, was appointed Principal of Mayo College in 1903 and held the post until 1917. Three of the Indian public-school headmasters were assistant masters at Marlborough at one time or another: F. A. Leslie Jones and V. A. S. Stow at Mayo, and E. C. Marchant at Daly College. Mangan: *Games Ethic*, p. 217. The annual report for Rajkumar College for 1904–5 emphasised that the staff had been considerably strengthened during the year: there was a new vice principal, P. Hide, with a degree from Oxford, working in conjunction with two assistant masters, both with degrees from Bombay University. Bhavasinhji: *Forty Years*, Vol. IV, p. 165.

159. *Progress of Education in India*, Sixth Quinquennial Review, 1907–12, p. 227.

160. Haynes, 'Alwar: Bureaucracy versus Traditional Rulership', in Jeffrey (ed): *People, Princes*, pp. 59–60.

161. Quoted Stern: *Cat and Lion*, p. 159.

162. The universities belonged to the middle class, the *babus*, about whose loyalties the British had increasing doubts. The princely colleges were meant to belong to those whose loyalties the British were courting.

163. Stern: *Cat and Lion*, p. 159.

164. Stern: *Cat and Lion*, pp. 159–60.

165. The secretary of state, Lord Hamilton, sympathised with the Rajput families, writing to the viceroy, Lord Elgin, in 1897, 'All the military authorities
seem to agree that in India at any rate coloured officers commanding white
men would do much to destroy the present prestige of the governing race.
Can we, however, maintain for ever this insuperable barrier against natives
rising to any position of responsibility in our Army? We allow them to rise
up to posts of great authority in civil work, yet to gentlemen of good family and belonging to fighting races, we deny the possibility of a satisfactory
military career. The test of examination is the ordeal for both services, we
admit equal competition in one case and deny it in the other'. Hamilton to
Elgin, 19 March 1897, Elgin Collection F84/15.

166. Hamilton to Curzon, 14 June 1901, R/2/30/288. See also Stern: *Cat and
Lion*, pp. 223–4.

167. Khan: *Ruling Chiefs*, p. v.

168. Khan: *Ruling Chiefs*, p. 1.

3. Marriage and Royal Women

1. 'Purdah' is a Persian word which literally means a 'curtain' or 'screen'. In
popular use it applies to the use of the veil among Muslim women as well
as seclusion within the household.

2. Metcalf: *Ideologies*, p. 94.

3. Lewis D. Wurgaft, *The Imperial Imagination: Magic and Myth in Kipling's
India* (Middletown, CT, 1983), pp. 51–3.

4. Rudyard Kipling, 'From Sea to Sea', *Rudyard Kipling's Verse: Definitive
Edition* (New York, 1940), Vol. I, p. 24.

5. Lepel Griffin, letter of 29 January 1887 in *The Pioneer,* Allahabad, 5
February 1887, pp. 4–5.

6. Varsha Joshi, *Polygamy and Purdah: Women and Society among Rajputs* (Jaipur,
1995), p. 56.

7. Ibid, p. 55.

8. The self-immolation of a Hindu widow on her husband's funeral pyre.

9. See Andrea Major, *Sati: A Historical Anthology* (Oxford, 2007).

10. Joshi: *Polygamy and Purdah*, pp. 141–2.

11. Offg. Pol. Agent Marwar and Jaisalmer to Offg. AGG Rajputana, 3
February 1873, R/2/182/359.

12. W. J. Cuningham, Sec. GoI, FD to T. Stoker, Chief Sec. to Govt. of NWP
and Oudh, 9 February 1898, R/2/783/18.

13. See R/2/801/3. Referring to a *muta* or temporary marriage permitted by the law of the Ithna Asharis, making up the majority branch of Shiites, but not sanctioned elsewhere in Islam. The temporary marriage is contracted for a fee received by the woman, rather than a dowry. In the 1977 Satyajit Ray film *The Chess Players* a British officer suggests that the real meaning of the word *muta* is 'enjoyment'.

14. A. Martindale, 1st Asst. AGG CI, to Res. Gwalior, 26 December 1888, R/2/750/14.

15. Major David Barr, Res. Gwalior, to F. Henvey, AGG CI, 17 January 1889, R/2/750/14.

16. Barr was 'a very large and somewhat sedentary man' who was sometimes described as the best political officer of his generation. He was resident in Gwalior, Kashmir and Hyderabad, as well as AGG in Central India. However his methods were somewhat unconventional: 'A criminal he was once pursuing took refuge in the fortified palace of a rani, a member of the Udaipur royal family, who refused to surrender him. Barr therefore exploited a Brahmin priest from the same family who went on hunger strike outside her door until she decided that causing the death of a Brahmin would be a worse sin than handing over a criminal'. Quoted Gilmour: *Ruling Caste*, p. 192.

17. Barr to Henvey, 12 January 1889, R/2/750/14.

18. Barr to Henvey, 17 January 1889, R/2/750/14.

19. Barr to Henvey, 27 January 1889 R/2/750/14.

20. Henvey to Barr, 24 October 1890, R/2/750/14. Obviously the royal families of Satara and Nagpur were still relatively socially acceptable despite the fact that the states were annexed by the British in the 1850s.

21. Aya Ikegame, 'Space of Kingship, Space of Empire: Marriage Strategies amongst the Mysore Royal Caste in the Nineteenth and Twentieth Centuries', *Indian Economic and Social History Review*, 46, 3 (July–September 2009), p. 358.

22. Col. Loch to W. Mackworth Young, Res. Mysore, 24 December 1896, R/2/29/273.

23. H. S. Barnes, GoI, to W. Mackworth Young, 30 April 1896, R/2/30/274.

24. Sir Donald Robertson, Res. Mysore, 'Secret Notes on Mysore', 25 September 1903, R/1/1/1064. The Ursu caste group, to which the Wadiyar family belonged, was very small.

25. Although the Government of India's Age of Consent Act of 1891 is not mentioned in Crown Representative Records, at the end of the nineteenth century it appears to have been rigidly adhered to by British officials in Indian *durbars*. Political officers insisted upon the prohibition of consummation of marriage for girls below the age of 12 when making post-nuptial

arrangements in royal households. The gaekwar initiated the Infant Marriage Prevention Act in Baroda in 1904. Even more impressive was the regulation pushed through the new Mysore Assembly in 1894 by Diwan Seshadri Iyer, which prohibited marriage for all Hindu girls below 8 and for girls below 16 to men over 50. See Barbara Ramusack, 'Women's Hospitals and Midwives in Mysore, 1870–1920: Princely or Colonial Medicine' in Ernst and Pati (eds): *India's Princely States*, p. 175.

26. Robertson to Elgin, 22 October 1897, R/1/1/195.

27. Confidential memorandum of Diwan of Mysore, 26 July 1898, R/2/30/278.

28. K. Seshadri Iyer, Diwan Mysore, to W. Lee Warner, 11 September 1895, R/2/29/272.

29. Robertson to the Hon. S. W. Edgerley, Sec. Govt. Bombay, 16 March 1898.

30. Aya Ikegame's claim that the enthusiasm of British residents and political agents for matrimonial alliances beyond traditional boundaries 'ultimately led them nowhere' underestimates British influence. Despite the fact that marriages between social and ethnic groups in the north and south were unusual, the British undoubtedly had success in helping to break new ground in the case of the Maharaja of Mysore. Ikegame: 'Space of Kingship, Space of Empire', p. 358.

31. Robertson to Sec. GoI, FD, 26 June 1899, R/2/44/413. See also R/1/1/1062. A match with a more 'obscure' wife could have its advantages. In 1878 a letter from the Political Agent in Kolhapur, Colonel F. Schneider, revealed that the Kolhapur *durbar* was deliberately looking for a bride 'of reduced circumstances' for the maharaja. Whereas brides from 'more exalted' backgrounds tended to 'become dissatisfied' and their dependents often gave much trouble to the *durbar*s concerned, those chosen from a humble source were 'proud of their elevation and more easily guided'. Col. F. Schneider, Pol. Agent Kolhapur, to C. Gonne, Sec. Govt. Bombay, 2 February 1878, R/2/1018/1006.

32. Editor, *Evening Mail* to viceroy, 14 October 1899, R/2/44/413.

33. Durisotto: 'Traditional Rule', p. 58.

34. R. J. Crosthwaite, AGG Rajputana to Elgin, 22 May 1897, Elgin Collection F84/70. The 'Oodeypore lady' eventually married the Maharaja of Kishengarh in February 1904. R/2/177/33 gives details of the extensive guest list, including at least 40 Europeans.

35. Elgin to Crosthwaite, 4 June 1897, Elgin Collection F84/70. See also Elgin to Crosthwaite, 12 May 1897, R/1/1/1054.

36. Crosthwaite to Elgin, 31 May 1897, Elgin Collection F84/70.

37. Durisotto: 'Traditional Rule', p. 62. The predecessors of Ganga Singh of Bikaner, although already ruling under British protection, were convinced

polygynists: Maharaja Sardar Singh, his grandfather, married more than ten times and Maharaja Dungar Singh, his father, seven times.

38. Ramusack: *Indian Princes*, p. 135. In the twentieth century the most prominent examples of marriages between ruling princes and non-Indian women involved the rulers of Kapurthala, Pudukkottai and Indore, who married Spanish, Australian and American wives respectively.

39. J. M. Douie, Chief Sec. Govt. Punjab to Sec. GoI, FD, 25 November 1900, R/1/1/264.

40. The sahibzada also features in the chapter on education.

41. Confidential memorandum by Political ADC India Office, Sir Curzon Wyllie, 17 October 1905, R/1/1/337.

42. GoI to John Morley, SoS, 11 October 1906, R/1/1/337.

43. Report of meeting between W. B. Jones, Res. Hyderabad, Major Trevor and Salar Jung, 21 December 1882, R/1/1/1226.

44. A Muslim marriage contract. A *nikah* ceremony does not need to take place in a mosque nor in the presence of a religious official, which may have contributed to the idea of its informal nature in the eyes of British officials.

45. Capt. John Clerk to Salar Jung, 4 January 1883, R/1/1/1226.

46. Sir David Barr, Res. Hyderabad, 'Confidential Note on Hyderabad Affairs', 8 February 1905, R/1/1/1281. Curzon also held a particularly low opinion of the lifestyle of the nizam, declaring that 'He cares only for the gratification of his personal whims and desires, and is ... wrapped up in sloth in the seraglio and scarcely capable of an intelligent conversation'. Curzon to Hamilton, 28 December 1899, Curzon Collecton F111, Vol. 158.

47. Sultan Jahan: *Account*, Vol. I, pp. 50–2.

48. Sultan Jahan: *Account*, Appendix B.

49. Sultan Jahan: *Account*, p. 56.

50. Lytton to Major General H. T. Ponsonby, 12 January 1877, Lytton Collection E218, Vol. 19. Lytton's efforts failed to bear fruit with any rapidity. In 1897 it was reported that the Maharani of Cochin was unwilling to leave the privacy of the palace to meet the Governor of Madras and Lady Havelock at the residency. There had been no instance of a female member of the Cochin royal family calling at the residency on such occasions and, due to her 'sensitiveness' the maharani found the idea of breaking tradition 'not quite agreeable' and 'too delicate for discussion'. Maharaja Rama Varma to J. D. Rees, Res. Cochin, 10 October 1897, R/2/9/47.

51. Ibid.

52. The Order of the Crown of India, which was given to governors' wives, to the vicereine and to the spouses of the Commander-in-Chief and the Secretary

of State for India, as well as high-ranking Indian women. David Cannadine, *Ornamentalism* (London, 2001), p. 90.

53. Lytton to queen, 28 August 1877, Lytton Collection E218, Vol. 19.

54. T. Madhava Rao achieved wide renown as the administrator who modernised Travancore during his appointment as diwan from 1858 to 1872. Later he migrated north to become diwan in Indore from 1873 to 1875, and in Baroda from 1875 to 1882.

55. Memorandum by T. Madhava Rao, Minister of Baroda, 13 May 1875, R/2/539/321. The role of Maharani Jumnabai reveals the power that wives of former rulers could possess. When Maharaja Sheodan Singh of Alwar died in 1874, his female relatives joined *jagirdars* to select his successor. See Edward S. Haynes, 'The British Alteration of the Political System of Alwar State: Lineage, Patrimonialism, Indirect Rule, and the Rajput Jagir System in an Indian "Princely" State, 1775–1920', *Studies in History*, 5 n.s. (1989), pp. 27–71.

56. *Kharita* from the senior maharanis of Mysore to Lord Lytton, 1877, R/2/27/241. This letter is somewhat at odds with the description of the *zenana's* efforts to sabotage the maharaja's education written by Colonel G. Malleson in September 1869 (see the chapter on education). It is hard to imagine that the royal women of Mysore had developed a considerably more liberated stance towards education in eight years. Perhaps Malleson was making assumptions about the evil intentions of the *zenana*.

57. Memoranda from Col. P. D. Henderson, Res. Mysore, to W. J. Cuningham, Sec. GoI, FD, 30 December 1894, 6 January 1895, R/1/1/143. See also R/2/29/264.

58. Ibid.

59. Ibid.

60. Henderson to Cuningham, 9 January 1895, R/1/1/143.

61. Report by S. M. Fraser, 21 November 1896, R/2/33/314.

62. Ibid.

63. Hamilton to Elgin, 26 November 1895, Elgin Collection F83, Vol. 13.

64. Col. Donald Robertson, Res. Mysore, to Elgin, 2 October 1897.

65. P. N. Krishna Murti, Diwan Mysore, to Robertson, 9 May 1902, R/2/31/293.

66. H. Daly, Deputy Sec. GoI, FD, to Robertson, 25 August 1902, R/2/31/293.

67. S. M. Fraser to Robertson, 13 July 1902, R/2/31/299.

68. Holkar to R. J. Crosthwaite, AGG CI, January 1891, R/1/1/129. Also Holkar to Crosthwaite, 16 March 1891, R/1/1/129. J. Duncan M. Derrett stresses that the British concept of law and litigation was alien to historical princely practice. The native ruler as the 'fountain of justice' had been supplanted

NOTES 243

by law courts used as a means of obtaining an advantage over an opponent. Legal administration with its artificialities and technicalities, the limitation of actions, the rule that plaintiffs must pay court fees and, finally, the law of evidence affronted the traditional notions of obtaining justice. J. Duncan M. Derrett, 'Tradition and Law in India' in R. J. Moore (ed), *Tradition and Politics in South Asia* (New Delhi, 1979), p. 45.

69. F. Henvey, AGG CI, to Sec. GoI, FD, 5 April 1890, R/1/1/117.

70. Ibid.

71. Holkar to Crosthwaite, AGG CI, January 1891, R/1/1/129.

72. Crosthwaite to Sec. GoI, FD, 21 August 1891, R/1/1/129.

73. Memorial from Varanasi Bai, Senior Maharani of Indore, to viceroy, 5 May 1899, R/1/1/229.

74. In contrast, in British Indian courts *zamindari* women felt no inhibitions in resorting to litigation to challenge male honour and authority, as is discussed in more detail in the chapter on succession. See Price: *Kingship and Political Practice*, pp. 47–76.

75. Memorials from Varanasi Bai to viceroy, 15 March 1899 and 5 May 1899, R/1/1/229. See also R/1/1/252 in which the senior maharani accuses Holkar of having 'a very imperfect knowledge' of the 'illustrious' position of women of reigning Maratha houses to make her the insulting proposal of Rs. 1,000 for monthly expenses. Varanasi Bai to Curzon, 14 February 1900.

76. Punzo Waghorne: *Raja's Magic Clothes*, p. 59.

77. Punzo Waghorne: *Raja's Magic Clothes*, p. 62.

78. Punzo Waghorne: *Raja's Magic Clothes*, p. 63. See also Frederique Apffel Marglin, *Wives of the God-King: The Rituals of the Devadasis of Puri* (Delhi, 1985), and Price: *Kingship and Political Practice*, p. 69. The *devadasis* stood in the direct line of one of the oldest professions in India, in which a woman entered the service of a deity for life. In the eleventh, twelfth and thirteenth centuries the Chola kings gave hundreds of *devadasis* to the temples they founded. These royal temples were conceived as palaces of the gods where the vast entourages added to the status of the rulers, whether heavenly or terrestrial. Not all temple women were necessarily dancing girls or concubines. Some appear to have been more like nuns with devotional and temple-cleaning duties, or to have been domestic and personal servants of the temple Brahmins. However in the nineteenth century, Hindu reformers, reacting to the criticism of Victorian missionaries, began to attack the institution of temple dancers and sacred prostitution. Successive waves of colonial and postcolonial legislation gradually broke the links between the *devadasis* and the temples, driving the women out of the temple precincts and eroding their social, economic and spiritual position. See 'The Daughters

of Yellamma' in William Dalrymple, *Nine Lives: In Search of the Sacred in Modern India* (London, 2009), pp. 66, 71.

79. Quoted Punzo Waghorne: *Raja's Magic Clothes*, pp. 59–60.

80. Punzo Waghorne: *Raja's Magic Clothes*, pp. 60–1.

81. Lansdowne to Cross, 19 May 1890, Lansdowne Collection D558, Vol. 3.

82. Ibid.

83. Interestingly the daughter-in-law of the despised Maharani of Rewah, who apparently had failed in her attempts to emasculate her son.

84. Note by Sir Charles Paul, 19 March 1898, R/1/1/217.

85. See Peter Hardy, *The Muslims of British India* (Cambridge, 1972), ch. 3.

86. Quoted Metcalf: *Ideologies*, p. 140.

87. Hardy: *Muslims of British India*, p. 85.

88. Quoted Metcalf: *Ideologies*, p. 141.

89. Metcalf: *Ideologies*, p. 144.

90. See extensive correspondence in R/1/1/32 and R/1/1/33.

91. Francis Robinson, Introduction to article by Princess Abida Sultan of Bhopal, 'The Begums of Bhopal', *History Today* 30 (October 1980), p. 31.

92. Claudia Preckel, 'The Roots of Anglo-Muslim Cooperation and Islamic Reformism in Bhopal' in Jamal Malik (ed), *Perspectives of Mutual Encounters in South Asian History, 1760–1860* (Leiden, 2000), p. 65.

93. In response to angry criticism by the viceroy, Lord Dufferin, of his treatment of the begam, Sir Lepel accused the Viceroy's Council of having no comprehension of 'the infinite intrigue of a native state, the absolute, and to an English mind, the inconceivable duplicity and unscrupulousness of the highest officials from the Chief downwards, the detected falsehoods, forgeries and perjuries, which occasion no shame or remorse'. Griffin to Durand, 27 May 1886, Durand Papers D727.

94. See R/1/1/35.

95. 'An Episode in Indian Government' in *The Times* (London), 27 December 1886, R/1/1/55.

96. Note signed D. [Earl of Dufferin], 5 February 1887, R/1/1/55.

97. Memorandum by FTH, 28 March 1886, R/1/1/33.

98. Lepel Griffin, AGG CI, to H. M. Durand, Sec. GoI, FD, 10 March 1886, R/1/1/33.

99. 'History of Bhopal', Lepel Griffin to Durand, September 1885, R/1/1/33.

100. Lepel Griffin to Durand, 29 October 1885, R/1/1/33.

101. Col. W. Kincaid, Pol. Agent, Bhopal, to Begam, 28 July 1885, R/2/453/71.

102. Lepel Griffin to Sec. GoI, FD, 21 February 1886, PSCI, 1875–1911, Box VI.

103. *Kharita* from Begam of Bhopal to viceroy, 28 July 1888, R/1/1/96.

104. Col. C. Ward to F. Henvey, AGG CI, 26 July 1888, R/1/1/88.

105. Ward to Durand, 10 September 1886, R/1/1/47.

106. R. W. Crosthwaite, Note of 24 October 1894, R/1/1/1225.

107. See the alleged attempted disinheritance of Sultan Jahan by her mother in the chapter on succession.

108. Sultan Jahan: *Account*, Vol. I, p. 200.

109. Lambert-Hurley: *Muslim Women, Reform and Princely Patronage*, p. 42.

110. Barbara Metcalf, 'Islam and Power in Colonial India: The Making and Unmaking of a Muslim Princess', *American Historical Review*, 116, 1 (February 2011), pp. 1–30.

111. See Gayatri Sinha, 'Women Artists in India: Patronage and Practice' in Deborah Cherry and Janice Helland (eds), *Local/Global Women Artists in the Nineteenth Century* (Aldershot, 2006), p. 73.

112. Metcalf: 'Islam and Power in Colonial India', p. 23.

113. Sultan Jahan: *Account*, Vol. I, p. 156.

114. Metcalf: 'Islam and Power in Colonial India', p. 26.

115. Sultan Jahan: *Account*, Vol. I, pp. 173–4.

116. Ibid, Vol. I, p. 225. Sultan Jahan also believed that the 'appointment of an absolute Minister can seldom be productive of good results. It is only in accordance with the natural order of things that a person so appointed should be jealous of his authority, and should endeavour to make his will the law of the land. He would need to be a man of exceptional loyalty who could, in such a situation, patiently defer to the wishes of the Chief when they happened to be in conflict with his own'. Sultan Jahan, *Account*, Vol. I, p. 224.

117. Ibid, Vol. I, p. 281.

118. Ibid, Vol. I, pp. 277–8.

119. Ibid, Vol. I, pp. 338–52. See also Sultan Jahan Begam, *The Story of a Pilgrimage to Hijaz* (Calcutta, 1909), pp. 19–127 and Siobhan Lambert-Hurley (ed), *A Princess's Pilgrimage: Nawab Sikander Begum's A Pilgrimage to Mecca* (New Delhi, 2007).

120. A form of traditional medicine, based on the teachings of the Greek physician, Hipppocrates, and the Roman physician, Galen, adopting the concept of the four humours: phlegm, blood, yellow bile and black bile.

121. Sultan Jahan: *Account*, Vol. I, pp. 317–25.

122. Shaharyar M. Khan, *The Begums of Bhopal* (London, 2000), p. 180. See also Siobhan Lambert-Hurley, 'Historicising Debates over Women's Status in Islam: The Case of Sultan Jahan Begam of Bhopal' in Ernst and Pati (eds): *India's Princely States*, p. 141.

123. Sultan Jahan: *Account*, Vol. I, p. 202.

124. Price: *Kingship and Political Practice*, p. 75.

4. Ruler of the State

1. Mayo to Argyll, 7 February 1870, Argyll Collection B380, Vol. I.
2. Mayo to Argyll, 10 May 1870, Argyll Collection B380, Vol. I.
3. Mayo to Argyll, 7 February 1870, Argyll Collection B380, Vol. I.
4. Mayo to Argyll, 25 November 1870, Argyll Collection B380, Vol. II.
5. Speech by Mayo, 21 October 1870 in *The Times*, 5 December 1870, quoted Sir W. W. Hunter, *A Life of the Earl of Mayo* (London, 1876), I, pp. 11–12.
6. SoS to GoI, No.153, 20 December 1871, PCI, 1792–1874, Vol. 14.
7. SoS to GoI, No. 57, 6 June 1872, PCI, 1792–1874, Vol. 15.
8. SoS to GoI, No. 211, 12 October 1869, PCI, 1792–1874, Vol. 12.
9. Lepel Griffin to Ripon, 15 June 1881, Ripon Collection ADD 43614.
10. SoS to GoI, No.13, 21 January 1870, PCI, 1792–1874, Vol. 13.
11. Copland: *British Raj*, p. 123.
12. SoS to GoI, No. 263, 11 October 1869, PCI, 1792–1874, Vol. 12.
13. Edward S. Haynes, 'Alwar: Bureaucracy versus Traditional Rulership' in Jeffrey (ed): *People, Princes*, p. 36.
14. Article from *Delhi Gazette* of 4 February 1871, enclosed with letter from Mayo to Argyll, 15 February 1871, Argyll Collection IOR Neg. 4236.
15. However this does not appear to have been the case in Western India. Copland makes the point that in the 1870s at grass-roots level it appeared that large areas technically under native rule (perhaps as much as a quarter in the case of princely Gujarat) were in fact administered by British political agents or their nominees. Justice was 'British' justice regulated according to a modified version of the Indian Criminal and Civil Procedure Codes, while police, public works, famine relief and other sorts of general expenditure were met by a direct levy from rulers who had no say as to how their money should be spent: 'Much of this *modus operandi* was illegal, as the government later realised, however in the early seventies few on the British side thought too deeply about the legal niceties, and the chiefs, of course, were in no position to argue'. Copland: *British Raj*, pp. 131–2, 137.
16. Although not a political officer, an exception was the ICS evangelical, Frank Lugard Brayne, a zealous commissioner in the Punjab, whose religious enthusiasm was rare among late Edwardian officials. See Clive Dewey, *Anglo-Indian Attitudes: The Mind of the Indian Civil Service* (London, 1993).
17. Copland: *British Raj*, pp. 130–1.
18. SoS to GoI, No. 2, 11 March 1875, PSCI, 1875–1911, Vol. 1.
19. Undated note by Sir Erskine Perry, attached to SoS to GoI, No. 78, 4 June 1873, PCI, 1792–1874, Vol. 16.
20. Undated note by Sir George Clerk, attached to SoS to GoI, No. 78, 4 June 1873, PCI, 1792–1874, Vol. 16.

21. SoS to GoI, No. 58, 30 April 1873, PCI, 1792–1874, Vol. 16.
22. SoS to GoI, No. 58, 30 April 1873, PCI, 1792–1874, Vol. 16.
23. Argyll to Northbrook, 23 December 1873, Northbrook Collection C144, Vol. 9.
24. Lytton to Lord Cranbrook, 5 November 1879, Lytton Collection E218, Vol. 21.
25. Ibid.
26. Ibid.
27. Lytton to Sir R. E. Egerton, 2 December 1879, Lytton Collection E218, Vol. 21.
28. Lytton to Cranbrook, 5 November 1879, Lytton Collection E218, Vol. 21.
29. Lytton to Sir Alfred Lyall, AGG Rajputana, 26 August 1879, Lytton Collection E218, Vol. 21.
30. Lord Randolph Churchill to Dufferin, 7 August 1885, Dufferin Collection F130, IOR Neg. 4352.
31. Hamilton to Curzon, 2 February 1899, Curzon Collection F111, Vol. 158. Despite persistent princely criticism of British political officers many rulers did not want Indians as their residents or political agents under the control of the Government of India, although they would employ Indians as ministers who were under direct princely control. There was as a result little impetus to speed up the Indianisation of the Political Service.
32. See the section on Bhopal in the chapter on marriage and royal women.
33. Letter from W. Bell, 17 April 1886, R/1/1/35. Sir Lepel was hardly a model of tact, writing in 1883 that it would be unwise for the British 'to descend from the high place which the genius of Englishmen has rightly won, and endeavour to persuade the people of India what, indeed, only the most credulous of them would believe – that they are intellectually or morally our equals, and that to them have been confided by fortune those secrets of government which in the modern world, are the inheritance of the Anglo Saxon race alone'. 'Indian Princes at Home', *Fortnightly Review*, 34 (October 1883), p. 495.
34. Curzon to Hamilton, 23 March 1899, Curzon Collection F111, Vol. 158.
35. Curzon to Hamilton, 25 September 1900, Curzon Collection F111, Vol. 159.
36. Ibid.
37. Minute by viceroy on 'The Appointment of a Political Agent to the Phulkian States', 11 October 1900, PSCI, 1875–1911, Box XXXV.
38. The outcome of much deliberation, detailed in the chapter on education.
39. Curzon to Hamilton, 3 October 1900, Curzon Collection F111, Vol. 159.
40. Curzon to Hamilton, 18 November 1900, Curzon Collection F111, Vol. 159. Since the first half of the nineteenth century the Bombay Political

Department had exercised a largely independent control over the states of western India, the sheikdoms of the Persian Gulf, the Sind frontier and the territories under the sovereignty of the Sultan of Zanzibar. These areas were jealously guarded as a Bombay preserve, despite intermittent efforts by the Foreign Department to break the local government's sphere of influence. However by 1876 the foreign secretary, Charles Aitchison, succeeded in having the overseas territories (including Baroda, following the deposition of the gaekwar, Malhar Rao) transferred to the jurisdiction of the Government of India. The Bombay Government fought longest and hardest against the shift of control of its states from the provincial to the central level, although in general the princes did not wish to be under the control of an Indian minister at provincial level and actively lobbied for a move to the Government of India.

41. Curzon to Hamilton, 28 November 1900, Curzon Collection F111, Vol. 159.

42. Curzon to Hamilton, 15 May 1901, Curzon Collection F111, Vol. 160.

43. Hamilton to Curzon, 28 March 1901, Curzon Collection F111, Vol. 159.

44. Fiona Groenhout 'Debauchery, Disloyalty, and Other Deficiencies: The Impact of Ideas of Princely Character upon Indirect Rule in Central India, c. 1886–1946', PhD Thesis, University of Western Australia, 2007, p. 298.

45. SoS to GoI, No. 109, 10 September 1874, PCI, 1792–1874, Vol. 17.

46. SoS to GoI, No. 273, 9 December 1869, PCI, 1792–1874, Vol. 12.

47. SoS to GoI, No. 8, 27 January 1870, PCI, 1792–1874, Vol. 13.

48. SoS to GoI, No. 1, 5 January 1871, PCI, 1792–1874, Vol. 14.

49. GoI to SoS, No. 5, 8 January 1884, PSCI, 1875–1911, Box IV.

50. Ibid.

51. Edward C. Moulton, *Lord Northbrook's Indian Administration* (London, 1968) devotes a whole chapter to the Baroda crisis, and S. Gopal, *British Policy in India, 1857–1905* (Oxford, 1953) also singles it out for attention.

52. Copland: *British Raj*, p. 150.

53. Northbrook to Salisbury, 21 April and 21 June 1875, Northbrook Collection C144, Vol. 12.

54. Northbrook to Salisbury, 19 March 1875, Northbrook Collection C144, Vol. 12.

55. Salisbury to Northbrook, 30 July 1875, Northbrook Collection C144, Vol. 12.

56. Minute dated 18 May 1876, quoted Copland: *British Raj*, p. 153.

57. Lytton to Cranbrook, 8 February 1879, Lytton Collection E218, Vol. 21.

58. Lytton to Sir R. E. Egerton, 2 December 1879, Lytton Collection E218, Vol. 21.

59. Ibid.

60. Oliver St. John to Ripon, 22 July 1883, Ripon Collection ADD 43613.

61. *The Times*, 4 May 1891.
62. Lansdowne to Cross, 19 August 1891, Lansdowne Collection D558, Vol. 4. The royal opinion of events in Manipur was undoubtedly heavily influenced by the view of Victoria's 'Indian Secretary', Munshi Abdul Karim, who, to the scorn of the court, had succeeded in ingratiating himself to an alarming degree with the monarch. In October 1896 the munshi wrote a minute declaring that 'There is well known a great amount of unhappiness among the Princes of the Native States of India arising from their being so subject to and under the control of Political Agents. These agents have raised themselves to such a height of power that they act as if they themselves were the head of the States ... and as if nothing could be done privately or publicly unless it was sanctioned and approved by them. They even exceed their own duty and do many things in the way of interference which have not the permission of the Government. Moreover these agents refuse to listen to any suggestion or advice from the old ministers and advisers of the States and when disputes arise between Native friends and relatives these agents allow the disputes to go on until some of the parties have been compelled to have recourse to violence and then it is that the agents interfere and report. There is no trial but Punishment is always inflicted on one side without a semblance of a hearing from the other. The Agent's report is never doubted ... Thus it is that the agents are more comfortably and richly placed than "the" Princes themselves'. Minute by Munshi Abdul Karim, October 1896, L/PS/8/61.
63. Lansdowne to Cross, 23 June 1891, Lansdowne Collection D558, Vol. 4.
64. Lansdowne to Cross, 15 April 1891, Lansdowne Collection D558, Vol. 4.
65. Lansdowne to Cross 30 June 1891, Lansdowne Collection D558, Vol. 4.
66. Lansdowne to Cross, 15 September 1891, Lansdowne Collection D558, Vol. 4.
67. Curzon to Hamilton, 5 July 1899, Curzon Collection F111, Vol. 158. The man dealing with the details of Holkar's deposition and the installation of the ruler's son was the current resident in Indore, Francis Younghusband, who was soon to depart on his infamous expedition to Tibet.
68. Fiona Groenhout, 'Loyal Feudatories or Depraved Despots? The Deposition of Princes in the Central Indian Agency, c.1880–1947' in Ernst and Pati (eds): *India's Princely States*, pp. 102–4.
69. GoI to SoS, No. 50, 18 March 1896, PSCI, 1875–1911, Box XXI.
70. Hamilton to Curzon, 17 October 1901, Curzon Collection F111, Vol. 160.
71. Not surprisingly, the British were particularly sensitive to the reactions of other princes to the deposition of one of their kind. Following an official visit to Orchha, during which the maharaja made 'offensive and uncalled for

allusion' to the deposition of the Maharaja of Panna, Curzon declared that no further viceregal visits should be made to the state during the lifetime of the present ruler. Note from viceroy's camp, Udaipur, 17 November 1902, R/1/1/287.

72. The recruitment of external administrators was already in existence by the second half of the nineteenth century. Barbara Ramusack suggests that 'These outsiders were sought for two reasons. First, the ruling elite and local land-controllers often did not possess the requisite skills. Second, newcomers would be more dependent on the ruler for their power and authority than kinsmen or locally based elites. Thus the Marathas employed Chitpavan brahmans; Travancore imported brahmans from Tamilnadu and north India; the nizams of Hyderabad recruited *kayasths* ... from north India'. Ramusack: *Indian Princes*, p. 42.

73. Stern: *Cat and Lion*, p. 23.

74. Robert W. Stern, 'An Approach to Politics in the Princely States' in Jeffrey (ed): *People, Princes*, p. 359.

75. Ashis Nandy, *The Intimate Enemy: Loss and Recovery of Self under Colonialism* (New Delhi, 1983), p. ix.

76. Robert Young, *White Mythologies: Writing History and the West* (London, 1990), p. 148. See also 'Of Mimicry and Man: The Ambivalence of Colonial Discourse' in Homi Bhabha, *The Location of Culture* (New York, 1994), pp. 85–92.

77. James Tod, *Annals and Antiquities of Rajasthan*, Vol. I (originally published 1829), pp. 223–4, quoted Stern: *Cat and Lion*, p. 32.

78. Alfred C. Lyall, 'The Rajput States of India', *Asiatic Studies: Religious and Social* (London, 1882), pp. 151–81, quoted Stern: *Cat and Lion*, p. 33.

79. Lyall: *Asiatic Studies*, pp. 204, 261–3, quoted Metcalf: *Ideologies*, p. 79.

80. For an opinion on the tendency for Britain to treat the Rajput states as foreign powers and to refuse to intervene to settle internal quarrels, see undated report by Sir Henry Lawrence, 'The Proposed Amalgamation of Central Indian and Rajpootana Agencies', attached to letter from Mayo to Argyll, 7 February 1870, Argyll Collection B380, Vol. I.

81. Rajat K. Ray, 'Mewar: The Breakdown of the Princely Order' in Jeffrey (ed): *People, Princes*, p. 206.

82. Ibid, pp. 211–12.

83. Ibid, p. 222.

84. Major A. F. Pinhey, Res. Mewar, 'Note on Mewar', 7 March 1901, R/2/147/97. In the same way, the Rajputana Agency proved only partially successful in bureaucratising the Jaipur *durbar*. To the Agency's dissatisfaction Maharaja Madho Singh evidently failed to acknowledge the 'self-evident superiority of European rule and system' and became the autocrat of his administration.

In theory a council of ten men assisted him, but most of them were 'sleeping members in the firm' and the council was unable to pass orders on the smallest matter without reference to the maharaja. Lt. Col. C. Herbert, Res. Jaipur, Note on Jaipur, 8 August 1905, R/1/1/328.

85. Pinhey: 'Note on Mewar', 7 March 1901, R/2/147/97.

86. Ray, 'Mewar: The Breakdown of the Princely Order' in Jeffrey (ed): *People, Princes*, p. 223. The Imperial Service Troops scheme is discussed in the chapter on the princely role as servants of the empire.

87. Ibid, p. 224. In 1912 Sidney and Beatrice Webb commented on the absence of a college or other educational establishment for the young men of Mewar. Webb: *Indian Diary*, p. 156.

88. Lt. Col. W. H. C. Wylie, AGG, Rajputana, to Sec. GoI, FD, 1 April 1901, R/2/147/97.

89. Pinhey, 'Confidential Note on Mewar Affairs', 8 March 1906, R/2/147/97.

90. In the same decade Jai Singh, the Maharaja of Alwar, influenced by his Mayo College education and aware that the implanted bureaucracy was undermining his role and prerogatives, made an attempt to regain the *jagirdars* as allies. However the outcome of the maharaja's proposed Jagir Council was not the emergence of a progressive nobility to counterbalance the weight of the bureaucracy. Instead the bureaucracy transformed the council into another department of government, effectively beyond the prince's control. Haynes, 'Alwar: Bureaucracy versus Traditional Rulership' in Jeffrey (ed): *People, Princes*, pp. 32–64.

91. Pinhey, 'Confidential Note on Mewar Affairs', 8 March 1906, R/2/147/97.

92. Asst. Sec. GoI, FD to E. G. Colvin, AGG Rajputana, 6 May 1907, R 2/147/97.

93. The Maharaja of Bikaner also managed to achieve an 'autocratic position'. In 1905 the political agent noted that instead of using a diwan or executive council the maharaja conducted the work of state personally through secretaries in charge of various departments. The 'essence of the scheme' was apparently to give the ruler a closer and more personal control over the affairs of his state. Major A. F. Bruce, Pol. Agent Bikaner, 'Note on Bikaner', 6 July 1905, R/1/1/328.

94. Bayly: *Indian Society*, pp. 95–7.

95. W. Lee-Warner to *The Times*, 18 August 1897, Lee Warner Collection F92, File 31. See also James Manor 'Princely Mysore before the Storm: The State-Level Political System of India's Model State, 1920–36', *Modern Asian Studies* 9 1 (1975), pp. 31–58.

96. Sharma Rao, *Modern Mysore*, Vol. II, p. 46, quoted Bjorn Hettne, *The Political Economy of Indirect Rule: Mysore 1881–1947* (London, 1978), p. 50.

97. Mayo to Argyll, 20 April 1870, Argyll Collection B380, Vol. I.

98. SoS to GoI, Draft No. 133, 3 October 1873, PCI, 1792–1874, Vol. 16.

99. Lytton to J. D. Gordon, 21 June 1878, Lytton Collection E218, Vol. 20.

100. Col. P. D. Henderson, Res. Mysore, to W. J. Cuningham, Foreign Sec. GoI, 30 December 1894, 22 January 1895, R/1/1/143. K. Seshadri Iyer, a Tamil Brahmin who was diwan in Mysore from 1883 to 1896, was reputedly responsible for inducting over 100 men from outside Mysore into the gazetted service of the state. Strong views on this matter were aired by the maharani regent, Vanivilas Sannidhana, quoted in the chapter on royal women.

101. Sir Donald Robertson, Res. Mysore, 'Mysore Narrative', 1902, R/2/14/92.

102. Henderson, 'Memorandum on Mysore Minority Arrangements', 17 January 1895, R/2/29/264.

103. Robertson, 'Secret Notes on Mysore', 25 September 1903, R/1/1/1064.

104. Robertson, 'Note on the Work of the General Secretariat', 30 April 1903, R/2/32/302.

105. Robertson to Krishna Murti, 13 April 1903, R/2/32/302.

106. Robertson, 'Secret Notes on Mysore', 25 September 1903, R/1/1/1064.

107. Robertson, 'Mysore Narrative', 1902, R/2/14/92.

108. Robertson, 'Note on Mysore', 5 November 1900, R/1/1/260.

109. Hettne: *Political Economy*, p. 365.

110. David Hardiman, 'Baroda: The Structure of a "Progressive" State' in Jeffrey (ed): *People, Princes*, p. 108.

111. Ibid, pp. 107–13. In his study of Baroda and Mysore, Manu Bhagavan makes the point that Malhar Rao inherited a significant number of problems from his predecessor and received the blame for them from the British. Bhagavan: *Sovereign Spheres*, p. 43.

112. Hardiman, 'Baroda: The Structure of a "Progressive" State' in Jeffrey (ed): *People, Princes*, p. 116.

113. R. L. Handa, *History of the Freedom Struggle in Princely States* (New Delhi, 1968), p. 61.

114. Hardiman, 'Baroda: The Structure of a "Progressive" State' in Jeffrey (ed): *People, Princes*, p. 117.

115. *Baroda Administration Report*, 1876–77, p. 101 and *Baroda Administration Report*, 1934–5, p. 85, quoted Hardiman 'Baroda: The Structure of a "Progressive" State' in Jeffrey (ed): *People, Princes*, p. 117.

116. Elliott's influence is discussed in greater detail in the chapter on princely education.

117. Lt. Col. N. C. Martelli, AGG Baroda to W. J. Cuningham, Sec. GoI, FD, 29 May 1895, R/1/1/162. See also Martelli to Cuningham, 30 May and 21 August 1895, R/1/1/162.

118. Oliver St. John, 'Memorandum on Baroda Affairs', 28 September 1888, R/1/1/1040.

119. See R/1/1/162.

120. Col. J. Biddulph, AGG Baroda, 'Report on Baroda Affairs', attached to No. 185, 18 September 1895, PSCI, 1875–1911, Box XX. See also R/1/1/1040.

121. Capt. W. Evans Gordon to Cuningham, 16 May 1894, R/1/1/140. See also report of interview between Res. Baroda, Col. M. J. Meade, and gaekwar, 14 February 1908, R/1/1/288, in which the gaekwar complains that 'The tendency is more and more to treat us like officers or servants in charge of districts, rather than the hereditary rulers of States'.

122. Cuningham to Evans Gordon, 21 February 1894, R/1/1/140. See also R/1/1/288.

123. Major C. Pritchard, Res. Baroda, to Sir L. W. Dane, Sec. GoI, FD, 16 December 1906, R/1/1/339.

124. Curzon to Hamilton, 29 October 1900, Curzon Collection F111, Vol. 159. Curzon's vitriol knew no bounds when it came to the gaekwar, 'the most disagreeable, contumacious and cantankerous of the whole of our Chiefs... The man, as you know, was the son of a cow-herd and his humble origin and antecedents are constantly, in spite of his considerable ability, coming out in his words and deeds'. Curzon to Hamilton, 4 June 1902, Curzon Collection F111, Vol.161.

125. Curzon to Hamilton, 25 June 1902, Curzon Collection F111, Vol. 161. Also Curzon to Hamilton, 12 March 1903, Vol. 162 and Curzon to Brodrick, 30 March 1905, Vol. 164. Despite viceregal protestations over the gaekwar's frequent visits to England, such visits afforded great opportunities for some hard bargaining. The viceroy, Lord Dufferin, pointed out that if the ruler attended Queen Victoria's Golden Jubilee celebrations in 1887, he might be persuaded to abolish transit duties and to find a solution to problems existing over a new telegraph line 'over which he wishes to have supreme jurisdiction'. Dufferin to Cross, 16 May and 3 June 1887, Dufferin Collection F130, Vol. 8A.

126. Hamilton to Curzon, 25 April and 1 August 1901, Curzon Collection F111, Vol. 160.

127. Hardiman, 'Baroda: The Structure of a "Progressive" State' in Jeffrey (ed): *People, Princes*, p. 114. A number of princes recruited western-educated Indians with nationalist credentials. Sayaji Rao employed Bengali nationalists, most notably Romesh Chandra Dutt and Aurobindo Ghose. Barbara Ramusack points out that 'When opportunities for Indians were limited in the ICS, some Indian nationalists joined the administrations of princely

states where they could demonstrate their administrative competence and exercise significant executive power'. Ramusack: *Indian Princes*, p. 184.

128. In Manu Bhagavan's opinion the gaekwar observed that western ideas could be 'modified in the Indian milieu to become distinctly Indian in nature' and turned into a 'tool of resistance' to counter colonialism. Bhagavan: *Sovereign Spheres*, pp. 51, 55. Using institutions of reform such as universities, the states of Baroda and Mysore could in the twentieth century be termed 'sites of native modernity', a state of affairs which was especially detrimental to colonialism since, in the colonial idiom, the princely states represented the 'fossilized past' that 'defined the modern-ness of the British in India'. Bhagavan: *Sovereign Spheres*, p. 178.

129. Bayly: *Indian Society*, pp. 94–5.

130. Karen Leonard, 'Hyderabad: The Mulki-Non-Mulki Conflict' in Jeffrey (ed): *People, Princes*, p. 67.

131. H. Fraser, *Memoir and Correspondence of General J. S. Fraser of the Madras Army* (London, 1885), Appendix, p. xxvi.

132. Leonard, 'Hyderabad: The Mulki-Non-Mulki Conflict' in Jeffrey (ed): *People, Princes*, p. 70.

133. Under the terms of the treaty of 1801 with the British, the Nizam of Hyderabad was obliged to maintain a military force at Hyderabad called the Nizam's Contingent. The subsequent treaty of 1853 renamed the force the Hyderabad Contingent.

134. See Thomas Henry Thornton, *General Sir Richard Meade and the Feudatory States of Central and Southern India* (London, 1898) and Richard Temple, *Journals Kept in Hyderabad, Kashmir, Sikkim and Nepal* (London, 1887), Vol. I.

135. Leonard, 'Hyderabad: The Mulki-Non-Mulki Conflict' in Jeffrey (ed): *People, Princes*, p. 71.

136. William Digby was a British author, journalist and humanitarian, who in May 1888 set up the Indian Political and General Agency in London for the purpose of raising awareness about Indian grievances in the British parliament and press. He became a strong advocate of constitutional reform and acted as an unofficial guide to Indian National Congress leaders visiting London.

137. Letter from William Digby to the editor of the *St. James's Gazette*, 16 May 1888, Dufferin Collection F130, Vol. 11A.

138. Nawab Jivan Yar Jung's English translation of his father's Urdu autobiography, Server-el-Mulk, *My Life* (London 1932), p. 92, quoted Leonard 'Hyderabad: The Mulki-Non-Mulki Conflict' in Jeffrey (ed): *People, Princes*, p. 71.

139. Leonard, 'Hyderabad: The Mulki-Non-Mulki Conflict' in Jeffrey (ed): *People, Princes*, p. 76.

140. Salar Jung died after eating canned oysters at a picnic. Since the minister had many enemies, poison was suspected.

141. Mahbub Ali Khan features strongly in the chapters on education and royal marriage.

142. GoI to SoS, No. 60, 9 May 1887, PSCI, 1875–1911, Box VII.

143. Dufferin to Lord Kimberley, 6 March 1886, Dufferin Collection F130, Vol. 5.

144. Trevor Chichele Plowden, Res. Hyderabad, 14 November 1895, R/1/1/165. See also R/1/1/1/51 and R/1/1/193.

145. Col. K. J. Mackenzie, Offg. Res. Hyderabad, to W. J. Cuningham, 6 October 1894, R/2/67/17. Mackenzie was intrigued by the fact that the nizam had had a photograph of him enlarged and painted: 'So I suppose the little beggar in a way does like me a bit – but it is deuced hard to say. I'm inclined to think he thinks us all a d-----d nuisance!' Mackenzie to Cuningham, 12 October 1895, R/1/1/1251.

146. Confidential note on Hyderabad affairs by Sir David Barr, Res. Hyderabad, 8 February 1905, R/1/1/1281.

147. Chichele Plowden to Sec. GoI, FD, 2 April 1894, R/2/66/10. See also R/2/66/13.

148. Chichele Plowden to Sec. GoI, FD, 9 February 1897, R/1/1/183.

149. Bawa: *Hyderabad under Salar Jang*, p. 220.

150. Sir David Barr, Offg. Res. Hyderabad, Report, 6 August 1900, R/1/1/1281.

151. Cuningham to viceroy, 28 January 1898, R/1/1/202.

152. See R/1/1/209.

153. Cuningham to viceroy, 28 January 1898, R/1/1/202.

154. Ibid.

155. See R/1/1/171 and R/1/1/202.

156. Hamilton to Curzon, 22 August 1901, Curzon Collection F111, Vol. 160.

157. Leonard, 'Hyderabad: The Mulki-Non-Mulki Conflict' in Jeffrey (ed): *People, Princes*, p. 66.

5. Servant of the Empire

1. A supplement to *Allen's Indian Mail* giving a gradation list of 'Chiefs of the Indian Empire' is attached to Salisbury to Lytton, 13 July 1876, Lytton Collection E218, Vol. 3A.

2. Hutchins: *Illusion of Permanence*, p. 199.

3. Cannadine: *Ornamentalism*, p. 9.

4. Ibid, pp. 123–5. See also C. Bolt, *Victorian Attitudes to Race* (London 1971), p. 186.

5. Proof of the determination to enforce the new social relationship between the Indian rulers and the paramount power appears in an official despatch of May 1873 concerning the Nizam of Hyderabad, the Gaekwar of Baroda and the Maharajah of Mysore, all of whom received in British territory a gun salute equal to that given to the viceroy and higher than that to which the governors of Madras and Bombay were entitled. It was decided that advantage was to be taken of the fact that the rulers of Hyderabad and Mysore were both minors, and that the gaekwar had just succeeded to the *gadi*, to reduce their salutes from 21 to 19 guns and, in so doing, to raise British officials in rank vis-à-vis the three major princes. SoS to GoI, No. 70, 8 May 1873, PCI, 1792–1874, Vol. 16.

6. Religious ceremony and princely largesse of a lavish nature was firmly discouraged in an attempt to instil methods of accountability into palace procedure. The change in ceremonial practice was not without its critics. In 1909 an impassioned letter from the Maharaja of Bikaner to the viceroy, Lord Minto, raised the question of 'restoring the *Izzat* and position of the Chiefs to their former glory' through the 'honours and courtesies' extended to ruling princes on official occasions. The maharaja stressed that 'our dignity and importance has gradually diminished to some extent and...we do not occupy the same position as we did some fifty years ago'. Some procedures had been allowed 'to drift away from the desirable and original line' and, since 'splendour and ceremonials' were special features of the East 'the importance of a person is gauged by the populace according to the compliments paid to him'. Maharaja of Bikaner to viceroy, 29 December 1909, R/2/752/36.

7. Edward S. Haynes, 'Rajput Ceremonial Interactions as a Mirror of a Dying Indian State System 1820–1947', *Modern Asian Studies* XXIV, 1990, p. 474.

8. Bhagavan: *Sovereign Spheres*, p. 17.

9. Cohn: 'Representing Authority in Victorian India' in Hobsbawm and Ranger (eds): *Invention of Tradition*, p. 168.

10. F. W. Buckler, 'The Oriental Despot', *Anglican Theological Review* (1927–8), p. 239, quoted Cohn: 'Representing Authority in Victorian India' in Hobsbawm and Ranger (eds): *Invention of Tradition*, p. 168.

11. Cohn: 'Representing Authority in Victorian India' in Hobsbawm and Ranger (eds): *Invention of Tradition*, p. 169.

12. Ibid.

13. Ibid, pp. 168–72. Hira Singh takes a rather different view, suggesting that 'It could be argued that the colonial rulers were simply imitating the Indian

rulers – casting the British Queen/King into the image of the Great Mughal – and making Indians pay for it'. Hira Singh, 'Colonial and Postcolonial Historiography and the Princely States: Relations of Power and Rituals of Legitimation' in Ernst and Pati (eds): *India's Princely States*, p. 20.

14. See R/2/750/12 for details of the installation of Madho Rao Scindia, Maharaja of Gwalior.

15. SoS to GoI, No. 74, 30 April 1873, PCI, 1792–1874, Vol. 16.

16. Cohn: 'Representing Authority in Victorian India' in Hobsbawm and Ranger (eds): *Invention of Tradition*, p. 172.

17. Lt.-Col. M. J. Meade, Offg. AGG CI, to H. S. Barnes, Sec. GoI, FD, 9 July 1901, PSCI, 1875–1911, Box XXXVI. R/2/28/261 itemises the articles making up the viceroy's *khilat* at the installation of the Maharaja of Mysore in January 1895.

18. Cohn, 'Representing Authority in Victorian India' in Hobsbawm and Ranger (eds): *Invention of Tradition*, p. 172.

19. Ibid, p. 180. R/2/783/20 deals in detail with the number of attendants permitted to accompany the Maharaja of Benares, the Nawab of Rampur and the Raja of Tehri at *durbar*s, in an effort to introduce 'a uniform scale classified according to salutes … to systematise the ceremonial observed at meetings between the H. E. the Viceroy and rulers'. R/2/69/52 discusses the 'ceremonials' to be observed on the occasion of official visits between the Governor of Madras and the Maharaja of Mysore, and R/2/880/48 looks at the vexed question of the 'garlanding' of British officials by Indian royalty.

20. A word of Persian origin which was assimilated into Hindustani during the period of Islamic rule. Sometimes translated as 'prestige', more usually as 'honour', *izzat* was both a source of power and a focus of obligation. While it turned the ruler into almost a demigod, it also predisposed him to act in a way which would maximise the glory of the state.

21. J. G. Kaye, Res. Udaipur, to E. G. Colvin, AGG Rajputana, 20 July 1911, R/2/161/206. The Rajput rulers were particular sticklers for protocol: R/2/168/267 is devoted to the procedure of Rajput princes at the wedding of the Maharana of Udaipur and a princess from Idar in 1875.

22. Charles Lewis Tupper, *Indian Political Practice: A Collection of the Decisions of the Government of India in Political Cases* (London, 1893), pp. 19–20.

23. E. M. Collingham, *Imperial Bodies* (Cambridge, 2001), p. 129.

24. Cannadine: *Ornamentalism*, p. 101.

25. See Ibid, pp. 45–6; Copland: *British Raj*, pp. 154–5; L. A. Knight, 'The Royal Titles Act and India', *Historical Journal* XI, no. 3, 1968, p. 488; M. Lutyens, *The Lyttons of India: Lord Lytton's Viceroyalty* (London, 1979), pp. 74–89.

26. Lytton to queen, 15 November 1876, Lytton Collection E218, Vol. 18.

27. Salisbury to Lytton, 7 July 1876, Lytton Collection E218, Vol. 3A.
28. Lytton to Benjamin Disraeli, 30 April 1876, Lytton Collection E218, Vol. 18. To define and regulation the 'native aristocracy' in India the viceroy also planned the establishment of a College of Arms in Calcutta. The college, which never came to fruition, was to be the Indian equivalent of the British College of Arms in London, to effect, establish and order a peerage for India. Coordinated with the idea of the College of Arms was a scheme to present 90 of the leading princes with large banners, emblazoned with individual coats of arms, at the Imperial Assemblage.
29. Salisbury to Lytton, 18 September 1876, Lytton Collection E218, Vol. 3B.
30. Salisbury to Lytton, 9 June 1876, Lytton Collection E218, Vol. 3A.
31. Lytton to queen, 4 May 1876, Lytton Collection E218, Vol. 18.
32. Lytton to Salisbury, 11 May 1876, Lytton Collection E218, Vol. 18.
33. Lytton to Disraeli, 3 October 1876, Lytton Collection E218, Vol. 18.
34. Miles Taylor contends that, due to her involvement in the affairs of Indian princely states during the 1840s and 1850s and the resulting 'exoticisation' of her Indian subjects, Victoria, in believing herself to be Empress of India, was 'not becoming complicit in a Disraelian world of pomp and theater, in which the new artisan voter of the second Reform Act would be given spectacle to divert his mind from social reform. Rather, she was looking back, almost to medieval Europe – certainly to European monarchy before the rise of absolutism under Louis XIV – where holy emperors ruled, statesmen obeyed, and princely subjects proved loyal'. Taylor: 'Queen Victoria', p. 272.
35. Lytton to queen, 23 December 1876 to 10 January 1877, Lytton Collection E218, Vol. 19.
36. Lytton to Salisbury, 11 October 1877, Lytton to Scindia, 23 November 1877, Lytton Collection E218, Vol. 19.
37. Holkar to Prince of Wales, 21 September 1876, Lytton Collection E218, Vol. 18.
38. Lytton to Salisbury, 11 May 1876, Lytton Collection E218, Vol. 18.
39. Lytton to queen, 23 December 1876, Lytton Collection E218, Vol. 19.
40. Lytton to queen, 10 January 1877, Lytton Collection E218, Vol. 19.
41. Lytton to queen, 4 May 1876, Lytton Collection E218, Vol. 18.
42. Lytton to queen, 23 December 1876, 10 January 1877, Lytton Collection E218, Vol. 19.
43. Ibid. See also Bawa: *Hyderabad under Salar Jang*, pp. 187–93.
44. Minute of 11 May 1902, quoted Metcalf: *Ideologies*, p. 197. See also note from H. S. Barnes, Sec. GoI, FD for a sample of the gargantuan amount of bureaucratic material involved in planning the Coronation Durbar, 16 July 1902, R/2/449/3. R/2/505/122 and R/2/505/123 deal extensively with

arrangements for the gaekwar and the Baroda party. R/2/13/86/1 deals with the Mysore party.

45. Speeches by Lord Curzon, Vol. 3, Curzon Collection F111, Vol. 559, pp. 60–7.
46. Hamilton to Curzon, 23 January 1903, Curzon Collection F111, Vol. 162.
47. Curzon to Hamilton, 13 January 1903, Curzon Collection F111, Vol. 162.
48. The Order was specifically aimed at non-Christian Indian princes, although Albert included himself in it. Albert 'probably hoped for India what he had hoped for Germany after the revolutions of 1848 – that is a national German diet, at which all the small states of the German Bund might be represented by their ancient ducal, princely and monarchical houses'. Taylor: 'Queen Victoria', p. 271.
49. Cohn: 'Representing Authority in Victorian India' in Hobsbawm and Ranger (eds): *The Invention of Tradition*, p. 181.
50. Cannadine: *Ornamentalism*, pp. 90, 100.
51. Cohn, 'Representing Authority in Victorian India' in Hobsbawm and Ranger (eds): *The Invention of Tradition*, p. 181. R2/50/894, *Installation and Investiture Durbars*, shows the great care for precedent and detail taken in investiture programmes.
52. Undated article from *The Pioneer* on Star of India investiture, Calcutta, 3 January 1870, Argyll Collection B380, Vol. I.
53. Cohn: 'Representing Authority in Victorian India' in Hobsbawm and Ranger (eds): *The Invention of Tradition*, p. 182.
54. See Stern: *Cat and Lion,* pp. 121–65.
55. Ibid, pp. 126–9.
56. Ram Singh's knighthood made him the second prince in Rajputana by giving him 'personal preference' over the Rathor Maharaja of Jodhpur. In the imperial order of preference the premier prince of Rajputana was the Maharana of Udaipur due to the antiquity and martial fame of the Sisodia clan dynasty.
57. Stern: *Cat and Lion*, p. 130.
58. Ibid, pp. 139, 145.
59. Ramusack: *Indian Princes*, p. 148.
60. Stern: *Cat and Lion*, p. 165.
61. Northbrook saw the willingness of the rulers of Jaipur and Gwalior to accept 'the very unpleasant duty of assisting in the enquiry as members of the Commission' as a token of their approval of general British policy in dealing with princely shortcomings, and was sadly disappointed to find that their allegiance to the Crown was not blind. See Northbrook to queen, 5 February and 7 June 1875, Northbrook Collection C144, Vol. 8.

62. Ram Singh's successor, Madho Singh, also had remarkable success in reaping honours, inducted as a Knight Grand Commander of the Order of the Star of India (GCSI) in 1888, a Knight Grand Commander of the Order of the Indian Empire (GCIE) in 1901, a Knight Grand Cross of the Royal Victorian Order (GCVO) in 1903 and a Knight Grand Cross of the Order of the British Empire (GBE) in 1918.
63. Mayo to Argyll, 7 February 1870, Argyll Collection B380, Vol. I.
64. Lytton to Cranbrook, 3 April 1879, Lytton Collection E218, Vol. 21.
65. Chief Sec. to Govt. of Madras to Sec. to GoI, FD, 11 January 1898, R/2/892/275. Travancore and Cochin did not have a tradition of kingly wealth and pomp. In contrast, kingship there was associated with austerity and dharmic morality. In his thesis on the two states Vikram Menon points out that, instead of a history of 'princely misgovernment, royal posturing and theatrical extravaganzas, there is a record of investment for growth, an educated and enlightened monarchy and a simplicity of lifestyle'. Menon: 'Popular Princes', pp. 20, 261.
66. Mayo to Argyll, 9 November 1870, Argyll Collection B380, Vol. II.
67. Lytton to Sir Louis Mallet, 9 June 1878, Lytton Collection E218, Vol. 20.
68. Dufferin to Kimberley, 5 June 1885, Dufferin Collection F130, Vol. 2. See also R/2/66/6 regarding the conferral of a native title by the nizam on Capt. John Clerk, superintendent of his education. A GoI despatch declared that there was no formal objection to Capt. Clerk receiving the title and form of address when within Hyderabad territories, however such a title should not be used by the resident or other British officers.
69. Capt. H. Daly, Dep. Sec. GoI, FD to Chief Sec. Govt Punjab, 12 April 1901, PSCI, 1875–1911, Box XXXVI. In Curzon's view the Raja of Kapurthala had 'never been the same man since he confabulated with the Czar of Russia and the Emperor of Germany', persisting in calling himself a maharaja, whereas he was 'only a Raja, and a very small one at that'. Curzon to Hamilton, 20 August 1902, Curzon Collection F111, Vol. 161.
70. Lansdowne to queen, 6 November 1893, Lansdowne Collection D558, Vol. 1.
71. Northbrook to Salisbury, 15 April 1875, Northbrook Collection C144, Vol. 12.
72. Lytton to Salisbury, 25 May 1876, Lytton Collection E218, Vol. 18.
73. Ibid.
74. Lytton to Lord Staplehurst, 1 May 1878, Lytton Collection E218, Vol. 20.
75. Sir F. J. Halliday, undated, attached to SoS to GoI, No. 6, 20 February 1879, PSCI, 1875–1911, Vol. 5.
76. Lytton to queen, 9 May 1878, Lytton Collection E218, Vol. 20.
77. Lytton to Cranbrook, 23 May 1878, Lytton Collection E218, Vol. 20.

78. Churchill to Dufferin, 22 September 1885, Dufferin Collection F130, IOR Neg. 4352.
79. Quoted Stern: *Cat and Lion*, p. 199
80. Roberts, appointed Colonel-in-Chief of the Empire Troops in France, having discovered on a visit to Ypres that the Indian sepoys lacked winter great-coats, declined to wear his own, contracted pneumonia and died in St. Omer on 14 November 1914.
81. Quoted Stern: *Cat and Lion*, p. 200. Political advantages were also obtained by the states concerned. By furnishing the empire with the first-rate Jaipur State Transport Corps, consisting of pony carts and carters, Maharaja Madho Singh was able to insist upon the aid of additional British arms to put down baronial unrest.
82. GoI to SoS, No. 206, 24 November 1888, PSCI, 1875–1911, Box IX.
83. GoI to SoS, No. 41, 13 March 1889, PSCI, 1875–1911, Box X.
84. Samiksha Sehrawat, 'Hostages in Our Camp: Military Collaboration between the Princely States and the British Raj, c. 1880–1920' in Ernst and Pati (eds): *India's Princely States*, p. 122.
85. Ibid, p. 125.
86. Ibid, p. 131.
87. Lytton to Disraeli, 30 April 1876, Lytton Collection E218, Vol. 18.
88. Salisbury to Lytton, 13 July 1876, Lytton Collection E218, Vol. 3A.
89. Lytton to Salisbury, 30 July 1876, Lytton Collection E218, Vol. 18.
90. Lytton to Salisbury, 25 October 1876, Lytton Collection E218, Vol. 18.
91. Salisbury to Lytton, 30 August 1876, Lytton Collection E218, Vol. 3B.
92. Salisbury to Lytton, 2 November 1876, Lytton Collection E218, Vol. 3B.
93. SoS to GoI, No. 59, 20 November 1876, PSCI, 1875–1911, Vol. 2.
94. James Fitzjames Stephen to Lytton, 30 November 1876, Stephen Collection MSS. ADD. 7349/14, Cambridge University Library.
95. Salisbury to Lytton, 10 November 1876, Lytton Collection E218, Vol. 3B.
96. Confidential minute from SoS to India Council, 2 November 1876, attached to No. 59, PSCI, 1875–1911, Vol. 2.
97. SoS to GoI, No. 6, 20 November 1876, PSCI, 1875–1911, Vol. 2.
98. Price: *Kingship and Political Practice*, p. 17.

Epilogue

1. Lamington to Minto, 9 October 1906, Minto Collection No. 12765, quoted Ashton: *British Policy*, p. 36.
2. Minto to Morley, 12 September 1907, Morley Collection D573, No. 12.

3. Butler's appointment was surrounded by controversy. The new Foreign Secretary had entered the Indian Civil Service in 1888 and reached the position of deputy commissioner at Lucknow in the United Provinces before taking charge of the department. He qualified for the position on the basis of neither his seniority nor his previous experience in the states or on the frontier. His appointment took many senior political officers on active service completely by surprise and they greeted it with open hostility.

4. Speech by Gaekwar of Baroda at viceregal reception, Baroda, 15 November 1909. Mary, Countess of Minto, *India, Minto and Morley 1905–10* (London, 1934), p. 351.

5. Copland: *Princes of India*, p. 30.

6. Quoted Ashton: *British Policy*, p. 195.

7. Quoted Philips (ed): *Evolution of India and Pakistan*, p. 427.

8. James Manor views the implementation of a *laissez-faire* policy towards the states as the major factor determining the downfall of the princes. James Manor, 'The Demise of the Princely Order: A Reassessment' in Jeffrey (ed): *People, Princes*, pp. 307–8. Other historians agree that the commitment by Minto to the 'minimum of interference' from the imperial government went far towards preventing the introduction of internal reforms within the states, and, unreformed, they stood little chance of positive participation in a new democratic India. Barbara Ramusack states that the adoption of an official *laissez-faire* policy towards the states in 1909 marked a point beyond which virtually nothing was done to secure the political future of the rulers (Barbara N. Ramusack, *The Princes of India in the Twilight of Empire: Dissolution of a Patron-Client System, 1914–1939* (Columbus, OH, 1978), pp. 233–5), and Ian Copland considers that during the 30 years from 1909 to 1939 the British 'did not do nearly enough to ready their clients for the time when they would have to stand on their own feet, without the support of imperial patronage' (Copland: *Princes of India*, p. 276).

9. Introduction to the *Manual of Instructions to Officers of the Political Department of the Government of India*, 1909, R/2/18/117.

10. Ashton: *British Policy*, pp. 45–7. Ironically, having removed 'the traditional barriers of isolation' Curzon's conception of a prince was a ruler who would remain in his state and submit to a superior British will.

11. Bhagavan: *Sovereign Spheres*, p. 176.

12. Ibid, p. 179. The rulers of Baroda and Mysore had the economic resources to pursue some progressive social and economic policies because they did not have extensive intermediaries, such as *jagirdars*, between their administration and the peasantry. The situation was the reverse in many Rajput ruled states.

13. Quoted Ashton: *British Policy*, p. 48. The insistence placed by British offi-
    cials on the employment of 'highly credentialled' outsiders in the form of
    diwans and senior bureaucrats, increasingly playing a more significant role
    in the state administration than a prince himself, had by the first decades of
    the twentieth century proved not to have been a good policy. Ian Copland
    stresses that as foreigners they were often unpopular with the people, and 'as
    mercenaries their primary loyalty was to their paymasters'. The rulers might
    have fared better in the denouement of 1947–8 if they had opted for less dis-
    tinguished but more patriotic 'servants with roots in the regions'. Copland:
    Indian Princes, p. 7.
14. James Mill: *British India*, Vol. V, p. 521, quoted D. A. Low, *Lion Rampant*
    (London, 1973), p. 51.

BIBLIOGRAPHY

Primary Sources

A. Unpublished Sources

1. Private Papers

British Library, Asian and African Studies

Argyll Collection	MSS Eur B380
Burne Collection	MSS Eur D951
Cross Collection	MSS Eur E243
Curzon Collection	MSS Eur Flll and F112
Dane Collection	MSS Eur D659
Dufferin and Ava Collection	MSS Eur F130
Durand Collection	MSS Eur D727
Elgin Collection	MSS Eur F83
Frere Collection	MSS Eur F81
Hamilton Collection	MSS Eur C125-6 and D508-10
Hartington Collection	MSS Eur D604
Lansdowne Collection	MSS Eur D558
Lawrence Collection	MSS Eur F90
Lee-Warner Collection	MSS Eur F92
Lytton Collection	MSS Eur E218
Morley Collection	MSS Eur D573
Northbrook Collection	MSS Eur C144
Pelly Collection	MSS Eur F126
Wood Collection	SS Eur F78

British Library, Manuscript Collections
Ripon Collection

Central Library, Leeds
Canning Collection

Cambridge University Library
Mayo Collection
Stephen Collection

National Library of Scotland, Edinburgh
Minto Collection

2. Official Papers

British Library, Asian and African Studies
India Office Records

a) Political and Secret Department
    L/P & S/6   Political Correspondence with India, 1792–1874
    L/P & S/7   Political and Secret Correspondence with India 1875–1911
    L/P & S/10   Political and Secret Subject Files, 1902–1931
    L/P & S/18   Political and Secret Memoranda
    L/P & S/20   Political and Secret Library
b) Proceedings of the Government of India
    P   Foreign Department Proceedings, 1857–1909
c) Crown Representative Records
    R1   Files of the Foreign Department of the Government of India
    R2   Residency and Agency Records

B. Published Sources

1. Official Publications

Chiefs and Leading Families in Rajputana (Calcutta, 1894).
General Report on Public Instruction in the N. W. Provinces of the Bengal Presidency for 1853–4, IOL V/24/905.
Hansard's Parliamentary Debates, Third Series, Vol. CCXXVII (London, 1876).
Parliamentary Papers, 1857–1909.
Progress of Education in India, Fourth Quinquennial Review, 1897–8 to 1901–2.

2. Collected Documents

Aitchison, Charles, *A Collection of Treaties, Engagements and Sanads Relating to India*, 11 Vols. Calcutta, 1862–92.

Philips, C. H., Singh, H. L. and Pandey, B. N. (eds), *The Evolution of India and Pakistan, 1858–1947: Select Documents*. London, 1962.

Tupper, Sir Charles Lewis, *Indian Political Practice: A Collection of the Decisions of the Government of India in Political Cases*, Vol. I. Calcutta, 1895.

Secondary Sources

A. Articles

Bingle, Richard, 'Changing attitudes to the Indian states, 1820–1850: a study of Oudh, Hyderabad and Jaipur' in C. H. Philips and M. Doreen Wainwright (eds), *Indian Society and the Beginnings of Modernisation, c. 1830–1850* (London, 1976), pp. 69–79.

Cannadine, David, 'The context, performance and meaning of ritual: the British monarchy and "the invention of tradition", c. 1820–1977' in E. Hobsbawm and T. Ranger (eds), *The Invention of Tradition* (Cambridge, 1983), pp. 101–64.

Cohn, Bernard S., 'Representing authority in Victorian India' in Hobsbawm and Ranger (eds): *Invention of Tradition*, pp. 165–209.

'Notes on the history of the study of Indian society and culture' in M. Singer and B. S. Cohn (eds), *Structure and Change in Indian Society* (Chicago, 1968), pp. 3–28.

'Recruitment and training of British civil servants in India 1600–1860' in Ralph Braibanti (ed), *Asian Bureaucratic Systems Emergent from the British Imperial Tradition* (Durham, NC, 1966), pp. 87–140.

Copland, Ian, 'The dilemmas of a ruling prince: Maharaja Sayaji Rao Gaekwar and "sedition"' in P. Robb and D. Taylor (eds), *Rule, Protest, Identity: Aspects of Modern South Asia* (London, 1978), pp. 28–48.

'The other guardians: ideology and performance in the Indian Political Service' in Robin Jeffrey (ed), *Princes, People and Paramount Power: Society and Politics in the Indian Princely States* (Delhi, 1978), pp. 275–305.

'The Baroda crisis of 1873–77: a study of governmental rivalry', *Modern Asian Studies* 2 2 (1968): 97–123.

J. Duncan M. Derrett, 'Tradition and law in India' in R. J. Moore (ed), *Tradition and Politics in South Asia* (Delhi, 1979), pp. 32–59.

Fisher, Michael H., 'The imperial coronation of 1819: Awadh, the British and the Mughals', *Modern Asian Studies* 19 2 (1985): 239–77.

Galtung, Johan, 'A structural theory of imperialism', *Journal of Peace Research* 2 (1991): 81–118.

Gordon, Stewart, 'Legitimacy and loyalty in some successor states' in J. F. Richards (ed), *Kingship and Authority in South Asia* (Delhi, 1998), pp. 327–47.

Griffin Lepel, 'Native India', *Asian Review* (April 1886): 452–5.

Groenhout, Fiona, 'Educating Govind Singh: "princely character" and the failure of indirect rule in Datia' in Peter Limb (ed), *Orb and Sceptre: Studies in British Imperialism and Its Legacies* (Melbourne, 2008), ch. 01.1.

'Loyal feudatories or depraved despots? The deposition of princes in the central Indian Agency, c.1880–1947' in Waltraud Ernst and Biswamoy Pati (eds), *India's Princely States: People, Princes and Colonialism* (London, 2007), pp. 99–117.

'The history of the Indian princely states: bringing the puppets back onto centre stage', *History Compass* 4 (2006): 629–44.

Hardiman, David, 'Baroda: The structure of a "progressive" state' in Jeffrey (ed): *People, Princes*, pp. 107–35.

Haynes, Edward S., 'Rajput ceremonial interactions as a mirror of a dying Indian state system, 1820–1947', *Modern Asian Studies* 24 3 (1990): 459–92.

'The British alteration of the political system of Alwar state: lineage, patrimonialism, indirect rule, and the Rajput jagir system in a Indian "princely" state, 1775–1920', *Studies in History* 5 (1989): 27–71.

'Alwar: bureaucracy versus traditional rulership: raja, *jagirdars* and new administrators, 1892–1910' in Jeffrey (ed): *People, Princes*, pp. 32–64.

Hurd, John, 'The influence of British policy on industrial development in the princely states of India 1890–1933', *Indian Economic and Social History Review* 12 4 (1975): 410–24.

Ikegame, Aya, 'Space of kingship, space of empire: marriage strategies amongst the Mysore royal caste in the nineteenth and twentieth centuries', *Indian Economic and Social History Review* 46 3 (July–September 2009): 343–72.

Ikegame, Aya and Andrea Major (eds), 'Princely spaces and domestic voices: new perspectives on the Indian princely states', *Indian Economic and Social History Review* 46 3 (July–September 2009): 293–300.

Inden, Ronald, 'Ritual, authority and cyclic time in Hindu kingship' in Richards (ed): *Kingship and Authority*, pp. 41–91.

Jeffrey, Robin, 'Travancore: status, class and the growth of radical politics, 1860–1940' in Jeffrey (ed): *People, Princes*, pp. 136–69.

'The politics of indirect rule: types of relationship among rulers, ministers and residents in a native state', *Journal of Commonwealth and Comparative Politics* 13 3 (1975): 261–81.

Kak, Shakti, 'The agrarian system of the princely state of Jammu and Kashmir: a study of colonial settlement policies, 1860–1905' in Ernst and Pati (eds): *India's Princely States*, pp. 68–84.

Kapila, Shruti, 'Masculinity and madness: princely personhood and colonial sciences of the mind in western India, 1871–1940', *Past and Present* 187 (May 2005): 121–56.

Knight, L. A., 'The Royal Titles Act and India', *Historical Journal* 11 3 (1968): 488–507.

Lambert-Hurley, Siobhan, 'Historicising debates over women's status in Islam: the case of Sultan Jahan Begam of Bhopal' in Ernst and Pati (eds): *India's Princely States*, pp. 139–56.

Leonard, Karen, 'Hyderabad: The Mulki-non-Mulki conflict' in Jeffrey (ed): *People, Princes*, pp. 65–106.

Low, D. A., '*Laissez-faire* and traditional rulership in princely India' in Jeffrey (ed): *People, Princes*, pp. 372–87.

Manor, James, 'The demise of the princely order: a reassessment' in Jeffrey (ed): *People, Princes*, pp. 306–28.

'Princely Mysore before the storm: the state-level political system of India's model state, 1920–36', *Modern Asian Studies* 9 1 (1975): 31–58.

Marshall, Peter J., 'Imperial Britain', *Journal of Imperial and Commonwealth History* 23 3 (1995): 379–94.

Metcalf, Barbara, 'Islam and power in colonial India: the making and unmaking of a Muslim princess', *American Historical Review* 116 1 (February 2011): 1–30.

Nuckolls, Charles W., 'The *durbar* incident', *Modern Asian Studies* 24 3 (1990): 529–59.

Preckel, Claudia, 'The roots of Anglo-Muslim cooperation and Islamic reformism in Bhopal' in Jamal Malik (ed), *Perspectives of Mutual Encounters in South Asian History, 1760–1860* (Leiden, 2000), pp. 65–78.

Qanungo, B., 'A study of British relations with the native states of India, 1858–62', *Journal of Asian Studies* 26 (February 1967): 251–65.

Ramusack, Barbara N., 'Women's hospitals and midwives in Mysore: princely or colonial medicine' in Ernst and Pati (eds): *India's Princely States*, pp. 173–93.

'Tourism and icons: the packaging of the princely states of Rajasthan' in Catherine B. Asher and Thomas R. Metcalf (eds), *Perceptions of South Asia's Visual Past* (New Delhi, 1994), pp. 235–56.

'Punjab states, maharajas and gurdwaras: Patiala and the Sikh community' in Jeffrey (ed): *Princes, People*, pp. 170–204.

Rashid, Shaikh Abdur, 'The Mughal imperial state' in Moore (ed): *Tradition and Politics*, pp. 128–50.

Ray, Rajat R., 'Mewar: the breakdown of the princely order' in Jeffrey (ed): *People, Princes*, pp. 205–39.

Robinson, Francis, Introduction to article by Princess Abida Sultaan of Bhopal, 'The Begums of Bhopal', *History Today* 30 (October 1980): 30–5.

Rudolph, L. I. and S. H., 'The political modernization of an Indian feudal order: an analysis of Rajput adaptation in Rajasthan', *Journal of Social Issues* 24 (October 1968): 93–128.

'Rajputana under British paramountcy: the failure of indirect rule', *Journal of Modern History* 38 (June 1966): 138–60.

Sehrawat, Samiksha, 'Hostages in our camp: military collaboration between the princely states and the British raj, c. 1880–1920' in Ernst and Pati (eds): *India's Princely States*, pp. 118–38.

Shulman, David D., 'On south Indian bandits and kings', *The Indian Economic and Social History Review* 17 3 (1980): 283–306.

Singh, Hira, 'Colonial and postcolonial historiography and the princely states: relations of power and rituals of legitimation' in Ernst and Pati (eds): *India's Princely States*, pp. 15–29.

Stein, Burton, 'Vijayanagara', *The New Cambridge History of India*, Vol. 1.2 (Cambridge, 1989), pp. 140–6.

Stern, Robert W., 'An approach to politics in the princely states' in Jeffrey (ed): *People, Princes*, pp. 355–71.

Taft, Frances, 'Royal marriages in Rajasthan', *Contributions to Indian Sociology* n.s. 8 (1973): 64–80.

Taylor, Miles, 'Queen Victoria and India', *Victorian Studies* 46 2 (Winter 2004): 264–74.

'Empire and parliamentary reform: the 1832 Reform Act revisited' in A. Burns and J. Innes (eds), *Rethinking the Age of Reform: Britain, 1780–1850* (Cambridge, 2003), pp. 295–311.

Tillotson, Giles, 'Orientalizing the Raj: Indo-Saracenic fantasies' in Christopher W. London (ed), *Architecture in Victorian and Edwardian India* (Bombay, 1994), pp. 15–34.

Trevithick, A., 'Some structural and sequential aspects of the Imperial Assemblages at Delhi: 1877–1911', *Modern Asian Studies* 24 3 (1990): 561–78.

B. Books

Allen, Charles, *Lives of the Indian Princes* (London, 1984).

Appadurai, Arjun, *Worship and Conflict under Colonial Rule: A South Indian Case* (Cambridge, 1981).

Argyll, Duchess of (ed), *George Douglas, Eighth Duke of Argyll 1823–1900, Autobiography and Memoirs*, 2 vols. (London, 1906).

Argyll, Duke of, *India under Dalhousie and Canning* (London, 1865).

Ashton, Stephen R., *British Policy towards the Indian States, 1905–1939* (London, 1982).

Bailey, F. G., *Stratagems and Spoils* (New York, 1969).

Balfour, Elizabeth, *Personal and Literary Letters of the Earl of Lytton* (London, 1900).

The History of Lord Lytton's Indian Administration, 1876 to 1880 (London, 1899).

Ballhatchet, Kenneth, *Race, Sex and Class under the Raj* (London, 1980).

Banerjee, Anil Chandra, *The Rajput States and British Paramountcy* (New Delhi, 1980).

Baroda, Maharaja of, and Fass, Virginia, *The Palaces of India* (London, 1980).

Barton, Sir William, *The Princes of India* (London, 1934).

Bawa, V. K., *Hyderabad under Salar Jung I* (New Delhi, 1996).

Bayly, Christopher, *Indian Society and the Making of the British Empire* (Cambridge, 1988).

Rulers, Townsmen and Bazaars: North Indian Society 1770–1870 (Cambridge, 1983).

Beames, John, *Memoirs of a Bengal Civilian* (London, 1961).

Bell, E., *The Mysore Reversion* (London, 1866).

Bence-Jones, Mark, *The Viceroys of India* (London, 1982).

Bennett, G. (ed), *The Concept of Empire from Burke to Attlee, 1774–1947* (London, 1953).

Bhabha, Homi, *The Location of Culture* (New York, 1994).

Bhagavan, Manu, *Sovereign Spheres: Princes, Education and Empire in Colonial India* (New Delhi, 2003).

Bhavnagar, Sir Bhavsinhji Takhtsinhji, Maharaja of, *Forty Years of the Rajkumar College 1870–1910* (London, 1911).

Bhopal, Sultan Jahan Begam of, *An Account of My Life* (London, 1912).

Blunt, Wilfred Scawen, *India under Ripon, A Private Diary* (London, 1909).

Bolt, C., *Victorian Attitudes to Race* (London, 1971).

Bowring, Lewis Bentham, *Eastern Experiences* (London, 1871).

Brittlebank, Kate, *Tipu Sultan's Search for Legitimacy: Islam and Kingship in a Hindu Domain* (Delhi, 1997).

Broughton, T. D., *Letters from a Mahratta Camp* (Calcutta, 1977).

Brown, Judith M., *Modern India: The Origins of an Asian Democracy* (Oxford, 1985).

Browning, O., *Impressions of Indian Travel* (London, 1903).

Cannadine, David, *Ornamentalism* (London, 2001).

Chailly, Joseph, *Administrative Problems of Princely India* (London, 1910).

Chevenix Trench, Charles, *Viceroy's Agent* (London, 1987).

Choksey, R. D., *A History of British Diplomacy at the Court of the Peshwas, 1786–1818* (Poona, 1951).

Collingham, E. M., *Imperial Bodies* (Cambridge, 2001).

Copland, Ian, *State, Community and Neighbourhood in Princely North India, c.1900–1950* (New York, 2005).

The Princes of India in the Endgame of Empire, 1917–1947 (Cambridge, 1997).

The British Raj and the Indian Princes: Paramountcy in Western India, 1857–1930 (London, 1987).

Coupland, Reginald, *The Indian Problem, 1833–1935* (Oxford, 1968).

Creagh-Coen, Terence, *The Indian Political Service: A Study in Indirect Rule* (London, 1971).

Dalrymple, William, *Nine Lives: In Search of the Sacred in Modern India* (London, 2010).

Daly, Hugh, *Memoirs of Gen. Sir Henry Dermot Daly* (London, 1905).

Das, M. N., *India under Morley and Minto* (London, 1964).

Derrett, J. Duncan M., *Religion, Law and the State in India* (London, 1968).

Devi, Gayatri and Rama Rau, Santha, *A Princess Remembers: The Memoirs of the Maharani of Jaipur* (London, 1976).

Dewey, Clive, *Anglo-Indian Attitudes: The Mind of the Indian Civil Service* (London, 1993).

Dilks, D., *Curzon in India*, 2 vols. (London, 1969 and 1970).

Dirks, Nicholas B., The *Hollow Crown: Ethnohistory of an Indian Kingdom* (Cambridge, 1987).

Dufferin and Ava, Marchioness of, *Our Viceregal Life in India* (London, 1890).

Eden, Emily, *Up the Country: Letters from India* (1886, reprint Oxford 1930).

Edwardes, Michael, *High Noon of Empire: India under Curzon* (London, 1965).

Elliott, R. H., *Gold, Sport and Coffee Planting in Mysore* (London, 1894).

Ernst, Waltraud and Pati, Biswamoy (eds), *India's Princely States: People, Princes and Colonialism* (London, 2007).

Ferguson, Niall, *Empire* (London, 2003).

Fisher, Michael H., *Indirect Rule in India: Residents and the Residency System, 1764–1858* (New Delhi, 1991).

A Clash of Cultures: Awadh, the British and the Mughals (London, 1988).

Forrest, G. W., *The Administration of the Marquess of Lansdowne as Viceroy and Governor-General of India, 1888–1894* (Calcutta, 1894).

Fox, Richard G., *Kin, Clan, Raja and Rule* (Berkeley, 1971).

(ed), *Realm and Region in Traditional India* (Durham, NC, 1977).

Fraser, H., *Memoirs and Correspondence of General J. S. Fraser of the Madras Army* (London, 1885).

Fraser, Lovat G., *India under Curzon and After* (London, 1911).

French, Patrick, *Younghusband: The Last Great Imperial Adventurer* (London, 1994).

Frykenberg, Robert E., *Guntur District 1788–1848: A History of Local Influence and Central Authority in South India* (Oxford, 1965).

(ed), *Land Control and Social Structure in Indian History* (Wisconsin, 1969).

Gallagher, J. and Robinson, R. E., *Africa and the Victorians: The Official Mind of Imperialism* (London, 1961).

Gilbert, M., *Servant of India: A Study of Imperial Rule from 1905 to 1910 as told through the Correspondence and Diaries of Sir James Dunlop-Smith* (London, 1966).

Gilmour, David, *The Ruling Caste: Imperial Lives in the Victorian Raj* (London, 2005).

Curzon (London, 1994).

Gopal, S., *British Policy in India 1858–1905* (Cambridge, 1965).

The Viceroyalty of Lord Ripon, 1880–4 (Oxford, 1953).

Guha, Ranajit, *Dominance without Hegemony* (Cambridge, MA, 1997).

Handa, R. L., *History of the Freedom Struggle in Princely States* (New Delhi, 1968).

Hardinge of Penshurst, Lord, *My Indian Years, 1910–16* (London, 1948).

Hardy, Peter, *The Muslims of British India* (London, 1972).

Harlow, Barbara and Carter, Mia, *Imperialism and Orientalism* (Malden, MA, 1999).

Haynes, Douglas, *Rhetoric and Ritual in Colonial India: The Shaping of a Public Culture in Surat City, 1852–1928* (Berkeley, 1991).

Heesterman, J. C., *The Inner Conflict of Tradition: Essays in Indian Ritual, Kingship and Society* (Chicago, 1985).

Hendley, Thomas Holbein, *Ulwar and Its Art Treasures* (London, 1888).

Hettne, Bjorn, *The Political Economy of Indirect Rule: Mysore 1881–1947* (London, 1978).

Hobsbawm, E. and Ranger, T. (eds), *The Invention of Tradition* (Cambridge, 1983).

Holiday, Henry, *Reminiscences of My Life* (London, 1914).

Horne, W. O., *Work and Sport in the Old ICS* (London, 1928).

Hunter, W. W., *A Life of the Earl of Mayo*, 2 vols. (London, 1876).

Hutchins, F. G., *The Illusion of Permanence: British Imperialism in India* (Princeton, 1967).

Jackson, Anna and Jaffer, Amin (eds), with Deepika Ahlawat, *Maharaja: The Splendour of India's Royal Courts* (London, 2009).

James, Lawrence, *Raj: The Making and Unmaking of British India* (London, 1997).

Jeffrey, Robin (ed), *People, Princes and Paramount Power: Society and Politics in the Indian Princely States* (New Delhi, 1978).

The Decline of Nayar Dominance: Society and Politics in Travancore 1847–1908 (London, 1976).

Jhala, Angma, *Courtly Indian Women in Late Imperial India* (London, 2008).

Joshi, Varsha, *Polygamy and Purdah: Women and Society among Rajputs* (Jaipur, 1995).

Kamerkar, Mani, *British Paramountcy: British-Baroda Relations, 1818–1848* (Bombay, 1980).

Kaye, John William, *The Life and Correspondence of Major General Sir John Malcolm* (London, 1854).

Khan, Narullah, *The Ruling Chiefs of Western India and the Rajkumar College* (Bombay, 1898).

Khan, Shaharyar M., *The Begums of Bhopal* (London, 2000).

Kipling, Rudyard, *Rudyard Kipling's Verse: Definitive Edition* (New York, 1940).

Lal, Ruby, *Domesticity and Power in the Early Mughal World* (New York, 2005).

Lambert-Hurley, Siobhan, *Muslim Women, Reform and Princely Patronage: Nawab Sultan Jahan Begam of Bhopal* (London, 2007).

(ed), *A Princess's Pilgrimage: Nawab Sikander Begum's A Pilgrimage to Mecca* (New Delhi, 2007).

Lee-Warner, William, *The Native States of India* (London, 1910).

The Protected Princes of India (London, 1894).

Llewellyn-Jones, Rosie (ed), *Portraits in Princely India, 1700–1947* (Mumbai, 2008).

Low, D. A., *Lion Rampant* (London, 1973).

Lutyens, Mary, *The Lyttons of India: Lord Lytton's Viceroyalty* (London, 1979).

Lyall, Sir Alfred, *Life of the Marquis of Dufferin and Ava* (London, 1905).

Asiatic Studies: Religious and Social (London, 1882).

Machonochie, Sir Evan, *Life in the Indian Civil Service* (London, 1926).

Maclagen, Michael, *Clemency Canning* (London, 1962).

Macnaghten, Chester, *Common Thoughts on Serious Subjects: Addresses delivered between the Years 1887–9 to the Elder Boys of Rajkumar College in Kathiawar* (London, 1912).

Major, Andrea, *Sovereignty and Social Reform in India: British Colonialism and the Campaign against Sati, 1830–60* (New York, 2011).

Malcolm, Sir John, *A Memoir of Central India*, 2 vols. (London, 1823).

Malleson, Colonel C. B., *An Historical Sketch of the Native States of India in Subsidiary Alliance with the British Government* (London, 1871).

Mallet, Bernard, *Thomas George, Earl of Northbrook* (London, 1908).

Mangan, J. A., *The Games Ethic and Imperialism: Aspects of the Diffusion of an Ideal* (London, 1986).

Mannoni, C., *Prospero and Caliban: The Psychology of Colonialism* (New York, 1956).

Manor, James, *Political Change in an Indian State, Mysore, 1910–55* (New Delhi, 1977).

Marglin, Frederique Apffel, *Wives of the God-King: The Rituals of the Devadasis of Puri* (New Delhi, 1985).

Mateer, The Rev. Samuel, *Native Life in Travancore* (London, 1883).

Menon, V. P., *The Story of the Integration of the Indian States* (Calcutta, 1956).

Metcalf, Thomas R., *Ideologies of the Raj* (Cambridge, 1995).

An Imperial Vision: Indian Architecture and Britain's Raj (London, 1989).

Land, Landlords and the British Raj (Berkeley, 1979).

The Aftermath of Revolt: India 1857–1870 (Princeton, 1964).

Minchin, J. G. C., *Our Public Schools: Their Influence on British History* (London, 1901).

Minto, Countess of, *India, Minto and Morley, 1905–1910* (London, 1934).

Moir, Martin, *A General Guide to the India Office Records* (London, 1988).

Moir, Martin I., Peers, Douglas M. and Zastoupil, Lynn (eds), *J. S. Mill's Encounter with India* (Toronto and New York, 1999).

Moore, Lucy, *Maharanis* (London 2004).

Moore, R. J., *Liberalism and Indian Politics, 1872–1922* (London, 1966).

Sir Charles Wood's Indian Policy, 1853–1866 (Manchester, 1966).

(ed), *Tradition and Politics in South Asia* (New Delhi, 1979).

Morison, J. L., *The Eighth Earl of Elgin* (London, 1928).

Morison, Theodore, *Imperial Rule in India* (London, 1899).

Moulton, G. C., *Lord Northbrooks's Indian Administration, 1872–1876* (London, 1968).

Nandy, Ashis, *The Intimate Enemy: Loss and Recovery of Self under Colonialism* (New Delhi, 1983).

Narullah, Syed and Nayaka, J. P., *A History of Education in the British Period* (Bombay, 1951).

Neogy, A. K., *The Paramount Power and the Princely States of India, 1858–1881* (Calcutta, 1979).

O'Dwyer, Sir Michael, *India As I Knew It, 1885–1925* (London, 1925).

O'Malley, L. S. S., *The Indian Civil Service, 1601–1930* (London, 1931).

Owen, R. and Sutcliffe, B. (eds), *Studies in the Theory of Imperialism* (London, 1972).

Pal, Dharm, *The Administration of Sir John Lawrence in India, 1864–1869* (Simla, 1952).

Paliwal, D. L., *Mewar and the British 1857–1921 A.D.* (Jaipur, 1971).

Pannikar, Kavalam M., *His Highness the Maharaja of Bikaner: A Biography* (London, 1937).

The Evolution of British Policy towards Indian States, 1774–1858 (Calcutta, 1929).

An Introduction to the Study of the Relations of Indian States with the Government of India (London, 1917).

Parry, B., *Delusions and Discoveries: Studies on India in the British Imagination, 1880–1930* (London, 1998).

Perham, Margery, *The Colonial Reckoning* (London, 1961).

Phadnis, U., *Towards the Integration of the Indian States, 1919–1947* (London, 1968).

Powell, Avril A., *Muslims and Missionaries* (Richmond, Surrey, 1993).

Powell, Avril A. and Lambert-Hurley, Siobhan (eds), *Rhetoric and Reality: Gender and the Colonial Experience in South Asia* (New Delhi, 2006).

Prasad, S. N., *Paramountcy under Dalhousie* (New Delhi, 1964).

Price, Pamela G., *Kingship and Political Practice in Colonial India* (Cambridge, 1996).

Punzo Waghorne, Joanne, *The Raja's Magic Clothes* (Pennsylvania State University, 1994).

Rai, Mirdu, *Hindu Ruler, Muslim Subjects: Islam, Rights, and the History of Kashmir* (Princeton, 2004).

Raleigh, Sir Thomas, *Lord Curzon in India: Being a Selection from His Speeches as Viceroy and Governor General 1898–1905* (London, 1906).

Ramusack, Barbara N., *The Indian Princes and Their States* (Cambridge, 2004).

The Princes of India in the Twilight of Empire: Dissolution of a Patron-Client System, 1914–1939 (Columbus, OH, 1978).

Rice, Stanley, *Life of Sayaji Rao III Maharaja of Baroda*, 2 vols. (London, 1931).

Richards, J. F., *Mughal Administration in Golconda* (Oxford, 1975).

(ed), *Kingship and Authority in South Asia* (New Delhi, 1998).

Ripon, Lord, *The Native States of India* (Leeds, 1886).

Rivett-Carnac, J. H., *Many Memories of Life in India, at Home, and Abroad* (Edinburgh and London, 1910).

Ronaldshay, Earl of, *The Life of Lord Curzon, Viceroy of India* (London, 1929).

Rose, K., *Superior Person: A Portrait of Curzon and His Circle in Late Victorian England* (London, 1969).

Rudolph, L. I. and S. H., *The Modernity of Tradition: Political Development in India* (London, 1967).

Said, Edward, *Orientalism* (New York, 1994).

Seal, A., *The Emergence of Indian Nationalism: Competition and Collaboration in the Late Nineteenth Century* (Cambridge, 1968).

Sen, Satadru, *Colonial Childhoods: The Juvenile Periphery of India, 1858–1945* (London, 2005).

Migrant Races: Empire, Identity and K. S. Ranjitsinhji (Manchester, 2004).

Sergeant, J. P., *The Ruler of Baroda* (London, 1928).

Sherring, H., *The Mayo College, Ajmere, 'The Eton of India': A Record of Twenty Years 1875–1895* (Calcutta, 1897).

Sleeman, W. H., *Rambles and Recollections* (London, 1844).

Smith, R. Bosworth, *Life of Lord Lawrence*, 2 vols. (London, 1901).

Sobti, Manu, *Urban Form and Space in the Islamic City: A Study of Morphology and Formal Structures in the City of Bhopal, Central India* (Ahmedabad, 1993).

Spangenberg, Bradford, *British Bureaucracy in India: Status, Policy and the Indian Civil Service in the late Nineteenth Century* (Columbia, 1976).

Stern, Robert W., *The Cat and the Lion* (New York, 1988).

Stokes, E., *The English Utilitarians and India* (Oxford, 1959).

Stow, V. A. S., *A Short History of the Mayo College, 1869–1942* (Ajmer, 1942).

Suleri, Sara, *The Rhetoric of English India* (Chicago, 1992).

Temple, Sir Richard, *Journals Kept in Hyderabad, Kashmir, Sikkkim and Nepal*, 2 vols. (London, 1887).

Men and Events of My Time in India (London, 1882).

Thompson, E. J., *The Making of the Indian Princes* (London, 1943).

Thornton, Thomas Henry, *General Sir Richard Meade and the Feudatory States of Central and Southern India* (London, 1898).

Tillotson, G.H.R., *The Tradition of Indian Architecture: Continuity, Controversy and Change since 1850* (New Haven and London, 1989).

Tod, James, *Annals and Antiquities of Rajasthan*, 3 vols. (1829, reprint Delhi 1993).

Tupper, Sir Charles Lewis, *Our Indian Protectorate* (London, 1893).

Vadivelu, A., *Some Mysore Worthies* (Madras, 1900).

Walrond, T. (ed), *Letters and Journals of James, Eighth Earl of Elgin* (London, 1872).

Wasti, S. R., *Lord Minto and the Indian Nationalist Movement, 1905 to 1910* (Oxford, 1964).

Webb, Sidney and Beatrice, *Indian Diary* (Oxford, 1987).

Wedderburn, D., *Protected Princes in India* (London, 1914).

Weeden, E. St. C., *A Year with the Gaekwar of Baroda* (London, 1912).

Wilkinson, Rupert H., *Gentlemanly Power: British Leadership and the Public School Tradition* (New York, 1964).

Wingfield Stratford, Barbara, *India and the English* (London, 1922).

Wink, Andre, *Land and Sovereignty in India: Agrarian Society and Politics under the Eighteenth-Century Maratha Svarajya* (Cambridge, 1986).

Wolf, Lucien, *Life of the First Marquess of Ripon*, 2 vols. (London, 1921).

Wolpert, S., *Morley and India, 1906–1910* (Berkeley, 1967).

Woodruff, Philip [Mason, Philip], *The Men Who Ruled India*, 2 vols. (London, 1953).

Wurgaft, Lewis D., *The Imperial Imagination: Magic and Myth in Kipling's India* (Middletown, CT, 1983).

Young, Robert, *White Mythologies: Writing History and the West* (London, 1990).

Younger, Coralie, *Wicked Women of the Raj* (New Delhi, 2003).

C. Unpublished Works

Durisotto, Paolo, 'Traditional Rule and Modern Conventions: The Maharajas of Bikaner and Their Relationship with the Raj, 1887–1947'. PhD Thesis, Royal Holloway College, University of London, 2001.

Groenhout, Fiona, 'Debauchery, Disloyalty, and Other Deficiencies: The Impact of Ideas of Princely Character upon Indirect Rule in Central India, c. 1886–1946'. PhD Thesis, University of Western Australia, 2007.

Gustafson, Donald R., 'Mysore 1881–1902: The Making of a Model State'. PhD Thesis, University of Wisconsin at Madison, 1968.

Menon, V., 'Popular Princes: Kingship and Social Change in Cochin and Travancore 1870–1930'. PhD Thesis, University of Oxford, 1998.

Shah, Alison Mackenzie, 'Constructing a Capital on the Edge of Empire: Urban Patronage and Politics in the Nizam's Hyderabad, 1750–1950'. PhD Thesis, University of Pennsylvania, 2005.

INDEX